HOSPITALITARIAN
Bruce White's Legacy

Kathi Ann Brown
Foreword by J. W. Marriott, Jr.

HOSPITALITARIAN: Bruce White's Legacy
By Kathi Ann Brown

Copyright © 2025 by Kathi Ann Brown

All rights reserved. No part of this book may be used or reproduced in any manner whatsoever without written permission from the publisher or author except in the case of brief quotations embodied in critical articles and reviews.
For information, contact: KathiBrown@aol.com.

Designed and published by
Spectrum Creative, LLC
Oakton, Virginia
www.spectrum-creative.com

Printed and manufactured in the United States of America.

First printing, February 2025

Cover photography: Bruce White; courtesy of the White Family.

ISBN: 979-8-9850582-1-5 (hardcover)
ISBN: 979-8-9850582-2-2 (paperback)

This book is dedicated to the White Family and every Hospitalitarian—past, present, and future.

> *"It burned in my psyche that if I ever had talent at anything, if I ever was good at anything, I was going to push the pedal to the metal."*

Bruce W. White
Founder, White Lodging

Table of Contents

> Popular "Bruce-isms" are shared throughout the book.*

Foreword by J. W. Marriott, Jr. vii

Introduction xi

Chapter 1: I Was Hooked! 1

Chapter 2: From Shelby, With Love 3

Chapter 3: The School of Life 29

Chapter 4: "BB" and "AB" 45

Chapter 5: Begin with the End in Mind 67

Chapter 6: Just Warming Up 91

Chapter 7: The White Lodging Way 111

Chapter 8: Four Walls 137

Chapter 9: Landscape of the Heart 167

Chapter 10: A Brand-New Star Up in Heaven Tonight 197

Afterword by Beth M. White 235

Acknowledgments 239

---

*Bruce-isms: The author has included a selection of "Bruce-isms" sprinkled throughout the book. Though many of these witty sayings are not Bruce White originals, he was notorious for peppering his conversation and memos with them.

"A great leader is not judged by the energy he creates with his immediate reports, but the energy he creates at the most entry levels of the organization, judged only by how effective the organization is in his absence."

A favorite Bruce-ism

Foreword

by J. W. Marriott, Jr.
Chairman Emeritus, Marriott International, Inc.

I first met Bruce White in 1990. He wasn't yet 40 and his company—White Lodging—was barely five years old. Marriott Corporation (as it was known then), by contrast, had been around since 1927, the year my parents opened a nine-seat root beer stand that launched The Hot Shoppes restaurant chain. By 1990, Marriott had grown into a major hotel company with more than 600 properties and about 160,000 rooms.

Despite differences in age and scale, Marriott and White Lodging shared one important thing in common: We were both wet-behind-the-ears when it came to hotel franchising.

Marriott had experimented briefly with franchising in the late 1960s, but we backed away when it became clear that we had jumped in too fast. We didn't have enough quality controls in place at the time to ensure that franchisees understood and embraced our standards. For the next two decades we viewed franchising with healthy skepticism. We decided to stick with building and operating hotels by ourselves. We were good at both. Why mess with success? In the 1980s, we began developing and operating select service brands like Courtyard by Marriott, Fairfield Inn, and Residence Inn.

At roughly the same time, Bruce White was busy launching his own small-scale brand of select service hotels in the Midwest: Carlton Lodge.

He was not a newbie to hospitality. Bruce had worked on and off at his father's Holiday Inn in Merrillville, Indiana since his teen years. He loved the fast pace and people-focus so much he sought a chance to train with Hyatt in California. By the time Bruce set up White Lodging in 1985, he had logged more than a decade of hands-on hospitality experience, including designing and running the 3,400-seat Holiday Star Theater in Merrillville.

So, what brought giant Marriott and tiny White Lodging together in 1990?

On our side, the impetus was a fierce economic recession that threw a colossal wrench into the engine of our hotel development juggernaut. Marriott's construction pipeline of managed hotels came to an abrupt standstill. On Bruce's side, he was beginning to see the limitations of trying to create a hotel brand without the resources needed to scale up. In fact, he was so frustrated that he was thinking about getting out of the hotel business entirely.

Then—call it fate, luck, or serendipity—Bruce bumped into Mike Ruffer, head of our young Fairfield Inn business. We had only recently decided that it was time to try franchising again. We wanted to keep growing our hotel business but couldn't see a path forward without enlisting partners in the effort. Mike invited Bruce to fly to our headquarters outside of Washington, D.C. to explore the idea. Bruce being Bruce, he leapt at the opportunity. Savvy and strategic, he recognized immediately that an affiliation with a well-established industry player like Marriott could be the ticket to White Lodging's future. In turn, Marriott would benefit from the nimble entrepreneurial mindset of a young and ambitious hotelier who shared our standards and values.

I was introduced to Bruce on his trip East to our headquarters. I still had my reservations about franchising, but meeting someone as smart, quick, and confident as Bruce helped convince me that taking the chance was worthwhile. In fact, we were all sufficiently impressed by Bruce that we granted him the *first* Fairfield Inn franchise—he opened Merrillville, Indiana's Fairfield Inn by Marriott in September 1990.

Bruce's stunning success with that property provided us with more certainty about franchising and established White Lodging as one of our most trusted partners. In short order, we granted Bruce's company additional franchises for Courtyard and Residence Inn—the first franchisee to operate all three brands—and I know he took pride in being a pioneer. For our part, we were able to help the tiny company win the confidence of banks whose willingness to provide financing was crucial, particularly during a recession.

By 1996, White Lodging was operating 25 properties under the Marriott umbrella—and doubled that number over the next three years. As we expanded our brands, Bruce and his team reveled in sniffing out the right locations in the right markets during a time of significant growth.

As time passed and I got to know Bruce, his executive team, and his family, I never questioned our decision to allow part of Marriott's success to rest in his capable hands. He understood that the hospitality industry is first, last, and always about *people*. He invested in building relationships not only with our leadership team, but also with his peers. You couldn't be a Marriott franchisee without knowing and benefiting from the knowledge, insights, and friendship of Bruce White.

Never one to shy away from blunt truths, Bruce often challenged our company's cautious approach to trying new ideas. He told us flatly on more than one occasion that our organization needed to listen—*really* listen—to the franchisee community. Sometimes his directness rankled our corporate leadership, but we recognized that Bruce's comments came from a place of genuine concern, collegiality, and a desire for mutual success. He wanted us all to win: Marriott, White Lodging, and hundreds of his franchisee peers. If that meant rattling our cages or pushing us to reconsider our policies, so be it. His heart was in the right place and his integrity was unquestioned.

Bruce even talked us into letting White Lodging become the first franchisee to develop, build, and manage one of our full-service convention hotels: the Indianapolis Marriott Downtown (February 2001). Once again, he hit the ball out of the park, exceeding expectations and opening the way for other franchisees to be entrusted with running our larger properties. Through the years, it surprised no one that White

Lodging won dozens of Marriott awards for everything from best-in-class property openings to stellar general managers.

White Lodging was not Bruce's only passion, by any means. He was devoted to his wife Beth, their three children, and a large circle of friends from every era of his life. Somehow, he found time to serve on several boards, including his alma mater, Purdue University. Following his tenure on Purdue's Board of Trustees, he doubled down on his support for the university. Bruce and his related family foundations have invested more than $100 million back into the school's hospitality and business programs. In honor of his philanthropic and in-kind support, they wanted to rename the hospitality program after White Lodging. Bruce refused to allow the program to be named for White Lodging alone. He insisted that the school be named The White Lodging—J. W. Marriott, Jr. School of Hospitality and Tourism Management—an unexpected, but deeply appreciated honor. Prior to his passing, Purdue also named its undergraduate business institute in his honor.

When Bruce passed away in January 2023, at the age of 70, the industry lost one of our greatest cheerleaders and most outspoken advocates, and I lost a dear friend. His encouraging voice was needed at times when we hesitated to shake up the status quo or required a boost to make it through an economic downturn. White Lodging will forge ahead without its founder at the helm, guided by his family and talented executive team, but Bruce's larger-than-life enthusiasm, his willingness to buck convention, and his unwavering faith in the future will be sorely missed by all of us.

The hospitality industry will long owe Bruce White a hefty debt of gratitude for more than three decades of leadership and loyalty. I know I do.

Introduction

In September 2024, White Lodging unveiled a sweeping renovation of its headquarters in Merrillville, Indiana. The multi-million-dollar project fulfilled a longstanding wish of White Lodging's founder, Bruce W. White. A few years earlier, he had proposed remodeling the single-story building, but the onset of COVID in 2020 and his passing in January 2023 delayed the start date. By late May 2024, the timing was right, plans were ready, and construction began. Corporate staff worked from home during the upgrade, while contractors wielded power saws, tarps, hammers, paint, lumber, and more for three months. When the project was finished, White Lodging's corporate headquarters echoed the flair and polish of the company's award-winning hotels and private ranches.

"Bruce challenged us five years ago to enhance our corporate office to better reflect who we are as a brand and an urban/lifestyle hospitality company," said CEO Jean-Luc Barone, when the refreshed headquarters was profiled in *The Times of Northwest Indiana*. "We are a very different company from 10–15 years ago."

Indeed, the transformation of White Lodging's headquarters reflects the company's stunning evolution from its founding in 1985 to today. During White Lodging's start-up phase in the mid-1980s, Bruce White and his tiny staff were housed in Merrillville's "Twin Towers," an office complex built by White's father Dean in 1972. The striking gold glass façade of the skyscraper at the intersection of I-65 and U.S. 30 could be seen for miles around. It was at the Twin Towers in Spring 1989 that White ran into a representative from Marriott—a chance meeting that set White and White Lodging on the road to success. In time, the franchisor-franchisee relationship between Marriott International and White Lodging would grow into a prosperous and enduring partnership spanning four decades.

During the 1990s, White and his team turned their bare-bones quarters in the Twin Towers into Command Control Central, the location from which they eagerly hunted for hotel properties that could be renovated and converted to one of Marriott's select service brands. At first, the game plan was purely opportunistic, driven by White's single-minded determination to gain traction in the booming hospitality industry. But as White Lodging demonstrated both the ambition and the discipline to operate first-rate hotels, the next growth phase kicked in: building select service properties from the ground up. By 2000—15 years after White Lodging's official founding—the company had mastered its approach to analyzing markets, locating prime real estate, designing hotels, and operating them at margins that often beat Marriott's own projections.

White Lodging kicked off the new millennium by accepting a challenge to design and build its first large-scale full-service hotel: the Indianapolis Marriott Downtown. The hotel's successful opening in the Spring of 2001 was a feather in White Lodging's cap. Then, just a few months later, the world shut down in the aftermath of the terrorist attacks of September 11, 2001. White and White Lodging buckled in and managed their way through one of the worst catastrophes the nation—and the travel industry—had ever experienced.

Fortunately, from the earliest days of White Lodging, White had envisioned building an organization for the long haul . . . one that would possess ample resilience to weather major events, from September 11 to a severe economic recession in 2008–9, to the COVID pandemic of 2020. White's deep belief in hiring the right people, training them well, and supporting them in their jobs paid off. White Lodging began to win dozens of industry awards for guest satisfaction, marketing, training programs, and more. The company took pride in developing and maintaining a corporate culture that rewarded excellence, creativity, collegiality, and hard work.

No one was prouder of the company's success than Bruce White. Born in Crown Point, Indiana on Christmas Day 1952, White grew up on South Park Avenue—a street straight out of the movie *American Graffiti*. He played basketball, baseball, 'kick-the-can', and more with neighborhood kids of all ages and different economic strata. He remained friends with many of them for his entire life. In his later years, he credited his South Park upbringing with teaching him to accept and respect everyone equally, a habit he never lost.

While in high school, White discovered his love of hospitality almost by accident, when he and a few buddies helped with the opening of his father Dean's Holiday Inn in 1969. During his college years at Purdue, White majored in business management and made more lifelong friends . . . at least two of whom later became treasured business partners. Following a successful two-year stint with Hyatt's executive training program in California, White returned to Merrillville to help upgrade his father's hotel operations. After a brief time working for his father's company—Whiteco Industries—the younger man opted for the opportunity to start his own hotel business. On November 7, 1985, White Lodging Services was born.

Another life-changing opportunity came White's way in the autumn of 1986: Purdue alumna Beth Maloney. The two were a perfect match and married in November 1987, a happy event followed a few years later by the births of Corinne, Conner, and Otis. White thrived on being a husband and father, never letting the pressure of building a business overshadow his devotion to his family. He enjoyed watching his three children and his 'fourth child'—White Lodging—grow up together for the next three decades.

By 2014, White Lodging was ready for new headquarters. Corporate staff was small compared to the thousands of White Lodging associates working in the company's hotels, but more and better space was needed. The company moved into a large single-story building on 83rd Avenue in Merrillville, a facility that once housed Whiteco's data operations. The utilitarian ambiance suited Bruce White, who wanted to encourage the company's Merrillville associates to keep their eyes focused on the field. White's own office was so low-key and unassuming that a visitor could be forgiven for not recognizing it as the command post for a large and far-flung workforce. It was a place to get work done, not impress visitors, period.

> Hospitalitarians—White Lodging's word for "someone who, in their DNA, feels good by making other people feel good."

White's keep-it-simple mindset was not to last, however. The company exited the select service market—its original business—and dedicated its energies to creating one-of-a-kind hotels and restaurants. The freedom to be more creative came courtesy of a landmark $1.7 billion deal between White Lodging and Black Entertainment Television (BET) founder Robert L. Johnson in 2006. The financial windfall from the transaction allowed White to dream bigger and better than ever. One dream led to the purchase of rundown Brush Creek Ranch near Saratoga, Wyoming. Another dream inspired the wholesale transformation of the Ranch into one of the top resorts in the world. Other dreams focused on White's alma mater—Purdue University. Multiple gifts from the White family have helped Purdue expand and strengthen its hospitality programs and transform the school's century-old Union Club Hotel into an incubator for the next generation of Hospitalitarians—White Lodging's word for "someone who, in their DNA, feels good by making other people feel good."

In 2019, White decided it was time for the company's headquarters to trade in its no-nonsense decor for a sophisticated style more in tune with White Lodging's growing portfolio of urban/lifestyle properties. When the COVID virus hit the nation in early 2020, plans for the upgrade were put on ice as the company grappled with the impact of a pandemic. Then, in April 2022, White was diagnosed with advanced pancreatic cancer; he died eight months later in January 2023. Fortunately for White Lodging, White had taken care a few years earlier to assemble an executive team capable of taking the company into the future . . . with or without him.

The handsome remodeling of White Lodging's headquarters in 2024 signals to the world that the White family and the company's leadership team fully intend to carry on the values and vision of the business's ever-restless, energetic founder. Within the company's headquarters, the Bruce W. White Memorial Library (and this book) will keep White's personal story, principles, and philosophy alive for future generations who will never have an opportunity to meet the man who started it all . . . the original Hospitalitarian: Bruce William White.

"A powerful past and an exciting future . . . the road between these two runs through you!"

**Bruce W. White
Founder, White Lodging**

CHAPTER 1

I Was Hooked!

> *My first night ever working in a hotel was ... when the Merrillville Holiday Inn opened. I fell in love with the hospitality industry that night.*
>
> Bruce W. White

Merrillville, Indiana. May 2, 1969

7:30 a.m. Sixteen-year-old Bruce William White stood gazing at the freshly painted lobby of the Merrillville Holiday Inn, his father Dean's latest business venture. After months of planning, bulldozing the land, construction, and clean-up, Dean White's brand-new Holiday Inn at the crossroads of I-65 and U.S. 30 in Merrillville, Indiana was about to make its public debut.

"Where do these chairs go?" White called out as the hotel's manager sped past him. The manager pointed to a doorway and hurried on.

White and a few high school buddies had been hired for the day to carry in furniture for the hotel's guest rooms and public spaces. The young men came dressed for a sweaty job: White wore old jeans and heavy steel-toed boots. Dozens of new bedframes, mattresses, tables, chairs and lamps filled the hotel's corridors. White and his friends spread out around the hotel to deliver the right furnishings to the right room.

Before they were finished, the property's new food and beverage manager approached the group with an urgent request. The hotel's first dinner service was just hours away.

"Oh my God, I forgot to hire bus boys," he said. "Do any of you want to work tonight bussing tables?"

The young men were dirty and tired but agreed. Even Jeff Conquest—a friend and neighbor of the White family—was game to pitch in despite

> How you do anything is how you do everything.

the bulky cast protecting his broken ankle. No one had time to go home and change into clean clothes. As the dinner service got underway, White and his pals did their best to keep up with the flow of empty plates and glasses.

"I fell in love with the hospitality industry that night," White later recalled. "The excitement, the fast pace, working with the waitresses, the kitchen. Even though it was a disaster. I mean, you have a food and beverage director that forgot to hire bus boys?! I soon found out that his previous experience consisted of running a cafeteria on a military base."

Even before White and his friends finished clearing tables, another emergency popped up. The manager had also failed to hire enough dishwashers to tackle the night's stacks of dirty dishes, cutlery, and glassware.

"So, after working all day, beginning at 7:00 a.m., I washed dishes until something like 4:00 a.m.," White said many years later. "But I didn't come home tired. I came home incredibly excited. I loved the energy. I loved working with the people. I loved being of service. In short, *I was hooked!*"

CHAPTER 2

From Shelby, With Love

> *A lot of what I've seen Bruce build—the principles, the concepts, the work ethic—started with our grandmother, Mary White.*
>
> **Terry Bird**
> Cousin

On December 25, 1952, Barbara Bayse White of Crown Point, Indiana, delivered her second child, a healthy blue-eyed boy. The newborn was a perfect Christmas gift for the White family. The year had been a busy one. Ten months earlier, Dean and Barbara White had packed up their belongings—and their five-year-old daughter Cynthia—and moved from an apartment in the tiny village of Shelby to a house in Crown Point, sixteen miles north.

In Barbara White's mind, the move was non-negotiable. She had told her husband that their family needed to relocate to a community that offered good schools and other amenities that rural Shelby lacked. Dean agreed, even though the move to Crown Point meant a longer commute for him. Shelby was home to White Advertising—the outdoor sign company incorporated by Dean's father in 1935. The village was also

Bruce White as a baby.

the permanent residence of Dean's parents, G. W. and Mary White. Barbara and Dean had been living in the Whites' home or nearby for several years. It was time to establish their own household.

Barbara might have had additional incentive for wanting to put a little distance between herself and her in-laws ... at least her *sisters-in-law*. Her long courtship with high school sweetheart Dean had been filled with ups and downs. When the pair finally agreed to tie the knot, Dean's three fiercely protective older sisters tried to talk him out of the marriage. He refused. In protest, the sisters grudgingly showed up at the wedding ... dressed in funereal black.

The birth of Dean and Barbara's son on Christmas Day 1952 managed to ruffle anew a few White family feathers. Nine days earlier, Dean's father G. W. had passed away of heart disease at age 73. As Barbara's sisters-in-law crowded into her room in the maternity ward, they offered congratulations ... and a chorus of unsolicited advice: surely the newest member of the family would be named in honor of their recently deceased father? Surely?

According to family lore, Barbara's well-known frankness carried the day: "No, I am *not* naming my son George ... Washington ... White," she calmly announced. "I've already picked a name: *Bruce William White.*"

When Bruce William White made his debut in 1952, he joined a family tree boasting deep roots in U.S. soil. His arrival in the world was the fruit of more than two centuries of White family courtships and marriages.

One of the most important events in newborn Bruce's life took place almost a half-century before his arrival. On December 29, 1909, White's future grandparents, George Washington "G. W." White, 30, and Mary Gertrude Barney, 26, exchanged vows at the bride's parents' home in Duff, near Boise, Idaho.[1] The couple's 1909 nuptials united two families who had arrived on the Eastern seaboard decades before the American Revolution. According to amateur family genealogist Dorothy Helen "Dot" White, the first members of the White family to set foot on U.S.

---

[1] G. W.'s older brother William and Mary's father Andrew acted as official witnesses for the ceremony. Pastor C. B. Dalton of the First M.E. Church in Boise officiated.

soil arrived at Baltimore, Maryland, sometime in the early 1700s. The Barneys emigrated even earlier, settling in Vermont in the late seventeenth century.

By the 1860s, at least one branch of the White family had moved West to Ohio. In 1863—in the middle of the U.S. Civil War—Samuel French White[2], one of the youngest members of the Ohio branch of Whites, married Margaret Ann Mahan (or Mahon). The couple moved several times, finally settling in Kansas in 1883 where the family farmed for more than two decades. They raised seven children, including G. W., Mary Barney's future husband.

> Dean White recalled that his parents—G. W. and Mary—were punctilious when it came to smoking, drinking, and going to church. The first two were forbidden; the third was mandatory.

Like the Whites, a few members of the Barney clan also headed West in the mid-nineteenth century. One of the most intrepid was Andrew Jackson (A. J.) Barney, born in Vermont to Edward and Eliza Barney in 1839. Unlike many of his Green State forebears, A. J. opted to travel and live outside of Vermont. A growing network of train routes crisscrossing the continent made it relatively easy to move from place to place in search of adventure, opportunity or a better life. Through the years A. J. Barney would make his home in locales as far-flung as Missouri, Iowa, Idaho, and California—far from his native Vermont.[3]

On December 21, 1869, 30-year-old A. J. Barney married 21-year-old Pennsylvania native Minerva Augusta Dietrich in Pettis County, Missouri.[4] Barney was working as a dry goods salesman at the time. In

---

[2]Samuel White was possibly a Dunkard preacher in the teetotalling Church of the Brethren. His 1918 obituary mentions that he was a "conspicuous figure at Salem [KS] revival meetings, his patriarchal appearance, coupled with a powerful pioneer preacher's voice, commanding the respect of all who heard him speak."

[3]When the California Gold Rush kicked off in 1849, several male members of the Barney family headed to French Creek, California to try their hand at mining. (A. J. Barney was 16 in 1849, but it's not yet known if he joined them.) According to Dot White, at least one of the Barney men died of illness in California during the Gold Rush. Whether any Whites likewise sought to make their fortune in the Golden State hasn't yet been discovered. The story of the two families' participation in the Civil War is also ripe for research.

[4]The location of the Barney-Dietrich wedding is interesting; both belonged to "Yankee" or Union families, but their nuptials were held in the South, just four years after the conclusion of the Civil War.

rapid succession, the couple produced several offspring, including G. W. White's future bride: Mary Gertrude Barney, born in 1883. The family was living in Cass County, Iowa at the time of Mary's birth, but moved to Boise, Idaho while she was young.

Smart, curious, and highly motivated, Mary Gertrude Barney[5] knew at an early age that she wanted a better education than Boise could offer. Before she was 17 years old, she traded life on the family farm in Idaho for the adventure of residing with her married sister Jennie Maud Brown on Bluff Street in Ponca, Nebraska, a community just north of Omaha.[6] In 1900, Mary Gertrude was a senior at Ponca High School, the only girl in a class of six. Teaching came naturally to her. Several articles in the local *Ponca Grit* newspaper that year noted that "bright and accomplished" Mary sometimes took over the classroom duties of absent teachers.

Mary Barney's pursuit of education didn't end with high school graduation. She enrolled in the University of Nebraska—affectionately nicknamed Uni—to continue her studies.[7] The Class of 1906 University yearbook teased her lightheartedly about choosing Ponca's high school "for no other purpose than to attend the Uni. Her future occupation is to be teaching Latin. Idaho will be the field for her labor. Why? Because there's money in it."

Mary Gertrude Barney did enter the field of education soon after receiving her degree in 1906, but her plans to teach Latin in Idaho took a detour when she was offered a job as assistant principal at a high school in Tilden, Nebraska. Within a year or two, an even bigger detour materialized: a dapper, hazel-eyed young man named George Washington White.[8]

The pair supposedly met by happenstance, somewhere in Washington State, where Mary Gertrude Barney was teaching on a

---

[5] Mary was also called Marie during her teen and college years.
[6] Jennie Maud Barney married James Brown in 1888 and the couple had produced two sons—Leo and Carroll—by the time Maud's young sister Mary joined the household.
[7] "Mama stayed with Aunt Maud [Jennie Maud Brown] and babysat the kids," said Dot White. "She went to the University and got her degree by being a companion to the kids."
[8] George Washington was a popular name for newborns in the 1800s, especially around the time of the 1876 Centennial. G. W. White was born in 1879.

temporary basis. Decades later, Mary's daughter Dot White recalled her mother's stories about living "in some town on the coast, wide open with saloons and everything." According to Dot White, one of George White's sisters was teaching in the same town, probably his younger sister Minerva.[9] The future couple might have met at a party hosted by George's sister.[10] Their courtship was not entirely smooth sailing. G. W. allegedly had a girlfriend in Colorado . . . until Mary Gertrude told him he had to choose between the two women. He chose Mary.

> Despite being gone for long stretches, G. W. was home often enough to father six children between 1911 and 1923: Paul, Ruth, Mary, Dorothy and Donald (twins) and Dean, Bruce's future father.

At the time the couple married in 1909, White was a real estate agent, helping to arrange homesteading opportunities for people looking for Western lands. He traveled extensively and for long periods throughout the western third of the country, living in hotels and lodging houses as needed. Handsome and ambitious, White would spend much of his adult life on the road, long after he courted and married Miss Mary Gertrude Barney.

Despite being gone for long stretches, G. W. was home often enough to father six children between 1911 and 1923: Paul, Ruth, Mary, Dorothy and Donald (twins) and Dean, Bruce's future father. The first five offspring were born in South Dakota, in or near the young town of Kennebec, founded in 1905.

"My mother Mary was born in South Dakota in a place that had maybe one or two trees," recalled Terry Bird, Bruce White's cousin. "It was pretty desolate. Our grandparents, G. W. and Mary, homesteaded there."

G. W. and Mary White's sixth and last child—Dean Victor White—was born in 1923, after the family moved to Lincoln, Nebraska. G. W.

---

[9]The sister might have been G. W.'s younger sibling Minerva, who taught school in Idaho and in Oregon. The connection to Washington State has not been established . . . yet. The author thinks Oregon is more likely.

[10]Details of the couple's courtship are fuzzy. G. W. White graduated with the Class of 1910 from the University of Nebraska's business school, less than a year after marrying Mary G. Barney. How he found time to attend classes while pursuing his real estate business isn't known. One White family story asserts that White's future bride tutored him in French so that he, too, could receive a bachelor's degree from the University of Nebraska.

Mary Gertrude Barney, Bruce White's grandmother, who was a strong presence in his life.

and Mary were both determined that their children would go to college. The family's residency in Lincoln paved the way for the young Whites to enter the University of Nebraska after completing high school.

Bird continued: "As the kids got older, our grandma said—probably not in these exact words—'To hell with this! We're going to Lincoln so the kids can get an education.' In Lincoln they could graduate from high school and then get four years of college—for free."

According to family stories, G. W. White made an excellent living from his real estate ventures—enough to allow him to be involved in promoting the ambitious Alaska-Yukon-Pacific Highway project. The A.Y.P. road campaign aimed to connect the far reaches of Alaska through western Canada and down the Pacific coast, possibly as far as Central America. With the advent of automobile travel in the 1910s and 1920s, a "Good Roads" movement swept the country as communities raced to construct smooth roads that promised to bring both people and prosperity. For a man who sold Western real estate for a living, good roads meant more customers.

> "The family was very poor then," said Bruce White. "My grandmother, Mary White, hawked her wedding ring. She also slept in a closet so she could rent out her room. My father Dean and his older brother Don would go sleep on the statehouse lawn in the summer so their rooms could be let."

"G. W. White was a big idea guy," said Beth White, who joined the White family in 1987 when she married Bruce White, G. W.'s grandson. "He was on the road all the time. We have letters in our family archive that he wrote to Bruce's grandmother, telling her that he thought she wasn't raising the children correctly. Poor woman!"

George Washington "G. W." White, Bruce White's grandfather.

"Our grandfather was tough on his kids," said Terry Bird. "Very tough. Tough on his wife, too—our grandma—in a lot of ways."

Some of White's crankiness was likely related to the reversal of fortune the family endured when the stock market crashed in October 1929, kicking off the Great Depression. Details of the family's financial misfortune aren't known, but stories from that period suggest that the Whites suffered right along with millions of fellow Americans who

> I always strive to improve on the things I don't do very well ... that's how I learn to do them well and without effort.

lost their jobs and their savings. At the height of the Great Depression, one in four Americans was unemployed.

"The family was very poor then," said Bruce White. "My grandmother, Mary White, hawked her wedding ring. She also slept in a closet so she could rent out her room. My father Dean and his older brother Don would go sleep on the statehouse lawn in the summer so their rooms could be let."

Dean White recalled that his father, G. W., commandeered his bicycle and pedaled around Lincoln after giving up the family car. Mary White scoured the local newspapers for potential work for her husband. One ad grabbed her eye. A sign-maker was looking for a salesman.

"My dad didn't want to be in the sign business," said Dean White, "but my mother said 'Well, you're going to do it, George.' So, he took the job and he started selling signs all over Nebraska and Iowa."

While her husband was on the road, Mary White kept the household intact, doing whatever was necessary to survive, while hammering home to her children the importance of education. Her persistence paid off. The oldest five of her six children enrolled in the University of Nebraska. Eldest son Paul studied law. Brilliant and blunt, Paul White eventually ascended to the post of Chief Justice of Nebraska's Supreme Court.

Before he attained such lofty heights, however, Paul White was a young partner in a small law firm in Lincoln: Matschulatt, Matschulatt & White. In July 1935, Paul filed incorporation papers on behalf of an unusual client: his own father, George Washington White. The details are fuzzy, but G. W. and two acquaintances—Joe Derkinderen and F. A. Gray—teamed up to create The White Advertising Company. Paul White prepared the necessary papers to formally register the new entity. Filing the paperwork cost $10 and recording the transaction required an additional $1.25—not small sums during the Great Depression. Derkinderen was named president and general manager. F. A. Gray was named vice president. Paul's father G. W. took the roles of secretary-treasurer and sales manager.

Why the firm was named after White and not Derkinderen or Gray has not yet been discovered. Perhaps White contributed the lion's share of start-up financing. Curiously, too, the three men lived hundreds of miles apart—not a convenient business structure in pre-Internet days. Derkinderen was based in Shelby, Indiana at the time. Gray lived in Kansas City, Missouri. G. W.'s home base remained in Lincoln, Nebraska. The new advertising company's lofty ambitions included leasing or buying real estate, erecting billboards, manufacturing signs, patenting any worthwhile inventions, and much more. The list of possibilities covered by the original corporate charter was thorough and left little to chance . . . or to wily competition.

The Great Depression was not an ideal time to launch a business, but the trio did their best: "They were making little signs with chalkboards for farmers, who could advertise their eggs or sweet corn or whatever," said Bruce White, G. W.'s grandson.

Although Lincoln was chosen initially to serve as the firm's headquarters, by 1939 the tiny burg of Shelby, Indiana—where Joe Derkinderen and his parents lived—became the *de facto* home of White Advertising, thanks to lower overhead.[11] The firm employed "six to a dozen men and women" in Shelby while doing "national business," according to a November 1939 article in The Hammond Times. The firm's specialty was "steel and blackboard road signs." The only other manufacturer in the tiny town was a Claussen pickle factory.

> Like the courtship of G. W. White and Mary Gertrude Barney, the path of true love was far from smooth for Dean and Barbara. One reason was the war, which pushed millions of young couples either to hustle to the altar or go their separate ways.

At some point, G. W. White arranged to transplant the rest of his family from Lincoln to Shelby, probably to kill two birds with one stone. He would be able to place orders and pick up signs directly from the company's printing facility in Shelby before heading out to see customers. And he would be able to spend a little time with his family. At first, the Shelby arrangement was for summertime

---

[11] The company retained its Nebraska incorporation status for many years.

only, recalled youngest son Dean. Lincoln remained the family's home base the rest of the year.

"We'd get a house in Shelby that we'd rent for four months or so," said Dean White. "We were working our rear ends off, building the signs and so forth. When my brother Don got his driver's license, he and I would go through Indiana and Illinois putting signs up. We got a dollar a day, six days a week."

"When he was on the road, our grandfather was constantly writing letters home," said Terry Bird. "Letters were really the only way to keep in touch in those days. He would use carbon paper to write the same letter to all the kids to let them know what he was doing."

The White Advertising Company squeaked by during the later years of the Great Depression, until World War II tossed a new wrench into the works.

"We did have some business, but not much, because in World War II, who wanted anything to do with billboards?" remarked Dean White in a 2011 interview.

After the attack on Pearl Harbor on December 7, 1941, the United States joined the global war. Factories shifted production from domestic goods to military wares. New automobiles and appliances disappeared from showrooms. Rationing of gas, tires, sugar, eggs, and other goods forced Americans to 'make do or do without.'

The men in the White family dutifully signed up for military service, including patriarch G. W., whose 1879 birthdate put him in a special class of 40-and-older registrants. Older sons Paul and Don enlisted. Daughter Mary took a job with the Red Cross and was sent to England. Don's twin sister Dot went to the University of Michigan to become a dietician. According to Beth White, Ruth White continued to teach school. Youngest sibling Dean was 18 years old and living at home on F Street in Lincoln when the Japanese attacked Pearl Harbor. He signed up officially in June 1942, when he was 19. His employer at the time was Beatrice Creamery in Lincoln.

Dean White didn't complain about enlisting—doing his duty was important to him—but the war put a crimp in his cherished plans to follow in his five siblings' footsteps at the University of Nebraska. He enrolled in the Fall of 1941, but soon dropped out. The war also disrupted his courtship of a pretty Lincoln Central High School classmate, Barbara Bayse.

> You are better off being approximately right than exactly wrong.

"Our mom and dad met when dad threw a snowball at her in school," said Craig White, Bruce White's youngest brother. The image of two fresh-faced teenagers flirting in the middle of a snowy Nebraska winter became a favorite White family story.

Like the courtship of G. W. White and Mary Gertrude Barney, the path of true love was far from smooth for Dean White and Barbara Bayse. One reason was the war, which pushed millions of young couples either to hustle to the altar or go their separate ways. For Dean, the war separated him from his sweetheart by thousands of miles and gave him homesickness to boot. He was first sent to the U.S. Merchant Marine Academy in Kings Point, New York for two years, where he learned not only military discipline, but how to handle a large ship and manage a crew. In due time he shipped out as Chief Mate on a Merchant Marine "Liberty Ship" in the Pacific—an eye-opening experience for the 21-year-old. The original Liberty Ships were large cargo vessels, powered by engines that were 21 feet long and 19 feet high. A few were secretly converted to floating repair depots for military aircraft. By the time White was assigned to one, many of the ships had been turned into troop transports.

"My captain was a great guy, a wonderful guy, but he was also a huge drunk," recalled Dean White decades later. The captain would go to his room and lock the door, leaving his young protege to command the ship.

"My dad had to deal with all these grizzled Merchant Marines," said Bruce White. "He was in charge of all of them. They were floating around in the South Pacific with Japanese subs taking shots at them."

"I grew up pretty fast," said Dean White.

In wartime letters home to his mother in Shelby, Dean shared his frustrations, his triumphs, and his worries about the future. In almost every missive, he talked about two things: his dreams of attending college and of convincing Barbara Bayse to marry him.

On the latter issue, Barbara proved less cooperative than the grizzled Merchant Marines. According to son Bruce, his mother felt no rush to settle down . . . and wasn't sure that the tall, blue-eyed boy she knew from high school was The One. When Barbara's family moved from Lincoln, Nebraska to the San Francisco area for her father's bank job, she attended a junior college and then went on to the University of California at Berkeley. Dean switched his sights from the University of Nebraska to Berkeley, hoping to join her there when his military service ended. Barbara wasn't sold on the idea. She brushed off Dean's long-distance phone calls and his offers to visit her: "Don't bother," was her nonchalant reply.

At one point, Dean purchased an engagement ring, perhaps hoping that a bit of sparkle would seal the deal. Instead, Barbara sent the ring back to him in a Dear John letter. Dean was angry and disappointed; one family story asserts that he threw the ring off the Golden Gate Bridge. Such episodes did not endear Barbara to the three White sisters: Ruth, Mary, and Dorothy. The women were highly protective of their baby brother.

Dean, on the other hand, had a staunch ally in Barbara's mother, Alta Bayse. Craig White credits his Bayse grandmother with Dean's success in finally winning over Barbara permanently as the war wrapped up in the autumn of 1945.

"My Bayse grandmother thought the world of my dad," said Craig. "She would invite him over for dinner, in Burlingame, California. She wouldn't tell my mom that she was inviting him."

Thanks to her mother's sly 'dinner date' tactic, Barbara finally realized that her blue-eyed boy from Lincoln was, in fact, The One. This time, an engagement ring went on her finger and stayed put. It was soon followed by a wedding ring.

The couple's decision to tie the knot required sacrifices for both. Barbara dropped out of Berkeley and Dean—albeit reluctantly—finally gave up on his dream of going to college. Instead, the newlyweds headed to Shelby, Indiana. The couple moved into an attic apartment in G. W. and Mary White's home. The house was "hotter than Hades" in the summertime, said Bruce White. Also, there was no indoor plumbing.

Whiteco Industries got its start in Shelby, Ind., by founder George W. White, second from left. The first goal George gave his son Dean was to "become a millionaire by the time you're 40." On Sunday, Dean sold the primary division of the family business for $930 million.

Dean White (standing, third from right) worked at his father's advertising and sign company during summers as a teenager.

It became a standing family joke that by marrying Dean, Barbara had moved "from the sorority house to the outhouse."

Moving to Shelby, a rural enclave on Indiana's Kankakee River, would not have been Dean's first pick, but he felt obligated. Many years later, Dean explained why he let his father sway him: "There was nobody else to take care of the sign company. Paul was doing his thing, all the girls—Ruth, Mary, and Dot—were doing their thing. I didn't want to do it. I really didn't. I had three employees and two broken down trucks."

"My grandfather strong-armed my dad into taking over the sign business, which was very small at the time," said Bruce White. "The first year that my father joined the business, it grossed $26,000 in total sales."

Besides being the only White family member available to take over the business, Dean was also keenly aware that his father—by now in his late 60s—had a heart condition and needed to slow down. In late 1952, G. W.'s cardiac troubles turned fatal. He died at home on December 16, age 73, a few days before his daughter-in-law Barbara gave birth to

Bruce William on Christmas Day. After G. W.'s death, his widow Mary opted to stay put in Shelby, rather than move to California where a few of her children and grandchildren lived. She also didn't want to move to Crown Point, where Dean, Barbara and their children resided. She had long taken care of the books for White Advertising and would continue to do so for her son. Dean visited the sign factory in Shelby regularly, including many Saturdays, so she knew she would see her youngest son most days.

Mary White's decision to remain in Shelby had a profound impact on her Crown Point grandchildren. For Dean and Barbara's four children—Cynthia, Bruce, Chris and Craig—their White grandmother was a steady, loving, and awe-inspiring presence.

> **In our family, our White grandmother is a deity. When she came to visit us on South Park Avenue, we couldn't wait to spend time with her.**
>
> Bruce W. White

"I'm pretty sure that my grandmother was the only person in Shelby who had a college degree," said Bruce White. "She was extremely well-read. She was also incredibly independent. Our grandmother loved us kids and we loved her. Dad would often bring her up to Crown Point on Fridays and she would go back to Shelby with him on Monday. You couldn't find a better babysitter than my grandmother. We kids behaved for her; we just respected her so much.

"In our family, our White grandmother is a deity," he continued. "When she came to visit us on South Park Avenue, we couldn't wait to spend time with her. Even my friends would ask if we could drive down to Shelby to spend time with her. They were mesmerized by her."

"My grandmother was such a fun person to be around," agreed White's youngest brother Craig. "When I went out on dates in high school, I would tell the girl that 'Hey, we're going to drive to Shelby and spend some time with my grandma.' They would look at me like, 'What kind of date is this?!' But after meeting her, they would always want to go back."

Bruce, who sometimes accompanied his dad to the sign factory in Shelby on Saturdays, loved hanging out with his grandmother on the weekends that she didn't come to Crown Point.

"One of my favorite childhood memories was Saturday mornings," wrote White in a White Lodging newsletter decades later. "If I did not have a ballgame, my father would take me with him to the plant . . . and let me roam around while he put in a few hours in the office. We always started off our day with a couple of doughnuts at the 'sweet shop' next door and finished with lunch, accompanied by my grandmother, at Sophie's Recreation and Cafe.[12] The food was only surpassed by the chance to be with my father and grandmother by myself."

Bruce White as a young boy.

White, who was notorious in Crown Point for his hijinks in the neighborhood and beyond, recalled an incident involving his beloved White grandmother his senior year in high school.

"My parents were out of town. It was Senior Ditch Day. And, trust me, I was not the teacher's pet. I grew up in kind of a rough and tumble steel-working area. And we had more than our fair share of 'fun.' So, I would typically be the one leading the Ditch Day parade. My friends couldn't believe it when I said, 'I'm not doing it.' And they're like, 'Why?!' I remember saying, 'My grandmother is staying with us and if the principal calls our home, my grandmother, who was a schoolteacher and a principal, answers that phone and hears that I'm not at school . . .' I said, 'Well, I would never do that to my grandmother. So, I'm going to school today.'"

White's classmates had good reason to be astounded by his decision. When the White family moved to South Park Avenue in Crown Point in early 1952, little did the neighborhood suspect that a gifted prankster would soon grow up in their midst. One of White's earliest escapades involved his newborn brother Chris. While family and friends were gathered in the Whites' backyard, Bruce decided he wanted to show off his two-day-old sibling.

---

[12]There is a listing in Shelby's bicentennial history for a Sophie's Recreation, run by Bill and Sophie Myers.

> "We often set fishing line across Greenwood Street with an egg taped to it at the height of a windshield. We would also put dummies with reflectors in their eyes just over a hill at night so motorists would think they hit someone in the road. We even got unsuspecting newcomers to pee on the electric fence that bordered a nearby field."
>
> — Bruce W. White

"We were visiting from California," recalled Terry Bird, Bruce's cousin. "It was the summer of the 17-year locusts. The weather was hot and muggy. Everybody was outside, eating at the picnic table. Then we kids went up to play in the house. The next thing we know, here comes Bruce!"

"I was four years old, and my parents had just brought Chris home from the hospital," recalled White. "I remember reaching into the crib and how hard it was to get him out of it. And I remember trying not to fall as I was walking down the hallway with him in my arms."

Fortunately, Larry Costin, an older neighbor kid, was in the house and spotted Bruce carrying Chris. He swiftly intervened, deposited the baby safely in his crib again, and—for good measure—yelled at Bruce. The adults joined the chorus when they heard the story. It wouldn't be the last time that young Bruce inspired an exasperated adult to holler at him.

As White got a little older, he and other kids around South Park discovered the joys of tormenting everyone from neighbors to innocent passersby.

"We used to put dog manure in a paper bag and leave it on old man Huseman's[13] front porch after we set it on fire," wrote White in a White Lodging newsletter many years later. "We often set fishing line across Greenwood Street with an egg taped to it at the height of a windshield. We would also put dummies with reflectors in their eyes just over a hill at night so motorists would think they hit someone in the road. We even got unsuspecting newcomers to pee on the electric fence that bordered a nearby field. You can imagine their reactions! We would release fireflies in the old theatre off the square . . . that used to get a lot of laughs. Once, we even put gasoline down the sewer to see what would happen if we

---

[13]In different versions of the story, Bruce used the names "Wizman" and "Huseman."

threw a match into it. You can imagine our fright when a column of fire threatened to burn not only us, but also the entire block."

White had plenty of good company for getting into trouble or having fun . . . or both. South Park was a dead-end street of only a dozen or so modest residences, but it was home to legions of kids. The WWII baby boom was in full swing in the 1950s—an uptick in births nationwide that filled schools, playgrounds and streets with millions of children. Suburbia boomed right along with the birth rate. South Park Avenue was no exception. The Costins, Besses, Taylers, Metcalfs, Smiths, Beemers, Conquests and Whites were among the families who contributed kids, bikes, basketballs, pets, homemade forts, baseball gloves, slamming screen doors, footballs, sledding parties, and cheerful noise to their street.

"In those days, you were raised by the neighborhood," said White. "If you were misbehaving, a neighbor would discipline you and your parents would thank them for it. You felt safe. I think South Park was a pretty typical blue-collar neighborhood. Families stayed put. They didn't move in or out. We kids might fight like dogs and cats amongst ourselves, but boy, if anybody from outside the neighborhood picked on you, the older kids stepped in. I was fortunate enough to grow up in a neighborhood where it was all for one and one for all."

"Crown Point was an idyllic place to grow up," said Patrick 'Pat' Costin, a South Park Avenue neighbor and member of White's tight circle of lifelong friends. "There was no crime. Everybody knew everybody. If you cut through somebody's yard, by the time you got home, your mother already knew about it."

"If you went anywhere, you left your doors unlocked," said White. "I remember my parents saying, 'Well, what if the Costins need some sugar?' We'd go away for a week and leave the doors open. You'd leave your bicycle out on the driveway overnight and you knew that it was going to be right where you left it."

South Park kids of all ages ran in and out of each other's homes after school and on weekends, often plopping down at a neighbor's dinner table just in time to inhale a meal and head back out to play until dark. During the summer, the Conquest family operated Crown Point's mobile ice cream business, selling popsicles and ice cream sandwiches from three-wheeled carts. They ran the business out of their garage on South Park. Neighborhood kids could bang on the Conquests' door, buy their treats straight from the freezers, and race back to whatever game they were playing.

> "Dean loved big cars, Cadillacs," recalled Pat Costin, who grew up across the street from the Whites. "He loved hot cars too. He had a 1959 Corvette. It was red with white fins. It was a hot car, I'll tell you."

"We used to have this special yell to alert everyone that it was time to play a game," said White. "'Frosteos!!' I can't tell you where that came from. Everybody brought their ball gloves out and we'd go play baseball together. Or in the wintertime we'd play basketball in someone's driveway. Kids of all ages played together in the summertime. We played kick-the-can every night. And the college kids would be right there with the five-year-olds."

Lynn Bird, who married White's cousin Terry, marveled at the 'American Graffiti' stories she heard about South Park. "It was straight out of a movie. The things those boys did! They actually had fist fights. It's like a piece of Americana that is disappearing."

The kids weren't the only ones who cut loose. Dean White had his moments . . . much to the astonishment and delight of the neighborhood kids. He loved fast cars, especially if he was behind the wheel. As White Advertising began to thrive under his management, he bought himself bigger and better cars.

"Dean loved big cars, Cadillacs," recalled Pat Costin, who grew up across the street from the Whites. "He loved hot cars too. He had a 1959 Corvette. It was red with white fins. It was a hot car, I'll tell you. He'd come racing down South Park Avenue in second or third gear doing about 60 mph with a cigar hanging out of his mouth. My mom would come roaring out of the house: 'Dean White, you're going to kill these kids! What do you think you're doing?!' That would happen a couple of times a day."

Dean didn't limit his need for speed to South Park Avenue. Crown Point was home to a long stretch of dead straight road that was too tempting to resist.

"Nine-Mile Stretch is straight as an arrow, but not as flat as you might think," explained Pat Costin. "Even though Indiana is flat, that road does have some hills on it. My brother Larry was probably 16 at the time when he rode with Dean. He said, 'I was never so scared in my entire life! I was white knuckled. Dean was going 110 miles an hour down on Nine-Mile Stretch. We were flying through the air!'"

Bruce White's parents, Barbara and Dean White.

"My dad would have fit into South Park as a kid," said Bruce White. "He was a troublemaker. He was not a stay-inside-the-lines type of guy."

Neither was his son Bruce. White became an ace at skipping out of things that bored him. He once ditched a piano recital in favor of playing ball. Bypassing Sunday School was also a specialty.

"My parents would bring us to church, but our Sunday School classes were in a separate building. Mom and Dad would say 'See you!' and head into the church for the service. I would walk down to what we called the smoke shop and read sports magazines and comic books. I'd get back to the church just as the service ended."

One event that White did not want to skip out on was the family's summer and holiday vacations to the West Coast. For the four White siblings, the cross-country treks by train or car to visit relatives were grand adventures. Southern California was as exotic as the moon to kids from Indiana. Houses with private swimming pools. Endless sunshine. IHOPs, Big Boy's and McDonald's everywhere. Disneyland. Cars cruising the boulevards. Palm trees. Live music.

"When we got back to Indiana, we knew the new music before it got played in Chicago, so we thought we were really the cool kids," White told his Bird cousins in a 2022 group interview in Wyoming. "It was a transformational experience for us to go out and stay with you guys.

"Our aunts and uncles treated us so incredibly well," continued White. "Aunt Mary [Bird] knew I loved sports, so she'd take me to a ballgame. She'd take me to the track meet down at Mt. San Antonio College—the Mount Sac Relays. They were the Olympic preliminaries. I remember seeing Bob Seagren, who set a new U.S. record for the pole vault. Aunt Marilyn and Uncle Don [White], too, were wonderful—the hospitality was just over the top."

"A lot of our lives as kids centered on the close family relationships that our mothers and fathers had," said Terry Bird, Bruce's cousin. "I grew up hearing about Nebraska all the time. I remember Uncle Don coming and showing off his Nebraska watch that played the Nebraska fight song. I remember Uncle Paul coming out and reciting his long poems and talking about being the Chief Justice of the Supreme Court of Nebraska. And I remember Grandma coming out to visit and talking about F Street where they lived in Lincoln. Everything that we heard about, at least from the Whites, was about the family."

Trips to California were also the only opportunity to visit with Alta and Lee Bayse, Bruce's maternal grandparents, who lived near San Francisco. Lee Bayse had suffered a massive stroke years earlier and was bedridden.

> Success breeds arrogance, arrogance breeds overconfidence which inevitably leads to making poor investment decisions.

"They lived in Burlingame, in a really small house," recalled White. "My Bayse grandmother worked as an elevator operator at the Emporium, a department store in San Francisco. I would go see her when she was on the job because I thought it was the coolest thing to have my grandmother give me rides up and down the elevator. She was a rabid Giants fan. And so, whenever I went out there, we would always go to Candlestick Park together and watch the Giants play, which I thought of course was just the coolest thing. I thought it was cool that my grandmother knew so much about pro baseball.

"Sadly, I never could talk to my grandfather because he couldn't talk and he couldn't walk," continued White. "You have to have respect for the Greatest Generation. My grandmother worked full-time commuting in and out of the city to be an elevator operator *and* took care of my grandfather. They had no outside help."

One development that White would have been happy to miss out on was the family's move from South Park Avenue to the new Holiday Creek subdivision in Crown Point when he was 15.[14] He was heartily sorry to leave South Park behind, even though he understood that the family's old house was simply too small for two adults and four kids.

"The three of us boys, we didn't have a bedroom in the house on South Park. Our 'room' was a hallway. And I have to admit, as we got older, it wouldn't have worked out. Because if I built a model airplane, one of my brothers would break it. We were all on top of each other. The new house was probably 5,000 square feet. Each of us boys had our

---

[14]The Whites' Holiday Creek home was showcased in a long article in the *Muncie (IN) Times* on February 10, 1970.

own small bedrooms, but we shared one bathroom with our sister. At the time it was built it was probably the biggest house in Crown Point."

Exciting as it was to be living in a brand-new and modern house—complete with a pool, tennis court and wall-to-wall shag carpeting—White commented more than fifty years later that his "center of gravity stayed at South Park." So much so, in fact, that he often headed back to his old neighborhood after school to hang out with friends like Pat Costin. Costin, on the other hand, was only too happy to spend time at the Whites' fancy new Holiday Creek house.

"We used to have marathon ping-pong death matches on the big screened-in porch," said Costin. "Bruce's dad would get out there and

Bruce's parents and siblings: (front, left to right) Cindy White, parents Dean and Barbara White; (back, left to right) Bruce White, Craig White, and Chris White.

play against us. He was quick on his feet and used to revel in kicking our asses. Then there was the basketball court, the tennis court and the pool. For a kid, it was paradise."

Craig White loved "having competitions for who could swim the longest underwater and for the best dives. . . . Sometimes on summer nights, our dad would sleep on the screen porch with us kids. We made a lot of great memories in that house."

> **My dad pulled me into his den the night before I started work. He says, 'You're the boss's son. So, whether you like it or not, everybody in the plant is going to be looking at you and judging you.'**
>
> Bruce W. White

The Holiday Creek house was a tangible sign of Dean White's success in growing his late father's small outdoor advertising business. In the two decades since returning from the war, Dean had transformed the struggling sign company into a player at the national level. Sheer hard work was one of the ingredients, but timing and moxie were every bit as important. In the mid-1950s, while driving through Louisiana to deliver signs to customers, White stayed at a brand-new hotel in Baton Rouge—one of the earliest Holiday Inns. Impressed by the hotel's fresh look and reasonable rates, he asked a manager about plans for the chain. The man pointed Dean in the direction of the company's Memphis, Tennessee, headquarters. White drove to Memphis, where he tracked down co-founders Kemmons Wilson and Wallace Johnson in a lumberyard and pitched them on buying signs from White Advertising. In no time, the men struck a deal and White Advertising jumped on the Holiday Inn juggernaut, creating and delivering signs all over the country as the chain built new properties. White Advertising went from small-town to big-time in no time.

Delighted by his good fortune, but determined not to rest on his laurels, Dean made sure his children—especially Bruce and Craig—absorbed his old-fashioned work ethic at an early age. The kids were assigned yardwork and other chores around the house. As soon as they were old enough to hold a broom, mop or hammer, Dean introduced them to the 'joy' of working at White Advertising or at Crown Point's Henderlong Lumber—one of his many acquisitions.

"Dad put us to work at a young age," recalled Craig White. "I have no memory of what I got paid, but my first job was at Henderlong, the lumberyard. The foreman had a little fun with me. The first task he assigned me was to go over to the cafeteria and ask the guys to borrow 'the board stretcher.' Of course, I was too young to know that there's no such thing as a board stretcher! They all got a chuckle out of that.

"I was the youngest kid by far, working there. I can't tell you how many times I swept out the barn where all the lumber was stockpiled. After I was there a couple of years, I was able to drive around the lumberyard and go on deliveries. When I got assigned to go on a delivery, whether at a home or a construction site, I couldn't have been more excited. Unloading doors or lumber beat sweeping out that barn!"

Bruce's first job was at White Advertising's sign company in Shelby when he was 11 years old.

"I went to work at the sign factory in the summer between sixth and seventh grades. The minimum wage that year was $1.25 an hour. I was used to cutting grass for probably 30 cents an hour. So, $1.25 an hour was incredible."

Even more memorable was the talk his father gave him before his first day on the job.

"My dad pulled me into his den the night before I started work. He says, 'You're the boss's son. So, whether you like it or not, everybody in the plant is going to be looking at you and judging you. . . . All I ask is that you work hard and that you always feel like you deserve your paycheck.'

"Dad went on, 'The other thing I'm going to tell you is there are going to be times when your boss is going to ask you something, and it's going to be easy for you *not* to tell the truth. Maybe you got something accomplished that you hadn't or whatever. You should never tell a lie or not tell the entire truth.' And, he said, 'Sometimes it's going to be incredibly difficult for you to do this, but always tell the entire truth to your boss or your coworkers. Because, to build trust with your coworkers is something that's going to benefit you greatly in the long run if you can achieve that.' So, he goes, 'Understand that trust is your most valuable currency.'

White said many years later that what his father told him that night "stayed with me the rest of my life."

Dean White either sensed or saw that his oldest son had both the brains and maturity to handle assignments that many kids might have shied away from. He sent young Bruce out on the road with White Advertising sign installation crews.

"I remember our per diem per day, including hotel and meals, was $12. We would sleep three to a room in some backwoods hotel. The guys that had the jobs of going out on the road, making close to minimum wage, putting up signs, were, for the most part, a pretty rough group of people. I appreciated that my dad had enough confidence in me that at a young age, I could go out there and be with those guys and handle myself, because I knew I was going to get ribbed a lot. Again, I was the boss's son, and more often than not, that didn't give you an advantage. In fact, they used every opportunity to cut you down to size. I just thought that was an incredibly maturing event in my life."

> **"My dad's childhood is what made him who he was,"** said Otis White, Bruce's youngest child. **"He valued being a Region guy. He always thought of himself as a Region Rat."**

A closely related "maturing event" for White during his childhood was learning the importance of being able to get along with people from all walks of life, not just the men at the sign factory. He was proud to be a Region Rat—a term used to pigeonhole the thousands of youngsters who grew up in the shadow of the huge steel-making plants that dominated Northwest Indiana's economy. Aware that the label was meant to be an insult, White instead wore it with special pride.

"My dad's childhood is what made him who he was," said Otis White, Bruce's youngest child. "He valued being a Region guy. He always thought of himself as a Region Rat."

Working construction jobs was especially appealing to White. He liked the hustle, teamwork, and honestly earned sweat that went with spending a day in hot sun and endless dirt, amid the roar of hammers, drills and backhoes. And he liked feeling that he had earned his paycheck.

Construction fit White's personality. He loved to build things—a passion that would become a defining theme of his approach to life, business and more. Construction also turned out to be the gateway to his future vocation: hospitality.

But, first, Mary Gertrude White's lifelong mantra rang out loud and clear for her grandson Bruce: "Education, education, education!"

Next stop: College.

CHAPTER 3

The School of Life

> "The one common religion in our family was education. Our parents basically said, 'Look, you're got to get an education. That's number one. We don't care what your major is.... After that, it was 'Your life is your life.'"
>
> **Terry Bird**
> Cousin

On June 8, 2011, Indiana Governor Mitch Daniels appointed alumnus Bruce White—Class of 1975—to Purdue University's Board of Trustees. People who knew White in his role as chairman of White Lodging likely weren't surprised by the news. But forty years earlier, few of White's classmates and fraternity brothers would have imagined that their fun-loving comrade would one day grace the university's prestigious and powerful Board.

At the head of the line of skeptics would have been White himself.

"I think I have fairly severe ADHD and I hated sitting in class," said White in a 2022 interview. "I hated the structure. When I went to Purdue, I rarely went to class. That's not an exaggeration. I only went to class before a test so I could cram or meet somebody who could share their notes with me. If we had had smart phones back then, I would have been scrolling and not paying attention to the professors. So, instead of classes, I spent my time playing basketball in Co-Rec, the main recreation building. The night before an exam, I could usually get a friend in the class to take me through some things and I could get a B or A.

"When I became a trustee at Purdue many years later, they wanted all us trustees to say how influential the faculty was on us and what a great experience we had and how it changed our lives. I felt really bad because I knew what they wanted me to say and why. But I'm a very candid, transparent person. I had to say, 'That's just not my story.'"

Instead, White's story can be neatly summed up with one of his favorite lines: "I never let my schooling get in the way of my education."

When Bruce White graduated from Crown Point's high school in the Spring of 1971, the next four years of his life were mapped out . . . at least in theory. He had been accepted into Purdue's management program and would begin classes at the main campus in West Lafayette, Indiana in the fall.

Purdue was a natural choice for someone who loved sports as much as White did. Applying for admission was an easy decision.

"Back then, you really didn't think about going out of state," said Beth White, Bruce's wife and a fellow Purdue alumna. "I think his mom wanted Bruce to look elsewhere, but he really didn't have much interest."

Like many Hoosiers, the White family were big fans of Purdue's sports teams and often tailgated at games. Bruce grew up knowing all the players' names and team stats. In 1967, the University unveiled Purdue Arena, a new 14,000-seat facility to replace Lambert Fieldhouse. In 1972—during White's undergraduate days—the popular arena was renamed Mackey Arena, in honor of longtime athletic director Guy "Red" Mackey. For a young sports fan, Purdue offered a slice of heaven.

> During White's time at Purdue, Beta House was known for its fun-loving attitude and parties. In the 1973 Purdue yearbook, the fraternity brothers—including Bruce White—are garbed in bath towels or bathrobes in their official portrait.

What Purdue did not offer—at least for Bruce White—was a curriculum capable of enthralling his restless mind. Conventional undergraduate coursework was tedious for him. A psychological profile of White done in the 1980s confirmed what he had known from early childhood: He was a non-conformist 'freewheeler'—a personality type that included people who are "stubborn, self-confident, very independent . . . [and] may enjoy bending the rules. . . . They are fierce competitors who do not like constant direction and will fight or resist someone looking over their shoulder. They find discipline and rules distasteful."

Another 'freewheeler' trait was White's natural friendliness. From childhood until the end of his life, White would make and keep friends from every era of his life. During his four years at Purdue, he thrived on meeting new people . . . especially if they could dribble a basketball. Hours of playing games in Co-Rec brought him into contact with dozens of classmates from Indiana and elsewhere. His time on the basketball court and in casual conversations with his Purdue classmates added to the life skills that he had begun to hone during his teen years working in construction and traveling with White Advertising's road crews. Getting along with people from different backgrounds and treating them with respect would become White's personal and professional mantra.

> Effective strategy is defined as much by what it leaves out as what it includes.

Another source of friendships for White was his fraternity: Beta Theta Pi. One of the oldest fraternities still in existence, Beta was founded in 1839 at Miami University in Oxford, Ohio. Purdue's Beta Theta Pi chapter was founded in 1903.

During White's time at Purdue, Beta House was known for its fun-loving attitude and parties. In the 1973 Purdue yearbook, the fraternity brothers—including Bruce White—are garbed in bath towels or bathrobes in their official portrait. Mike Wells, a fellow Beta, chuckled as he recalled the boisterous devil-may-care atmosphere of Beta House during his term as house president fifty years ago.

"Bruce found a beautiful old-time bar from a place that was being torn down somewhere in Northwest Indiana. He installed it at Beta House. So, we had our own bar. We had keggers and were partying all the time. Remember, this was during the Vietnam War. People were smoking dope, which was illegal. It was a full-time job as house president trying to deal with some of what went on."

White lived in Beta House his sophomore and junior years and then opted to spend most of his senior year in an off-campus apartment. During his junior year, he met freshman Steve Poe, a fellow Hoosier and avid basketball player. Bruce paved the way for Poe to join Beta Theta Pi.

"I played basketball at Co-Rec, so that's how I met Bruce," said Poe. "Betas were very good academically, but they were also known for taking pride in their athletics. I got recruited to Beta Theta Pi during a game on the basketball court. They wanted me on their basketball team. At that point, I didn't know really anything about Bruce. He and some other guys picked me up at my dorm and took me through the rushing process. Bruce was my pledge 'pop.' He sponsored me and then mentored me. We went through pledge shift for a whole semester and then you became a full member after that. My first semester of my sophomore year, Bruce and I roomed together in the fraternity."

Becoming friends with White introduced Poe to the world beyond Indiana. The younger man hailed from sparsely populated Crawford County and had rarely traveled out of state. So, he was thrilled to take up White's invitation to join him on a trip out to California in the summer of 1974.

"Bruce was going to fly out West to help move his Bayse grandmother. He said, 'You want to come help me and we'll go hang out in California for a while?' That trip was the first time I'd ever been on an airplane. We met his mom Barbara out there and helped with the move. Then for the next month or so Bruce and I literally hitchhiked from Los Angeles to San Diego to Tijuana to San Francisco. We just meandered around the state.

"We would go to college campuses to see if their Beta House—if they had a chapter there—was open, and we would stay there," continued Poe. "If not, we would just change our fraternity affiliation to whichever house was open. Free food, free place to stay. At UCLA, we were able to stay at the Beta House; in fact, we stayed there twice on that trip."

The UCLA stop was particularly memorable for both men. While playing hoops near campus, the pair met a few students from the school who shared their passion for basketball. UCLA was home to Pauly Pavilion, an 11,000-seat arena, built in 1965. It

> **"For Bruce and me, Pauley Pavilion was a temple, a church, a cathedral. So, for two Indiana boys to get to play basketball there was unbelievable. We walked in and Bruce actually got down on his knees and gestured toward heaven!"**
>
> Steve Poe
> Friend + Business Partner

was also home to legendary head coach John Wooden—the "Wizard of Westwood"—who took the UCLA Bruins to ten NCAA national championships in twelve years, including seven championships in a row. Two of his players were widely idolized: Kareem Abdul-Jabar and Bill Walton. The icing on the cake for White and Poe? Wooden was a Beta Theta Pi brother, who had played for the Purdue Boilermakers from 1929 to 1932.

"The guys we met told us that they played pick-up games at night in Pauley Pavilion," said Poe. "For Bruce and me, Pauley Pavilion was a temple, a church, a cathedral. So, for two Indiana boys to get to play basketball there was unbelievable. We walked in and Bruce actually got down on his knees and gestured toward heaven!"

> "We poured Bruce into the back seat and he threw up all the way home. We carried him down to the basement to what we called The Cave. He was kept on major concussion protocol for about a week and a half."
>
> Pat Costin
> Friend

Basketball was White's number one sports passion, but not the only one. In high school he played on both the basketball and football teams. He continued playing basketball for many years, but his football career came to a crashing halt—literally—a year before he graduated from high school.

"Bruce was really passionate about football in high school," said brother Craig White. "He loved the sport. But he endured not one, not two, but THREE concussions while playing. The third time was so serious that the doctor stayed at our house."

"Bruce had a massive concussion when he was a junior in high school," said Pat Costin, a childhood friend. "He got hit so hard by a linebacker he was literally knocked out. So, his father and I came down from the visitor's side as fast as we could. Dean saw Bruce throw up on the field and said, 'I'm taking my son home.' He sent me to get his car, a big old Lincoln Mercury. I pulled up on the track, while the opposing team was booing us! We poured Bruce into the back seat and he threw up all the way home. We carried him down to the basement to what we called The Cave. He was kept on major concussion protocol for about a week and a half."

> Always take the high road... it is much less crowded!

White recovered from the blow, but the family doctor told the Whites that Bruce should never play football again—news that Barbara White knew would deeply disappoint her son.

"Mom made it a mission to find something to replace football for Bruce," said Craig White. "She told the family that we were going to go up to Boyne Mountain, Michigan to go skiing. None of us wanted to go. In Crown Point, it was all football, basketball, and baseball. Our dad was also reluctant to go, but finally agreed with one proviso: the family had to stop on the way back to Crown Point and watch the Chicago Bears game. So, we went and the rest is history. We all fell in love with skiing."

The Whites bought a condominium in Snowmass, Colorado, a resort tucked within Aspen. All four White kids—Cindy, Bruce, Chris, and Craig—enjoyed their time on the slopes. Craig White recalled spending "every Christmas and every spring vacation" there. "Some of the absolute best memories of our family together were made at Snowmass."

South Park neighbor Pat Costin recalled his introduction to skiing with the Whites... not at a ski resort, but in Crown Point:

"Bruce's father cleared out a small hill in Crown Point and got an old Ford engine and fired it up. So, we had a rope tow to hang onto to get back to the top. You had more fun going *up* the hill with the rope than you had going *down* because going down was four seconds of lickety-split. Then you grabbed onto the rope tow, held on, and went right back up to the top."

Swapping out football for skiing was a win-win for White. Thanks to his mother, he discovered a new passion that would occupy him for decades, one that he could share with friends and family. Purdue pal Steve Poe recalled visiting the Whites' Snowmass condo during his sophomore year.

"Bruce took a group of us to stay at his parents' condo. I can't believe his dad allowed us to stay there. I wouldn't let a bunch of 19- and 20-year-olds use *my* place!"

The ski slopes played to White's highly competitive nature. Any sport that offered a chance to measure his skills against others appealed to him. He loved to yodel at top volume as he hurled himself down the ski runs. In later years he enjoyed taking friends and colleagues skiing . . . especially if they couldn't keep up with him. Deno Yiankes, who joined White Lodging in 1990, had almost no ski experience when he went along on one of White's trips West.

"I had skied only two other times in my life before going skiing with Bruce," said Yiankes. "This was in 1992. A group of us flew out to Big Sky, Montana. I had skied on a couple of bunny hills in Indiana. I didn't know what black, blue, red or green markers meant. So, we go up on one of the black trails. I get off the lift. It was something like negative 20 degrees up there! I couldn't even see the run clearly."

Yiankes soon learned the hard way that a black trail marker meant "very difficult."

"Everybody else takes off, so I started to ski down. There's no instructor or any kind of help. I lost everyone in the group. I got about a third of the way down the run and my skis popped off. I literally slid down the mountain carrying my skis. At the bottom there's Bruce and the rest of them. Bruce laughed and asked, 'Hey, Dude, did you make it?' I replied, 'That's NOT funny, Bruce!' I was miserable. But it really *was* funny. He was competitive, to say the least."

As much as White loved to ski, basketball remained nearer and dearer to his heart. On South Park, he had played hoops for hours on end in neighbors' driveways and local playgrounds. When he was 12 years old, White and three other Crown Point boys were selected for a pre-high school basketball camp at DePauw University in the summer

Bruce loved playing basketball and was intense on the court at Purdue.

of 1965. His Crown Point junior high basketball team steamrolled its competitors, hosted sell-out crowds, and was covered in glory by local newspapers.

White admitted that his team's success went to their heads: "Confidence morphed into arrogance. We thought we ran the school." But the upside was having a "great coach who taught us how to win and achieve at the highest levels. I think that stuck with me all my life. I never had any expectation that anything I was involved in would be less than the best."

By the time White set foot on Purdue's campus in the fall of 1971, basketball was deeply embedded in his DNA. He was so intense on the court that playing against him—or even being on his team—guaranteed plenty of trash talking and relentless pressure to win. Woe to anyone who hankered for a low-key game of b-ball if Bruce White was on the court.

> "My friend Lacy Johnson, who is black, used to say, 'People are people,'" said White. "That was our deal, and it's why we got along so well. We didn't look at each other as black or white; we just looked at each other as friends."

But basketball's appeal for White went beyond free throws, fast breaks, and slam dunks. Unlike skiing, which is usually a solo activity, basketball involves teams. For White, one of the principal charms of the game was meeting and playing with anyone from close friends to total strangers. Well into his adult years, White always kept basketballs and gym clothes in the trunk of his car, ready to play wherever, whenever and with whomever was available.

During his four years at Purdue, White cemented several close friendships at Co-Rec, his favorite hangout. His circle included African American classmates who loved basketball as much as White did. In his eyes, the game was a natural equalizer. At a time when race was still a powerful force in many aspects of American life, Co-Rec's basketball court was a place where all that mattered was playing hard and winning fairly.

"My friend Lacy Johnson, who is black, used to say, 'People are people,'" said White. "That was our deal, and it's why we got along so well. We didn't look at each other as black or white; we just looked at each

Bruce with his friend Lacy Johnson, who reveled in the sense of equality he felt being on the basketball court.

other as friends. Lacy would say, 'I'm just pounding basketballs.' When you get on a court and all you've got on is a pair of shorts, a pair of Converse sneakers and a jock strap, everybody's equal. I love that idea of equality."

Johnson, who remained a dear friend of White for fifty years, recalled a pivotal moment when race could have derailed the easy camaraderie between black and white players at Co-Rec.

"Bruce and I played on the same team sometimes, but we often ended up on opposing teams," said Johnson. "Even when we were freshmen and sophomores, Bruce was already a leader in his fraternity. And I was a leader in mine. Bruce had a fiercely competitive streak, I mean *fiercely* competitive. At the same time, he was one of the fairest people that you could ever meet. Many times, these intramural games would be really close and the two sides would argue over a ref's call.

"In 1975, my all-black Omega Psi Phi fraternity's team and Bruce's all-white Beta Theta Pi team faced off in the finals of the fraternity league," continued Johnson. "The Omegas got

> The fraternity exchange showcased White's growing maturity, leadership skills, sense of fair play, and collaborative mindset—all of which would help to fuel his later success. On the basketball court and at Beta House, White was gleaning valuable lessons for finetuning his approach to business and life.

..Members from Beta Theta Pi and Omega Psi Phi have initiated a member exchange program that is a unique step forward in interracial relations.

Purdue first

Betas, Qs have 1st interracial exchange

By JOHN ARNOLD
Staff Writer

Fraternity brothers from Beta Theta Pi and Omega Psi Phi are exchanging several members this week.

The situation is unique in that the exchange is between a white fraternity, Beta Theta Pi, and a black fraternity, Omega Psi Phi, the first time a project like this has been attempted at Purdue.

The originators of the concept are Bruce White, from Beta Theta Pi, and Freddy Burrus, from the Qs, as Omega Psi Phi is

the issue out in the open If it's all talk and no action, nothing is achieved. We need to communicate."

The exchange will involve five members of the Beta house and eight members of the Q's. Both White and Burrus will participate with the members involved.

"Fraternities are not just country clubs. We want to do something for the community. You can never tell where this thing can go after this," White said.

Prior to the exchange,

dinner with the Q's little sisters and Indianapolis Mayor Richard Lugar.

A banquet, which will be attended by President Hansen and his family, John Jeffries from the dean of admissions office, and various faculty members, will be held Thursday night. WLFI-TV will cover the events, according to White.

Later in the year, a dance is scheduled between both houses and will serve as a finale to the exchange to hopefully

> The fraternity exchange was so novel it was featured in the local newspaper.

the worse end of the deal. We said that it was because all the refs were white. Of course, it's human nature to blame a loss on calls that don't go your way. Well, the two teams started arguing and we barely stopped it. The matter got referred to the Dean of Student Affairs, who called in the fraternity leaders. Bruce and a couple of guys showed up for Beta House. Freddie Burrus and I represented Omega Psi Phi fraternity. After some discussion we agreed that if we got to know each other better, a lot of things would resolve themselves."

"Thanks to Bruce's diplomacy, we agreed that the two fraternities would do a house exchange for a week," continued Johnson. "Several members of Omega moved into Beta's house on Littleton Street; a few Betas moved into our Omega house."

The Beta-Omega fraternity house exchange was so novel—and successful—that the local *Purdue Exponent* and *The Lafayette Courier and*

Journal both featured the story as a breakthrough moment for race relations at Purdue.

"I really don't know where I got the idea of the exchange," White explained to the newspapers. He noted that it took a couple of months to get everyone on board and organize the week-long experiment, which included hosting social functions every night. The fraternity exchange showcased White's growing maturity, leadership skills, sense of fair play, and collaborative mindset—all of which would help to fuel his later success. On the basketball court and at Beta House, White was gleaning valuable lessons for finetuning his approach to business and life.

White told the press that he had "people coming up to me on campus the next day I didn't even know telling me how neat they thought the whole thing was. It was just unreal, it really makes me feel great."

"What came out of that week were friendships," said Lacy Johnson in a 2023 interview. "After that, we were welcome into each other's houses. The most beautiful thing about the exchange was getting to know other cultures."

> **Bruce had the IQ and the ability to recollect the most incredible minutiae. He rarely—if ever—forgot someone's name. ... He had the ability to go into a situation and communicate easily with *anyone* regardless of age, race, creed, whatever.**
>
> Pat Costin
> Friend

Childhood friend Pat Costin wasn't surprised that White paved the way for the two groups to get to know one another: "Bruce had the IQ and the ability to recollect the most incredible minutiae. He rarely—if ever—forgot someone's name. . . . He had the ability to go into a situation and communicate easily with *anyone* regardless of age, race, creed, whatever."

White credited his lifelong ease with meeting people from every walk of life to his upbringing in The Region. Going on the road with White Advertising's rough-and-gruff sign installers in his early teens taught him to get along with people whose background was markedly different from his own. On South Park, his neighbors included steel mill workers, a carpenter and utility company employees—mostly blue-collar families mixed with a few white-collar families. Despite moving to a different neighborhood, Dean and Barbara never lost touch with their

South Park neighbors. Bruce followed suit, often hanging out with his old South Park friends on weekends during his last years in high school. At Purdue, he added a whole new circle of friends, including two future business partners: Beta Theta Pi fraternity brothers Steve Poe and Mike Wells. Three decades later, White's appointment to Purdue's Board of Trustees would channel his affection for his alma mater and fraternity brothers into initiatives to boost Purdue's business programs for future generations of Bruce Whites.

In the meantime, as graduation from Purdue approached in the spring of 1975, White looked forward to two major changes: no more classes and his first post-college job. The latter, he hoped, would take him "away from Indiana. Not because I hated Indiana, I just wanted a grand adventure."

He didn't have to wait long. White had been chosen by one of his management program professors to be a 'campus host' for guest lecturers. Dr. J. Fred McLimore, former head of human resources at Ralston Purina, organized a program to bring CEOs and other C-suite level leaders to speak to business students at Purdue. Campus hosts were responsible for taking the day's guest to lunch after the class.

> After Cindy's friend gave him a tour of the bustling hotel, White could not stop himself from comparing the prospect of a cubicle in St. Louis with the allure of living in sunny California and working in a busy hotel.

"They didn't give us any specific instructions," said White, chuckling. "We were just supposed to not be idiots and act like we were responsible young people."

White received numerous job offers from the executives he met, including one invitation from the CEO of Ralston Purina. Based in St. Louis, Ralston Purina had been founded in 1894 as an animal feed supplier. By the time White was offered a job in 1975, the company had expanded into multiple markets and product lines. Sales for the diversified conglomerate tripled from $1 billion to more than $3 billion between 1964 and 1974. The icing on the cake for White was the Keystone ski resort in Colorado, purchased by Ralston Purina his junior year.

"The job I was offered was incredible for 1975," said White. "The salary was $15,500. I would have been in the company's fast-track executive development program in corporate finance."

> I never let school get in the way of my education.

Despite the opportunity, White wasn't jazzed by the idea of sitting in a cubicle in St. Louis. Being glued to a desk reminded him of going to class. But the offer from the CEO was too good to refuse. White accepted the Ralston Purina job, aware that many of his classmates would have given "their right arms to get the same offer."

In mid-April of his senior year, Alta May Bayse—his maternal grandmother—died at age 86 on the West Coast. Purdue pal Steve Poe and White had moved her to a new residence just a year earlier. White flew to California for the funeral. While there he met an acquaintance of his sister Cindy, a man who was a beverage manager at the Hyatt Regency San Francisco Airport.

After Cindy's friend gave him a tour of the bustling hotel, White could not stop comparing the prospect of a cubicle in St. Louis with the allure of living in sunny California and working in a busy hotel. As a kid, he had visited his Bird cousins several times at their home near Los Angeles on family vacations. One of his favorite memories was the Corvette owned by his Aunt Dot White, who sometimes let Terry Bird—the oldest of the cousins—drive. For 22-year-old White, California was exotic, tantalizing, and promised the kind of "grand adventure" he was looking for.

"I was staying at the Burlingame Hyatt, right next door to Hyatt's corporate headquarters," said White. "On Saturday morning I went over and knocked on the door. The senior vice president of human resources was getting ready to play tennis at the courts across the street. He gave me a half hour of his time, at the end of which he offered me a job as a corporate management trainee. The salary, I think, was $8,400 annual—half of what Ralston Purina had offered me."

White accepted Hyatt's offer. Goodbye, St. Louis; hello, Monterey.

"If not for my grandmother's funeral, I never would've gone to work for Hyatt," said White many years later. "I probably would've gone to work for Ralston Purina and been miserable the rest of my life."

One small hiccup: White didn't tell his parents about his change of mind. When the family returned to Indiana after the funeral for Barbara's mother, Hyatt called to confirm Bruce's arrival date. Barbara White answered the phone and told Hyatt matter-of-factly that there must a be mistake: her son had taken a position at Ralston Purina. Fortunately, the miscommunication was quickly corrected, and White began packing his bags.

When he arrived at the Del Monte Hyatt House in Monterey in his trusty blue Econoline van, he discovered that the hotel was completely full. He had been promised two weeks of free housing in the hotel. His new boss, Jerry Gleason, had an idea.

"He noticed my van and asked if I had a sleeping bag," said White. "'Yeah,' I said. Gleason replied, 'If you'll live out of your van, we can let you use the employee bathroom, which has a shower.'"

White was game: "So, for the first two weeks in Monterey, I slept in my van in a hotel employee parking lot!"

> *It was nothing for me to open the kitchen at four o'clock in the morning to bake off the bacon and do the sauces, set up the line, work until 2:30 p.m., go home for two hours, come back at 4-4:30 p.m. and work banquets till 9:00 at night. And I loved it. ... Because it was all learning. I was drinking from the fire hose. I would have worked there for nothing, I learned so much.*
>
> — Bruce W. White

Gleason had more in store for his newest recruit. Management trainees were put through a kind of 'boot camp' to cure them of any illusions about their status. When White reported to Gleason's office in the new sport coat that his father had bought for him, his boss looked him over.

"Nice coat," said Gleason, reaching for an item on his desk. "But here's your uniform. Put this on."

Gleason handed White an orange jumpsuit, the standard uniform of Hyatt housemen.

"He called in a fellow named Eddie, whose role was the public area houseman," said White. "His job was to keep the public areas, bathrooms and toilets clean. My boss said, 'For the first week you're going to be working with Eddie.'"

Gleason waited for White's reaction. Certain that his boss was testing him, White undressed on the spot and slipped into the uniform. Gleason's office had glass walls, so White's wardrobe change was visible to anyone walking down the hallway.

"I think I won him over right then and there," said White, chuckling at the memory. "I never complained or asked for anything. My boss became a strong advocate for me."

For the next few months, White's schedule was non-stop . . . and he loved every minute of it. The hours were brutal, but nothing he was asked to do came close to the hard construction work of his teen years.

"I was working 80 hours a week at the hotel, making $700 a month. My van broke down, so I had to ride my bicycle to work for about six months. It was nothing for me to open the kitchen at four o'clock in the morning to bake off the bacon and do the sauces, set up the line, work until 2:30 p.m., go home for two hours, come back at 4-4:30 p.m. and work banquets till 9:00 at night. And I loved it. . . . Because it was all learning. I was drinking from the fire hose. I would have worked there for nothing, I learned so much."

> **"This is absolutely true: my mother threatened to divorce him, because we kids weren't going to have money to go to college. I remember our minister, Reverend Wright, coming over to talk my dad . . . I hid on the stairs, and I heard the whole conversation: 'Dean, we need to pray about this.'"**
>
> Bruce W. White

Many years later, White advised hospitality students at Purdue to forget about starting salaries: "I know it's easy for me to say, but I would not care about what my starting salary was in my job getting out of school; I would look at what the opportunity was in the company. Obviously, a growth organization presents a lot more opportunity than a non-growth organization, particularly an organization that's growing organically as opposed to mergers and acquisitions. I would look at the one that allowed me to get a very broad background because that's what it's going to take if you really aspire to a senior management position."

At the end of his year-long training program, Hyatt offered White a promotion and transfer to New Orleans. But he had already decided he should go back to school to earn an M.B.A. He applied to and was accepted into the graduate business program at Indiana University's School of Business.

Rather than head to New Orleans, only to quit 90 days later to go back to school, White decided to return to Crown Point. He figured he would use his union card to work construction and earn good money for the summer.

Dean White, however, had other ideas. In 1969, he had let himself be talked into building a Holiday Inn—one of his many small side ventures. The spot he picked was at the junction of I-65—which was just being built—and U.S. 30 in Merrillville.

"Dad bought a farm," said White. "This is absolutely true: my mother threatened to divorce him, because we kids weren't going to have money to go to college. I remember our minister, Reverend Wright, coming over to talk my dad . . . I hid on the stairs, and I heard the whole conversation: 'Dean, we need to pray about this.' And I remember my dad's investment club members literally begging him not to do it."

Dean went ahead anyway. In time, the location would prove to be an excellent choice. But there was a major hitch. Eight years after construction, the Merrillville Holiday Inn had yet to turn a profit. Dean knew nothing about managing hotels. But his Hyatt-trained son certainly did.

"My dad figured I had a college degree and a year at Hyatt. So he asked me to try to clean it up and at least generate a positive cash flow," said White. "So, I agreed to look into it. They hemorrhaged money in food and beverage. They didn't have any labor control. I had enough knowledge I could fix a lot of this stuff. It was not rocket science, it was just basic wage and purchase order control. But they had none of these things in place."

White's decision turned out to be life-altering.

"Fixing the hotel's problems delayed graduate school first by one semester . . . then two semesters . . . then three semesters," he said years later.

White's search for a "grand adventure" after college was slowly leading him where he least expected: home.

CHAPTER 4

"BB" and "AB"

> "My dad called me up. I was in Houston. Dad said, "You get your ass home. Now! If it wasn't for your mother, I'd fire you over the phone."
>
> Bruce W. White

On the evening of December 6, 1979, the brand-new Holiday Star Theatre in Merrillville, Indiana, officially opened its doors to the public for the first time. Hundreds of well-wishers turned out for the soft opening, delighted to gawk at the fancy new theater and congratulate its principal backer: Dean White. Guests were treated to a performance of "4 Girls 4", starring Rose Marie, Rosemary Clooney, Helen O'Connell, and Margaret Whiting.

For the previous twelve months, drivers passing by the intersection of U.S. 30 and I-65 had watched the skeleton of the 3,400-seat theater slowly rise from the empty cornfield next to the Whites' ten-year-old Holiday Inn. The scale of the new building was not the main attraction. Residents of the Region were accustomed to far more massive structures: U.S. Steel's sprawling Gary Works were only 18 miles to the north of Merrillville. What was intriguing about the new theater was its novelty. For the first time, residents of the Region no longer had to drive 40 miles into downtown Chicago to attend a major concert. Now the

Holiday Star Theater (renamed Star Plaza Theater)

area's music fans would have a theater to call their own—one designed with sightlines and acoustics so perfect that music lovers from all over would come to Merrillville.

When disco diva and global megastar Donna Summer rocked the stage for a standing-room-only crowd on the theater's grand opening night—December 19, 1979—the Holiday Star's bright future was assured.

◆◆◆◆◆

Unlike the Holiday Inn project a decade earlier, Dean White's idea to build a large theater in Merrillville did not inspire threats of divorce or visits by the family clergy. By the late 1970s, Dean White had plenty of cash flow from his principal business. White Advertising was booming.

If Dean White wanted to build a theater on his own dime, to benefit Northwest Indiana, why not?

> **Donna Summer was the biggest star in the world at that time. And here I was—26 years old—sitting talking with her after a show in her dressing room!**
>
> Bruce W. White

The idea for the Holiday Star sprang directly from an earlier effort to bring summertime theater to nearby Valparaiso. Dean White's friend and contemporary Bill Wellman had launched the Bridge-Vu Theater in the summer of 1968. A large green and white tent that seated 450 people was set up in a town parking lot. Wellman booked well-known talent, including Count Basie, Duke Ellington, Victor Borge and comedienne Phyllis Diller to perform in the small outdoor theater. Opening night was memorable. A torrential downpour revealed multiple leaks in the new tent and prompted the actors on stage to applaud the audience at the end for sticking with them through the storm.

"[The tent] was too cold, too hot, it leaked, and we had mosquitoes," recalled Wellman a decade later. Still—leaks and all—it was live theater and brand-name acts. Even after several summers of losing money, Wellman continued to believe that the area deserved a real theater. He approached his pal Dean White with an idea for a permanent performance space . . . right next to White's Merrillville Holiday Inn. A key point: the theater would help fill up the hotel every weekend.

White was an easy sell.

"My dad always liked having an adventure," said Bruce White. "He grew up poor and remembered the traveling Chautauqua shows of his childhood in Nebraska."

Dean initially entertained visions of a dinner theater, but his son did his best to talk his father out of the idea. The younger White knew that the appeal of dinner theater was mainly limited to an older crowd and would probably fare no better financially than Wellman's Bridge-Vu theater. To be successful, any year-round theater would need to offer a variety of shows, with a heavy emphasis on music. It was also critical that the theater match or exceed the standards of other well-known concert venues. Ticket sales would depend on the eagerness of out-of-town music fans to come long distances to experience state-of-the-art acoustics and amenities.

> Success is not owned … it is rented and the rent is due every day!

It was a tall order for anyone, but especially so for Dean's multifaceted business enterprise—Whiteco Industries—which had built condominiums and apartments but had no experience with something as complex as a large performance space.

"None of us knew what we were doing," Bruce White recalled. "We designed it out of a textbook with the help of an architect. We were winging it. I knew nothing about theaters."

Many people might have thrown up their hands and walked away or done their best to scale back the project. For White, the theater had the opposite effect: it appealed to his appetite for taking on a big challenge—a trait that would become one of his trademarks for the rest of his life.

In a Summer 1988 profile of White in Purdue's *Krannert Portfolio*,[15] he noted: "We had to learn quickly, because gaining experience in the entertainment business can be a very expensive learning curve, much more than that of an MBA degree. Believe me, our 'tuition' was very high whenever we made a mistake."

---

[15]"Bruce White's Rising Star," *Krannert Portfolio,* Purdue University, Summer 1988. https://earchives.lib.purdue.edu/digital/collection/kmag/id/1208/rec/2

The planned theatre was comprised of two seating levels in a semicircle around the stage. The main floor seated 2,000 people; the mezzanine level accommodated 1,400. The furthest seat in the auditorium was only 120 feet from the stage.

"It was incredibly hard work," said White. "I mean, the hours we put in were just unbelievable. But what a learning experience. I enjoyed it thoroughly."

By the time ground was broken for the theater in late 1978, a revamp of the Holiday Inn was also on the drawing board. The makeover included creation of a public space dubbed the Holidome, complete with tropical trees brought in from Florida, a sauna, indoor pool, whirlpool and children's play area. A convention center was available for meetings.

An enclosed walkway connected the hotel to the theater, so concertgoers did not have to go outside.

> But it wasn't long before Bruce found himself tasked with a new job that many would consider a dream assignment: booking acts for the theater.

The 1988 *Krannert Portfolio* profile of White touted the Holiday Star hotel-theater combination as Bruce's brainchild and "the first of its kind in the U.S." White explained that the novel concept was "created to solve what we saw as a problem—the lack of weekend business to balance the strong weekday business generated by area industries." Like his appetite for taking on big challenges, White's willingness to innovate would become one of his trademarks.

Two days after the soft opening in December 1979, *Chicago Tribune* reporter Larry Kart pronounced the new Holiday Star Theater "the kind of entertainment 'menu' the Chicago area has long needed."

Kart continued: "The only drawback (and for many it might not be a drawback at all) is that the theater is located in Merrillville . . . about an hour's drive from the Loop. Residents of Chicago's North Side or the northern suburbs may find the trek a bit forbidding, which would be a shame because the line-up of forthcoming acts . . . is almost as appealing as the theater itself."

Dean White's friend Bill Wellman was named General Manager of the Holiday Star and White stayed put in his role as director of room operations of the adjacent hotel. But it wasn't long before Bruce found himself tasked with a new job that many would consider a dream assignment: booking acts for the theater.

"At first, we hired a company to help us book the theater," recalled White. The arrangement didn't last long. The Whites discovered that the agency was skimming money off the contracts. After firing the company, Bruce jumped into the role.

"That's how I got involved in booking. It wasn't because I wanted to do it, it was out of necessity."

White brought to the job a deep love of music of all genres—ranging from well-known musical groups to obscure niche artists. In high school he had learned to play the saxophone well enough to land first chair in the band. Listening to all kinds of music and singing along with gusto—on-key or off—became a life-long habit.

"Bruce was a savant when it came to music," said his childhood friend Pat Costin. "He had a collection of hundreds of albums and thousands of CDs. He introduced me to all kinds of music that I would never have heard otherwise. Reggae, for example. When we were ten years old, it was Stevie Wonder. When we got to high school, Sly and the Family Stone, The Fifth Dimension, and the Doors. In college, the Doobie Brothers, Bee Gees, and the Beach Boys."

White was soon on the road to places like Nashville and New York City, meeting booking agents, attending concerts and auditions, and going backstage to meet musicians. He also had the pleasure of introducing friends to the big-name stars who played at the Holiday Star.

"I called Bruce up one day and asked him if he could get me tickets to the Luther

Liberace accepts the Holiday Star Theatre Award from Bruce White for ticket sales exceeding $1 million.

> While on one of his out-of-town trips, White received an irate call from his father, ordering him back to Merrillville. The infamous call entered the White family annals as one of the most loved and laughed-about stories.

Vandross show at the theater," recalled Lacy Johnson, a Purdue classmate. "Of course, he said yes, so my wife Patti and I were able to go. Then, Bruce being Bruce, he took us backstage to meet Vandross. 'Come on back, I'm going to introduce you to Luther.' Totally comfortable. Amazing."

"For me personally, it was an exciting business," said White. "What's not fun for a young person to be able to go to Los Angeles, New York and other cities every month and hang out with the Nederlander brothers or go to dinner with the head of William Morris? It's a business based on relationships, so I built bonds with every primary agent I could."

In addition to booking acts for the Holiday Star, White was still responsible for the ever-expanding Holiday Inn complex, as well as checking up on several small hotels that his father had added to his company's tiny hospitality division. Locations required road trips to Evansville, Bloomington, and Warsaw—all in Indiana—plus Louisville, Kentucky.

"I had no corporate support, just one secretary and a car," he recalled. "I was driving from town to town in my Toyota. Talk about multitasking! Besides being on the road, I was still running the Holiday Inn most days from dawn until late and then handling the theater on show nights. I might leave the theater at 12:30 a.m. and then hit the road early to spend the day at one of our hotels."

While on one of his out-of-town trips, White received an irate call from his father, ordering him back to Merrillville. The infamous call entered the White family annals as one of the most loved and laughed-about stories.

> "Who in hell are the Doe-bee Bros?" Dean demanded, butchering the band's name.

"I was in Houston," White recounted. "Dad said, 'You get your ass home! Now! If it wasn't for your mother, I'd fire you over the phone.'"

White was used to his father's gruff manner, but he was taken aback by Dean's outburst. What could possibly be the problem?

"Who in hell are the Doe-bee Bros?" Dean demanded, butchering the band's name. The elder White had seen a list of acts that Bruce had lined up for the Holiday Star; he had no clue who or what this Doe-bee bunch might be, but Dean was pretty sure that they had no business playing at *his* theater.

"*Doobie* Brothers, Dad," replied Bruce. Trying to calm his father, he patiently explained who the Doobie Brothers were—one of *the* biggest rock bands of the day. The Grammy-award winning group had a huge fan base and would be a major draw for the new theater. Dean grumbled but backed off. Bruce was proved right when a long line appeared at the Holiday Star box office the following day and the show sold out in a flash. Additional shows did likewise.

"That call from my dad was my coming out day," said White many years later. "I told him, 'I know what I'm doing. Why don't you just keep the hell out of my business?' And you know what? He did leave me alone after that. To my dad's credit, he was willing to listen when I told him that we needed to expand our market. He built the theater thinking mainly of acts like Perry Como and Paul Anka. Those days were over. We needed to be doing rhythm and blues acts too. We needed Marvin Gaye and The Four Tops. We needed rock stars."

Under White's direction, the Holiday Star annual calendar became a virtual who's-who of big names and big acts. On show nights, restaurants near the theater were packed—a boon to Merrillville's economy. During one four-month stretch in 1980, the star-studded line-up included Lou Rawls, Mel Tillis, Hall & Oates, Jan & Dean, Paul Lynde, Gordon Lightfoot, and Johnny Cash, among others. Other marquee stars included Three Dog Night, Emmylou Harris, Doc Severinsen, Tony Bennett, Merle Haggard, Gloria Estefan and the Miami Sound Machine, Everly Brothers, and Reba McIntire. Anyone who was anyone in the music business eventually played at the Holiday Star.

"Bruce treated every entertainer like they were an honored guest in his house," said Mike Williams, who started working for Bruce White in 1982 and managed the theater at one point. "He got to know every entertainer and had fun with them. In those days, entertainers didn't play just one show and move on. They often stayed two or three days

> White's hospitality came naturally—as did his passion for music—but rolling out the red carpet was also a savvy business move.

and played four to six shows. We would put on a special dinner called the Star Cabinet, which included key leaders of the hotel, the band, and their entourage. There might be 100 people in attendance."

White's hospitality came naturally—as did his passion for music—but rolling out the red carpet was also a savvy business move. The Holiday Star wasn't located in a major city, so the task of convincing major performers to spend a couple of days in quiet Merrillville required sweetening the deal.

"Bruce and the theater got the reputation of offering great hospitality, where stars could be themselves, nobody was going to bother them," continued Williams. "At one point, we were the most heavily programmed country music theater in the nation six years in a row. We had stars from every genre: The Oak Ridge Boys, Liberace, Tom Jones, Johnny Mathis, Bob Hope, Jay Leno. We were booking more than 200 shows a year. The Oak Ridge Boys played every New Year's Eve for 25 years. They became close friends of Bruce. So did many of the other stars who performed at the theater."

White knew that he couldn't continue to do all the booking himself, so he handed off the main responsibility to music industry veteran David Frey. Frey and Holiday Star staff together coordinated bookings for the Vic Theater in Chicago, an old cabaret venue in the Lakeview neighborhood dating back to 1912. The 1,100-seat theater fell on hard times during the Great Depression and survived for the next half century as a movie house for X-rated and foreign films. Following a major restoration in the early 1980s, the glamorous Vic reopened in 1985. In pre-Internet days, Holiday Star staff often had to drive an hour or more back and forth between the two theaters to hand-deliver tickets and other documents. Eventually, responsibility for booking acts was handled by Star Productions.

Inconveniences aside, the strategy of booking stars for two theaters—one in Chicago and one in Merrillville—made it easier to entice major entertainers to agree to play at both venues.

One Holiday Star regular, singer Tom Jones, praised the theater in an interview with the *Chicago Tribune* in September 1985: "They built the theater like they used to build theaters: it's a place specifically designed for entertainment. It's a perfect place for the kind of show I do, and I like the balcony, it reminds me of vaudeville. . . . I would rather do three shows here for 10,000 fans than one show for the same number, say, in an ice hockey arena."

The popularity of the Holiday Star spurred additional expansions of the adjacent hotel complex during the next two decades. The hotel switched affiliations from Holiday Inn to Radisson, prompting a name change for the theater to the Star Plaza. In 1990, the Radisson announced plans to add a $2 million ballroom to the hotel's conference center—a move to increase the complex's convention space to more than 30,000 square feet. Meetings and conventions became a staple of the hotel's business. On weekends, theatergoers filled the rooms. From Wednesday through Sunday, guests could enjoy stand-up acts in the Comedy Cottage, a small nightclub tucked into the complex. Ginger's Garden restaurant offered buffet dining.

"It's just great to walk into a sold-out theater and know your work has brought about some creative things," White told the *Krannert Portfolio*. "Or having the Doobie Brothers and Kenny Loggins together on stage, George Burns and Bob Hope on the same weekend, and hearing people on their feet clapping and saying, on the way to their rooms, how great it was. Growing up in Crown Point, Indiana, I would never have thought I would preside over Chicago's premier entertainment destination."

Despite the outward appearance of financial success, Bruce White knew that the Star Plaza Theatre was never going to be a major profit center.

"The theater business was intoxicating, but at the end of the day, it's a business—and a difficult business at that. We entered the market at a time when middle-of-the-road acts—which was the business case that the theater was predicated on—were dying. And I mean that literally: many of those stars were in their 70s and 80s. The entertainment industry was changing radically."

> Avoid talking about what we want to accomplish but shift focus on how we are going to do it!

Among the big changes was the advent of state-authorized gambling, which began in 1988 after the legislature approved a state lottery for the first time in more than 130 years. By the 1990s, the gambling landscape in the Hoosier State included off-track betting parlors, racetracks, and riverboat casinos. Live entertainment had to share the market.

New concert venues were also an omen. Many facilities were much larger than the 3,400 seats that the Star Plaza offered. In 1989, the Deer Creek Music Center (now Ruoff Music Center) opened in Noblesville, Indiana—a giant outdoor venue that included more than 6,100 reserved seats under a pavilion and 18,000 general admission lawn seats. Other communities in Indiana and around the country built new stadiums and theaters to attract ever larger crowds. Added to the mix was the advent of cable television and affordable large-scale color television sets—both of which offered consumers mass entertainment in the comfort of their own homes.

As late as 1989, Dean White was still toying with the idea of adding an old-fashioned dinner theater to the Star Plaza, but Bruce argued strongly against it in an April 4 memo to his father.

"At the risk of being a 'pest' or worse, I feel compelled to address this issue one last time," wrote White. "I hope you understand that this is not to prove a point, or have my way, but because I strongly feel it is not in Whiteco's best interest to proceed. . . . We have a tremendous amount of development going on. I strongly believe our focus should be on exploring existing opportunities and improving the customer experience. If we succeed at this, our profits will be greater than any of us have projected."

With or without Bruce's nudging, Dean did eventually abandon the dinner theater concept.[16] The Star Plaza Theatre continued to provide top-flight entertainment on its main stage for many years, becoming

---

[16]In 1982, Dean White flirted, briefly, with building a second 6,000-seat theater and hotel complex at White River Park. The project never proceeded beyond concept and preliminary planning.

a beloved cultural icon in Northwest Indiana in the hearts of generations of music lovers, including Bruce. White was delighted that the Star Plaza's impact on Merrillville and beyond could be felt and heard in thousands of stories about the theater before and after it closed its doors for the last time in December 2017.

Even so, in hindsight, Bruce would have encouraged his dad to invest Whiteco's money differently: "From a pure economic viewpoint, we would have been better off taking that money and going to Austin, Texas or Denver, Colorado to build multiple hotels."

In the early 1980s, Whiteco's hospitality division was tiny—just a handful of hotels—but the potential to grow was there. The first step, in Bruce's mind, was to fix or get rid of properties that his father had casually invested in. In January 1979, his father had appointed him President of Wachim Corporation, Whiteco's hospitality arm. White dove into the weeding process.

"We had leased a Ramada Inn in Evansville and got burned," said White. "We also had a Holiday Inn in Warsaw, Indiana that probably broke even at best. Then we had this monstrosity in Merrillville—the Holiday Inn/Radisson—that was way overbuilt for the market. Whiteco had also bought the Breckinridge Inn in Louisville, Kentucky, and the Fireside Inn in Bloomington, Indiana. Dad was an entrepreneur and an opportunist. Great negotiator. Knew how to make a deal, but he wasn't a finance guy."

Given the lackluster performance of the properties, Dean White had soured on hotels—at least for the moment—leaving the way open for his oldest son to figure out what to do. Bruce tapped Mike Williams, who had joined Whiteco in 1982, to try to fix two of the hotels.

"My job was to go in and clean them up," Williams explained. "The goal was just to get them operational and try to squeeze a nickel out of them. Bruce would come see me once a week, but I talked to him all the time too by phone. Every so often I'd have to make what I termed a 'cash call' to Bruce, who then had to go to his dad to get enough money to make payroll at the hotel that week. I started to really understand the business side of it. And it also made me understand the long and arduous road that Bruce was on to start a company."

To outsiders, it might have been seen as an odd choice for young Bruce. The answer to why Bruce didn't simply join his father's advertising company was both simple and complicated.

"My dad always thought I was out of my mind," White explained. "Of course, he never thought I was IN my mind either. He had inherited the business from his father, when it was tiny, and he built it up. I think because of my ADHD (attention-deficit/hyperactivity disorder), I needed to do something with a much faster pace. Signs were inanimate objects to me."

To boot, father and son were not an executive match made in heaven. White felt his dad was a micromanager who would never allow him a free hand to develop his own ideas.

"He was always going to be Papa Bear," said White.

"Dean was larger than life," said White's childhood friend and neighbor Pat Costin. "He and Bruce were a lot alike, but their styles were different. Bruce was a velvet glove, Dean was a hammer. Dean's upbringing in Nebraska and then his time in the Merchant Marines had a lot to do with it."

The relationship between Dean and Bruce was solid outside of the office, but inside the walls of Whiteco, the differences loomed large. Among other things, Bruce believed in disciplined financial management, while Dean was more opportunistic and free-wheeling.

"My dad had more than 40 businesses," recalled White. "He had a health club. He had a health food store. He had a public relations agency. He had a lumber yard. He had a residential construction company. He had an insurance agency. He owned a grocery store in Shelby, just so they'd have a grocery store. He would buy these small pieces of land that we ended up not even being able to give away after he died. It added up to something like 43 different companies. I really can't explain it, but he enjoyed it."

The challenge for the two men boiled down to opposite approaches to business: "Dad was opportunistic; I wanted to be strategic," said

White. "I wanted processes in place. I wanted HR policies. My dad at that time didn't even have an HR department. No surprise, my dad and I were soon very frustrated with each other. He wanted to make the final decisions on everything, right down to telling me how much to pay a receptionist. We had 1,500 employees at the time! I finally got to the point that I was going to quit.

"My mother intervened and told my dad in no uncertain terms: 'You've got a son who is very capable. He's here, close to home. He's going to get married someday and have kids. He's going to go somewhere else. You're NOT going to let that happen. You've got to figure out how to make this work.'"

Dean White hired a management consultant to assess the problems and suggest solutions. One of his principal recommendations was brief and blunt: Dean and Bruce should not work together.

"I went through two days of testing and interviews," said Bruce. "The consultant said to us, 'The problem between you is easy to identify: Your profiles are identical. You're both incredibly domineering and controlling. You can't work together. The issues you have today will only get worse.'"

On the upside, the consultant told the two men that Bruce's profile was "outstanding"—a comment that echoed Barbara White's assessment of her son's talents. The test results listed traits that would not have surprised anyone who knew him: "analytical; creative; authoritative; freewheeler; stubborn; ambitious; competitive drive; risk-taker; very independent; very self-confident."

Although Dean would never completely cure himself of wanting to tell Bruce how to do things, he did his best to accept that he should let his highly capable son handle business and life his way.

> Unlike Bill Marriott, Bruce White wasn't going to be stepping into his father's shoes. But he didn't want to cut ties to Whiteco entirely. Instead, he came up with a plan that he thought would benefit both men.

"Bruce was driven to make his own mark, I think," said Tim Ozark, a friend and colleague from the Young Presidents Organization (YPO). "He did work with his father on a number of projects, and they helped each other, but Bruce wanted to chart his own path."

That path included avoiding what White considered the pitfalls of his father's approach to staffing, planning and more.

"Mr. White (Dean) filled management roles with some of his friends," said John Januszko, former head of human resources, who joined White Lodging in 1989. Not all of those who were hired were well-suited to the job.'

Dean White's informal approach to hiring people was not unique. Many first-generation entrepreneurs have leaned on family members and friends to fill roles. If the company is small or the business is uncomplicated, the decision might work . . . at least in the short-term. Marriott International—which started out as the Hot Shoppes restaurant chain in 1927—began the same way. Many of the executive positions were filled with founder J. W. Marriott's brothers and other relatives.

> "I had a pretty strong negotiating position," White told Purdue's hospitality business students in a guest lecture in 2014. "The deal was that I would work for a percentage of the improvements that I could make on the properties. Dad had a no-risk deal. He agreed and that was the beginning of White Lodging."

But as a business grows, dependence on non-professionals in key roles can have a crippling effect. Dean White's frustration with the uneven performance of his first hotel—the Merrillville Holiday Inn—was a textbook case of the perils of hiring people with no direct experience in the field. In Marriott's case, second generation leadership—J. W.'s son Bill—came into the business equipped with a degree in banking and finance from the University of Utah. Among Bill Marriott's earliest and toughest assignments was easing out family members and filling roles with experienced professionals. He maintained many of his father's values but updated the company's processes for a modern era.

Unlike Bill Marriott, Bruce White wasn't going to be stepping into his father's shoes. But he didn't want to cut ties to Whiteco entirely. Instead, he came up with a plan that he thought would benefit both men. He had learned that Marriott was beginning to separate its real estate holdings from its hotel management business. Why not try a similar approach to Whiteco's hotels?

"I had a pretty strong negotiating position," White told Purdue's hospitality business students in a guest lecture in 2014. "The deal was that I would work for a percentage of the improvements that I could make on the properties. Dad had a no-risk deal. He agreed and that was the beginning of White Lodging."

On November 7, 1985, White Lodging Services Corporation was incorporated in Indiana. Bruce White was named Chairman. The office consisted of Bruce, a finance executive named Bill Erdmann, and an administrative assistant.

White Lodging immediately assumed official management of the Whiteco hotels and dove into remodeling them. White was on the road, as usual, checking on progress and keeping an eye on the budget. He had financial incentive: his future income depended on fulfilling the hotel management agreements with his dad.

Despite working crazy hours, White found time here and there to stay in touch with friends from Crown Point and Purdue. In Fall 1986, Bruce and two of his Beta House brothers—Steve Poe and Bob "Bullet" Brown—plus non-Purdue pal Tony Fleming—borrowed a stretch limo from the Star Plaza and headed to Purdue for Homecoming. The casual outing turned into much more than a party on wheels.

White Lodging Services Corporation was incorporated in Indiana on November 7, 1985.

"I wouldn't have gone if Steve hadn't strong-armed me," said White many years later. "I really didn't have any interest in going back to campus."

"So, we pull up to Beta House and get out," recalled Poe. "The limo seemed like a good idea before we got there, but it was almost embarrassing. The trunk was full of beer. One of the guys at Beta House—probably

20 years old—looked at the limo and said, 'Man, if I had a car like that, filled with booze, I could pick up all kinds of girls!' And Bruce says, 'Have at it!'

"So, Tony and this kid and a few others climbed in and took off. When they came back, the car was filled with girls from the Phi Mu sorority. This was hours before the game. So, everybody was just having fun, drinking, getting ready to tailgate."

A Phi Mu sister had made the finals for Homecoming Queen, so the sorority women didn't want to miss half-time. After a fun afternoon, they waved their goodbyes to White and the others and headed to the stadium to see who would be crowned. Sometime after the game, the four men drove the limo back to Merrillville, said their own goodbyes and parted ways.

> Poe didn't miss a beat. He had noticed at the Homecoming pre-game festivities that one of the Phi Mu women had made an impression on Bruce. One problem: neither man could recall her name.

That might have been an end to it if White had not headed to Louisville, Kentucky a week later to visit one of White Lodging's small hotels, the Breckinridge Inn. Steve Poe was living in the Louisville area.

"I met Steve for dinner and afterward we drove around Louisville to look at possible sites for another hotel," said White. "He had one of those Motorola box phones in his car—one of the first mobile phones. I don't think I'd ever seen one before. I said, 'I'd love to call somebody on your phone, but I don't have anyone to call.'"

Poe didn't miss a beat. He had noticed at the Homecoming pre-game festivities that one of the Phi Mu women had made an impression on Bruce. One problem: neither man could recall her name. Fortunately, they remembered other details about her: blond, very pretty, from the Evansville area, and studying dietetics.

"So, I used Steve's phone to call the Phi Mu house and asked for a fifth-year dietetics major from Evansville," said White. "Whoever picked up the phone answered: 'Oh, sure, that's Beth Maloney.' So, I hung up, called back and asked for Beth."

White was heading to Evansville in a day or two to check on White Lodging's Ramada hotel there. Beth would be at home then, on fall break.

"So, he asked me out," said Beth. "And he gave me three choices. One of them was to go with him to the Country Music Association awards. But I was in college and didn't really like country. Another option was simply to have dinner in Evansville, so I said yes to that one."

Beth hung up and told her friends that she had accepted a date with "that guy Bruce White."

"Which one was that?" asked one of the women.

Beth started describing White, but a friend stopped her. "No, no, no," she said. "That's a different guy. Bruce was the one who had a beard and was balding."

When Beth arrived home for fall break, she squirmed at the idea of White picking her up at her parents' house in Mount Vernon. Among other things, she knew he was a bit older than she was.

"My parents were old-fashioned, and I thought, 'What have I done? They're going to think I'm crazy!' So, I told Bruce to pick me up at my brother's apartment in Evansville. I didn't want my parents to meet him because I had no idea what he was going to be like. I went over to my brother's, and we were looking out the window together when Bruce pulled up in his rental car and got out. 'That must be him,' I said as I headed out the door. I didn't even let him come into the apartment! I told my brother, 'I won't be long.'"

The pair ended up at River House, one of Evansville's nicer restaurants.

"We had a great time," said Beth. "He had me call my brother to see if he wanted to meet us for a drink afterwards. My brother said no. But that was the beginning. We immediately connected. We talked a lot about our families. We both loved sports. I saw in Bruce a maturity and zest for life. I had dated a little but hadn't had many serious relationships. On the other hand, he had been engaged at least twice.

"At that time, I wanted to go into the Peace Corps, so I wasn't thinking that I was going to get serious. And he was a Region Rat, which I had always been told to stay away from. So, here I was . . . dating a Region Rat! He lived in Crown Point at the time, in a condo at the Four Seasons with his friend Marty. He also had a bit of a reputation, so friends would ask me if he had a 'bachelor pad.' He didn't. His apartment was a hodgepodge of his mom's old furniture. Maybe I was naïve, but I really didn't care."

Sports quickly became their favorite date. White had season tickets to the Chicago Bulls, White Sox, and Bears. Beth quickly learned about the basketballs and gym clothes in the trunk of his car—ready for a casual pick-up game at a moment's notice.

Two months after their first date—October 14, 1986, at River House—White introduced Beth to his parents. Looking back, Beth said Bruce knew before she did that their relationship was the real deal.

"From the moment Bruce met Beth, he would call me up mooning over her," said childhood friend Pat Costin.

Beth was more cautious, worried by what her parents—Tim and Joanne Maloney—might think of a man eleven years older than their daughter.

"My parents were a bit suspicious," noted Beth. "He came to Evansville for a weekend. I finally told them that we were seeing each other. Of course, they had questions about him. My mom wanted to know how old he was. At the time, I honestly didn't know for certain, so I said, 'I think he's around 30.' I guess she asked more than once because she said, 'Every time I ask, he gets a year older!'"

> **"Dean pulled Bruce aside and gave his hearty seal of approval,"** said Pat Costin. "Dean said, 'This girl has a backbone of steel. She'll never back down. You should be with her.' Beth's independence made he special."

The age difference didn't bother Beth. Her parents also took it in stride. Beth's mother told her that she always thought her daughter would marry someone older.

The couple's courtship was a quick one. White never formally proposed, but at a White Sox game in May 1987, he turned to her: "We know we're getting married, but we haven't told anyone because we aren't actually engaged." Beth got out her check register and they looked at the calendar.

"We set a date of November 28th and that night we started telling everyone," said Beth.

Beth Maloney graduated from Purdue in June 1987 and accepted a dietitian job in Palos Heights, Illinois. She didn't want to move in with

Bruce until after they were married. At that point, White suggested that she live with his parents in their Holiday Creek house in Crown Point. The commute between Crown Point and her new job was an hour. What might have been an awkward arrangement for many couples was perfect for Beth and her future in-laws.

"It was great," said Beth. "I lived in one of the guest rooms and got up every morning to commute to my job. Bruce was traveling a lot for his work, so the arrangement gave his parents and me a chance to get to know each other. It was really wonderful. Barbara became like a second mother to me."

"Probably two weeks after she moved in, Dean pulled Bruce aside and gave his hearty seal of approval," said Pat Costin. "Dean said, 'This girl has a backbone of steel. She'll never back down. You should be with her.' Beth's independence made her special."

As Beth's parents got to know White, they likewise saw the rock-solid relationship between their younger daughter and her future husband. Unlike the Whites, the Maloneys were not wealthy, but the two couples shared the same middle-class Midwest values. Timothy Maloney, Beth's father, was one of nine children and had grown up on a farm in Illinois. He worked for General Electric almost his entire career. Beth's mother, Joanne, was a full-time homemaker and raised Beth, her older sister Bridget, and her older brother James.

"Mount Vernon, where I grew up, had maybe 8,000 residents," recalled Beth. "Both of my parents were very hard-working and provided me with a very idyllic, nurturing upbringing. But we didn't travel, so I didn't see the ocean until I was 19, until I had worked and saved money to drive with a few college friends to Florida.

"Education in our family was always a top priority, as it was in Bruce's. My brother, sister, and I were always expected to go to college and my dad worked hard to make that happen. I started out at Western Kentucky University, which was close to home. But after two years I transferred to Purdue because it had a better program."

Bruce William White and Elizabeth Ellen Maloney married on November 28, 1987 in Mount Vernon. The groom was 34, the bride, 23. The wedding was big—almost 300 guests. Beth had been raised Catholic,

Bruce and Beth celebrate on their wedding day.

so a priest officiated. Bob "Bullet" Brown—the tall, dark, handsome man that Beth thought she was talking to on the phone after Purdue's Homecoming—was one of White's groomsmen.

"Out of town invitations were mailed, but for nearby friends and relatives, we simply put an announcement in the local newspaper," said Beth. "By today's standards it was a simple wedding, but to us it was beautiful. Mike Williams, who was managing the Evansville Ramada for White Lodging at the time, helped to plan our reception at the hotel."

After the festivities, the newlyweds headed to Colorado to enjoy a quiet honeymoon and time on the ski slopes. The trip turned out to be more adventurous than either one envisioned.

"I was showing off for my bride," said White many years later. "I jumped off a cliff while skiing and landed on rocks that had no snow covering. I broke my shoulder."

Fortunately, the pair had loaded up on videotaped movies for the condo's VCR and turned their ski trip into an impromptu film fest. But White wasn't content to sit on the sofa full-time. Demonstrating his trademark can-do attitude, he skied with one arm in a sling for the rest of their stay and for the rest of the season.

When the couple returned to Crown Point, Beth worked for the Veterans Administration Hospital in Chicago for a year and then went back to school for her master's degree at Indiana University Northwest. By then, White decided that he needed to be on-site 24/7 to turn around the struggling Radisson at Star Plaza.

"So we lived in the hotel for a year," explained Beth. "Friends thought it must be fun to live in a hotel, but I assured them it wasn't all it was cracked up to be. Most of my classes were in the evening so when I got back to the hotel at 9:30 or 10:00 p.m., I would drive my little Plymouth Horizon under the porte cochère, beep my horn and flash my headlights so Bruce would know I was home. His office was right above the entrance. He'd meet me back at our room and we'd order room service for dinner."

Bruce and Beth skiing.

When Beth discovered she was expecting a baby, the couple agreed it was time to find a house. Beth graduated with her master's degree in May of 1990 and the Whites moved into their new home in Valparaiso, just one month before the arrival of daughter Corinne in early July.

White once again tapped Mike Williams, this time to take his place managing the Radisson.

Williams was flattered that White picked him to take over the general manager job, but he was also amused: "Bruce says to me, 'I can't do this anymore. I'm having a baby, a family!' I had three kids of my own by then, so I chuckled a little at Bruce's worrying about the impact of one baby."

Many of White's closest friends were amazed—and delighted—to see the effect that Beth had on their pal. "Mr. Fun" of South Park and Beta House days now took second place to Bruce, family man.

Steve Poe, whose Motorola car phone had started the ball rolling, was thrilled by what he saw: "Beth is a very genuine, sweet person, with

> "Bruce really came into his own when he married Beth. I refer to the change in him as BB and AB: Before Beth and after Beth. There was then a whole different level of focus and drive after that."
>
> Steve Poe
> Friend + Business Partner

a strong backbone. It was obvious early on that she was really important to him. And the more they were together, the more obvious it was that he was extremely happy. Bruce really came into his own when he married Beth. I refer to the change in him as BB and AB: Before Beth and After Beth. There was then a whole different level of focus and drive after that."

Bruce's younger brother Craig likewise marveled at the couple's partnership: "My brother had the best marriage I've ever known. It took them to higher levels than they would probably have achieved separately. They were an incredible team. Beth was truly Bruce's equal."

"Beth brought out every best quality in him, there's no doubt about that," said White's childhood friend Pat Costin. "She rounded out his peaks and valleys and kept him grounded."

Thanks to marriage, a new house, and fatherhood, Bruce White was delighted by the positive changes in his personal life. The only serious frustration was on the professional side. White Lodging was approaching its fifth birthday in 1990. Thanks to a real estate market meltdown, tiny White Lodging looked likely to remain just that . . . tiny.

Then, one afternoon in early 1990, White pushed the elevator button to go up to his father's office in the Twin Towers, an impressive office complex Dean had masterminded two decades earlier. White Lodging was also a tenant in the building. When the elevator doors opened, he stepped into the car. Another man was already on board. White immediately recognized him, smiled, and stuck out his hand.

"I'm Bruce White," he said.

The other man smiled.

"I know who exactly you are," he said, taking White's outstretched hand as the elevator doors slid shut.

◆◆◆◆◆

CHAPTER 5

Begin with the End in Mind

> "'Begin with the end in mind.' That was always one of Bruce's big things. In other words: What are we trying to achieve here? Let's figure that out and then we can figure out how to begin."
>
> **Mike Wells**
> Friend + Business Partner

The familiar face in the elevator belonged to Mike Ruffer, head of Marriott's three-year-old Fairfield Inn brand. Bruce recognized Ruffer from photos in hotel trade magazines.

"He was going up to my father's office to buy outdoor billboards," recalled White.

The two men exchanged pleasantries, then White told Ruffer that he was thinking about getting out of the hotel game. He was tired of struggling to make a real business from the assortment of small hotels that his father Dean had acquired. White had entertained high hopes for the new limited-service Carlton Lodge concept that Whiteco had launched in January 1985. Loosely modeled on a ski chalet, Carlton Lodge was designed to tap into the same business traveler market that Courtyard by Marriott was wooing. The lodges were making money, but not enough to convince White—a pragmatist—that the concept had a solid future. He recognized the tough challenges of trying to create a hotel brand from scratch.

"It's too hard," White told Ruffer, in a rare moment of pessimism. "I can't make any money. I can't grow the company. I can't compete with Marriott. I have a site where I was going to build what we call a Carlton Lodge. Instead of us continuing, I want to sell it to you."

> **It took all of a millisecond for me recognize the opportunity,** said White. **"My attitude about my future in the hotel industry changed from worst to first and I said, 'Of course I would love to come out and do that.'**
>
> — Bruce W. White

Ruffer listened to White's lament and then offered a counterproposal. Marriott was mulling over the pros and cons of franchising its Fairfield Inn brand. How about flying to Washington, D.C. to meet Bill Marriott? Maybe even become the brand's first franchisee?

White could hardly believe his ears. The invitation reminded him of his father's good fortune in connecting with Holiday Inn just as the tiny chain was taking off. White Advertising had boomed ever since. Maybe Marriott would be his 'Holiday Inn'?

"It took all of a millisecond for me to recognize the opportunity," said White. "My attitude about my future in the hotel industry changed from worst to first and I said, 'Of course I would love to come out and do that.'"

White and a couple of colleagues flew to Marriott's headquarters, where they were met by Chairman Bill Marriott and more than a dozen company executives. Although White was welcomed graciously, it became obvious to him during the meeting that the idea of franchising was not viewed with a friendly eye by at least some in the room. In the late 1960s, Marriott had taken a stab at hotel franchising, only to back away when it discovered that franchisees would not or could not adhere to Marriott's standards. The properties had risked giving the Marriott brand a black eye. The Marriott Inn franchise program was small, so the company simply pulled the plug and returned to its tried-and-true strategy of building, managing and owning all its hotels.

"Franchising was an aspect of the business that we had serious disagreements about in senior leadership," said Liam Brown, who worked extensively with Marriott's select-service brands before being named Group President, U.S. & Canada. "Should we embrace franchising? There were people in the company who just did not like franchising, felt it was giving up all control and the ability to control our own destiny and maintain our standards."

Marriott's plans in the early 1980s had included a big push to develop select-service brands for business travelers. Courtyard by Marriott debuted in Atlanta in 1983 and then expanded nationally. Courtyard's success led to plans for Fairfield Inn, a no-frills economy brand for budget-minded travelers. The first Fairfield Inn opened in Atlanta in October 1987. Four more followed in quick succession. In March 1988, Marriott committed to spend $500 million over five years to take the concept nationwide. The plan was to construct 40 Fairfield Inns within 18 months and to have 100 opened by the early 1990s. By September 1989, 39 Fairfield Inns were up and running.

Marriott's do-it-all-in-house approach worked well until a major recession hit in the late 1980s, followed quickly by a savings and loan debacle, and a war in the Persian Gulf (1990–1991). Overbuilding in the hotel industry was also a thorn in the side. The economic uncertainty threatened the company's huge development program. Marriott had to cut expenses drastically and leave half-built hotels in limbo while weathering the downturn. Treading water, however, was not a long-term solution. How could Marriott keep growing in the face of tight financial markets? For the first time in two decades, the taboo word 'franchise" surfaced. When Mike Ruffer invited Bruce White to Washington, D.C., the stage was set for a lively debate about the wisdom of letting the independent White Lodgings of the world try their hand at building and managing a Marriott hotel.

> **"When I came in the door—possibly to become the first Fairfield Inn franchisee—I could feel a level of hostility. Not from Bill Marriott or the executives who were all-in on franchising, but from others who weren't on board yet. They thought I was the Antichrist!"**
>
> Bruce W. White

"If you hung around Marriott headquarters back then, they were the kings of the industry," said White in a 2022 interview. "And they knew it. When I came in the door, I could feel a level of hostility. Not from Bill Marriott or the executives who were all-in on franchising, but from others who weren't on board yet. They thought I was the Antichrist! They thought that as soon as Marriott started franchising their hotels, the quality was going to go down and it would be the end of the company. We were going to kill the golden goose."

White noted the mix of attitudes in the room but didn't let it throw him. He was there mainly to listen and learn. White felt he won Bill Marriott's confidence with his response to a skeptic's question about tiny White Lodging's ability to manage hotels as well as Marriott did.

"I said, 'If—with our own capital invested, working on a smaller scale, and being an entrepreneur—if we can't outperform a large global organization in a small business like select-service hotels, then you *are* making a mistake.'"

White went a step farther when asked what concerns he had about becoming a Marriott franchisee. His blunt answer likely raised eyebrows among those in the room who were surprised to hear a potential franchisee schooling Marriott in brand management.

"My concern would be that you bring in the right franchisees, because the value of the brand is only as good as the equity that the customer sees," White told the group. "You've built up incredible equity, but your people are right: It is at risk. But if you play it right, franchising should enhance your equity. What will be key is who you select and the relationships you build. It has to be a collaboration. It can't be us *versus* them."

Collaborators in the first Fairfield Inn by Marriott franchise: (left to right) Bruce White, J. W. Marriott, Jr., and Dean White.

White's straight talk won the day. Bill Marriott gave the nod. White Lodging was awarded the first Fairfield Inn by Marriott franchise in the Spring of 1990. White immediately set his team to work. Or, more accurately, he scrambled to put a team in place . . . and then set them loose.

"When I joined White Lodging in the summer of 1990, we were about 90 days away from opening up that first Fairfield Inn franchise," said Deno Yiankes, a member of the company's original core executive team. "I was Manager of Development, but in reality, those first 90 days were all-hands-on-deck. We didn't have enough structure to have divisions or different business units."

Marriott sent staff to train White Lodging in using the company's reservation system—a reflection, said Yiankes, "of their long-held belief that training is so important."

"We had at least a couple of Marriott people in our offices, training our general manager and assistant general manager, who also went on a week-long training course," said Yiankes. "When we got closer to the opening date, Marriott had people on-site to help our staff learn the check-in system."

The sprint paid off. In September 1990, the 132-room Merrillville Fairfield Inn by Marriott opened across the road from the Star Plaza theater complex. The new hotel hit its numbers in no time, recalled Yiankes.

"Based on my background in appraisal and feasibility studies, the rule of thumb was that a new hotel takes three to four years to ramp up and stabilize occupancy. The Merrillville Fairfield Inn did well immediately. In less than a year the numbers were well ahead of average."

The White Lodging team promptly recognized the power of the Marriott brand and Marriott's reservation system. The number of room nights booked for the Merrillville property using Marriott's system was astounding.

"Over half of our business was coming through their reservation system," said Yiankes. "We had never seen anything like that with our own hotels."

Bruce White was thrilled. And eager. Partnering with Marriott for the long haul could only benefit White Lodging. Within two months of the opening of the Merrillville Fairfield Inn, White was already looking into more opportunities. The most economical route was to buy struggling hotel properties, spruce them up, and convert them to the Marriott brand.

"There are many hotels with problems that threaten their very existence," wrote White in the November 1990 White Lodging newsletter. "Owners have tried stopgap measures and failed. They are looking for and willing to pay for highly regarded turn-around specialists."

White fully intended to be one of those specialists. But he needed to be savvy about which properties were worth buying and converting to a Marriott brand. On the plus side, there were plenty of distressed properties available. Overbuilding in the hotel industry in the 1980s meant that many hotels were struggling financially even before the savings and loan crisis and economic downturn. Many of the hotels had been built by limited partnerships looking to take advantage of generous tax loss provisions of the Economic Recovery Tax Act of 1981. "Hometown Hero" hotels were especially vulnerable. Such properties tended to be one-off projects built by a local doctor, dentist, or attorney as an investment and were viewed locally as a boon to the area's economy. The banks that repossessed the properties when they failed were eager to get rid of them, even at a loss.

> Debt financing markets were tight and interest rates were high. Some banks were overextended and would soon go out of business themselves. Figuring out how to strike deals for distressed hotel properties—quickly—was top priority.

"Banks by charter couldn't own real estate long-term," said Deno Yiankes. "So they were motivated to get it off the books as fast as possible. We would go to the banks and make them an offer, because they were motivated to sell."

On the minus side, five-year-old White Lodging didn't have the budget to go out and snap up properties willy-nilly. Debt financing markets were tight and interest rates were high. Some banks were overextended and would soon go out of business themselves. Figuring out how to strike deals for distressed hotel properties—quickly—was top priority.

Fortunately for White and White Lodging, he had Deno Yiankes on board and would soon add Larry Burnell—both of whom possessed solid backgrounds in finance. Yiankes was a Purdue graduate and had worked at hospitality consultant HVS International in New York City, evaluating hotel appraisals and feasibility studies before joining White Lodging. Burnell's deep expertise was in accounting, but he was also talented in evaluating deals and finding money to pay for them. Between Yiankes and Burnell—plus Bruce's own business background—the critical core of White Lodging's scrappy development side was in place.

> The easiest way to fool ourselves is to judge ourselves by our intentions as opposed to results.

"We called it Dialing for Dollars," said Yiankes. "I hired Mike Flannery from Purdue's hotel program. He would come into our office three days a week for four or five hours at a time. His assignment was to go through a big database of bank names located all over the country, make calls, and ask if the bank had any hotel assets in their portfolios. Then, once a week, I would sit down with Bruce and go over the results."

"The idea was to scour the country and look for hotels that were in trouble," said Larry Burnell. "They had either been taken over by a bank or were about to be. The bank was happy to sell properties for pennies on a dollar. And then they were happy to hold the paper, so they would be your finance company."

The effort paid off. Leads generated by the calls weren't huge in number, but the ones that White Lodging pursued turned out to be great opportunities for the small company. Some involved buying properties from banks; others required dealing with the Resolution Trust Corporation (RTC), the federal government program created in 1989 to clean up the $400 billion savings and loan mess. Marriott helped by putting the weight of its reputation behind White Lodging when White and his team needed to guarantee debt.

"We could buy properties for almost nothing, put a little bit of money into them, and convert them to one of three Marriott brands: Courtyard, Fairfield Inn, Residence Inn," noted White. "We were able to leverage our projects up to 100 percent of cost and we were able to create enough value quickly enough that we could get them off that debt, refinance, and pull out the proceeds. We built our company with no outside investment. It was all through bootstrap financing."

"We went way faster than we should have," said Yiankes. "Bruce and I were literally putting together the offers. We would go out, review the property and the market. We were driving around with Hertz maps and yellow highlighters, reviewing the opportunities."

The ability to move quickly was key. In one case—in South Bend, Indiana—White received a call from a Marriott contact who passed along a tip about an independent hotel called the East Race Inn that had just been handed over to a bank for liquidation. Marriott didn't have the financing to go after it and thought White Lodging might be a good fit.

White eagerly agreed and said he would take a look at the property that evening. There was just one problem. He had promised his wife that he would babysit their tiny daughter Corinne so Beth could attend a meeting. Beth pumped milk for Corinne while Bruce loaded the stroller and baby into the family car.

> White Lodging was not only the first Fairfield Inn franchisee, but also the first Marriott franchisee to operate properties for all three select-service brands: Fairfield Inn (September 1990), Courtyard (January 1991) and now the Residence Inn (March 1991).

"I toured the property with the general manager and together we would carry the baby stroller up and down the staircases," recalled White. "Then I went to the full-service Marriott in downtown South Bend to have dinner and recap my thoughts about the tour. Well, I was the belle of the ball—every woman in the dining room came over to see Corinne while I was trying to write up my notes!"

The following morning White met the CEO of the local bank that owned the hotel.

"We were able to buy it for no money down because the property was in bankruptcy," said White. "But it came with environmental issues that we had to clean up. Years earlier, there had been a gas station on the site. It was in an awful location, but it was cheap, no money up front. That's what I could afford. It took us three or four months to convert it to a Residence Inn by Marriott—our first hotel of that brand. I think we spent about $125,000 to convert it."

Always a fan of being first, White was delighted to be able to tell the world that White Lodging was not only the first Fairfield Inn franchisee, but also the first Marriott franchisee to operate properties for all three select-service brands: Fairfield Inn (September 1990), Courtyard (January 1991) and now the Residence Inn (March 1991).

With so much going on, the tiny company could easily have bitten off more than it could chew. If White Lodging went overboard buying up properties, it might spread itself too thin. If the company goofed up on even one acquisition, there wasn't much financial cushion to fall back on.

A set of brakes came in the form of Bruce's father, Dean. His experience launching Merrillville's Holiday Inn in 1969 had been frustrating. Only after he talked Bruce into coming home from California in 1977 did things improve. For better or worse, Dean had purchased a handful of additional hotels, none of which were financial home runs. So, he looked upon his son's hotel ventures with a skeptic's eye. He was willing to put up some money, but his loan terms were tough—often far tougher than any financial institution.

"My dad was involved only as an investor, not an operator," said White. "But he demanded onerous terms, almost mob loan shark terms!"

Deno Yiankes agreed: "Dean demanded a very high return—very high, almost unheard of. What that did, though, was create a very high threshold for us, to the point that it basically prevented us from doing any bad deals. We were only able to go after the biggest opportunities."

Many people no doubt thought that the younger White's success was being bankrolled by his wealthy and well-known father. But people who were involved in building White Lodging from the start are quick to make clear that Dean White's role was carefully defined by both father and son.

> **"** Mr. White—Dean—was very helpful, don't get me wrong, but this company was Bruce's. I mean, he built it. He made it happen. It helped to have his dad's guarantees on some things, but it was 99.9% Bruce. **"**
>
> **Mike Wells**
> Friend + Business Partner

"People often ask me if Bruce really built White Lodging on his own or was it because he was a billionaire's son?" said Mike Wells, a Purdue fraternity brother and occasional business partner. "Mr. White—Dean—was very helpful, don't get me wrong, but this company was Bruce's. I mean, he built it. He made it happen. It helped to have his dad's guarantees on some things, but it was 99.9% Bruce."

The two constantly butted heads over business issues large and small. Dean would procrastinate for months over signing a simple contract, but on any given day, he might agree on the fly to finance a small business he knew almost nothing about.

"If you really look at my dad's business, he was a kind of venture capitalist," said Bruce White. "He would only talk about his home runs. But his winners were big, particularly the outdoor sign company and some of the apartments he built."

"Dean was our main partner in the beginning," said Larry Burnell, who joined White Lodging in 1992. "There were many meetings where Dean would pound on the table, 'When are you going to pay Whiteco back?!' By 1995, we had accumulated enough money that I told Bruce the first thing we were going to do was pay back his father. So, we did. From that point out, Dean was a partner in some of our projects, but we—White Lodging—had gotten to the point financially where we could walk on our own."

During a three-year sprint (1990–1993) to scoop up properties at bargain rates, White Lodging successfully added almost a dozen properties to its portfolio. Nearby locations included Merrillville, Goshen, Fort Wayne, Valparaiso and South Bend—all in Indiana. Farther afield were hotels in Key West, Florida; Benton Harbor, Michigan; Denver, Colorado, and Austin and Houston, Texas.

Switching properties to Marriott brands wasn't difficult. When a hotel went into foreclosure, the original franchise agreement was automatically terminated. White and his team could reflag the property as a Courtyard, Fairfield Inn or Residence Inn with no legal issues. Banks with whom White did business were also reassured when he could show proof of White Lodging's ability, say, to take a bankrupt Ramada Inn and convert it in a year or less to a profitable Courtyard by Marriott.

Some bankrupt properties were easier than others to renovate or revamp. The independent East Race Inn in South Bend had been modeled on Marriott's Residence Inn, so fixing it up to meet franchise specs was straightforward. Others weren't so simple. In 1991, White Lodging purchased the Inn at the Wharf in Key West, Florida—a hotel that Beth White later said was the worst she had ever stayed in. The company put in a hefty $1 million to renovate the property and reflag it as a Fairfield Inn and Suites. The challenge? The property was composed of 100 rooms and 26 suites . . . divided by Highway 1A, the main road into Key West. White couldn't do anything about the highway, so housekeepers had to push their heavy carts back and forth across the road.

By mid-1994, White Lodging had 18 hotels in its portfolio, representing more than 2,400 rooms. Most were Marriott brands, but not all. Among them were the six Carlton Lodges—the brand that Whiteco had masterminded in 1985. The lodges were holding their own, but it made sense to incorporate them into the growing stable of Marriott-flagged properties managed by White Lodging. With Marriott's blessing, the properties were converted to Courtyards.

Because White Lodging had to act fast to get first dibs on desirable properties, the company didn't have the luxury of working from a strategic plan. For the moment, simply nabbing available properties, converting them, and making them profitable was the game plan. Bruce's experience at Hyatt and then running his father's Holiday Inn in Merrillville equipped him to figure out how to turn a failing or mediocre hotel into a winner.

White, however, couldn't do it alone. While running around looking at potential acquisitions, he also had to begin creating a

> Two who joined the corporate team early on were Deno Yiankes and Larry Burnell, whose financial savvy was critical to the start-up phase. Both would stay at White Lodging for decades, supplying not only their expertise, but institutional memory.

permanent organization. Key to the company's success would be the recruitment of talent—not just to execute goals on a daily basis, but to think in Big Picture terms about White Lodging's future. Finance was a priority.

"Bruce had only four people on board, I think, at the beginning," said Steve Poe, a Purdue classmate, fraternity brother, and later a partner in several ventures. "That was it. People forget that fact."

Two who joined the corporate team early on were Deno Yiankes and Larry Burnell, whose financial savvy was critical to the start-up phase. Both would stay at White Lodging for decades, supplying not only their expertise, but institutional memory.

Yiankes had an unusual story. He worked as a line cook at the Merrillville Holiday Inn[16] when he was in college in the mid-1980s. At the time, Yiankes was in the Restaurant, Hotel, and Institutional Management program at Purdue University Northwest. He met Bruce White one evening when the boss came through the hotel kitchen to shoot the breeze for a few minutes with staff. While keeping an eye on the broiler he oversaw, Yiankes watched as White kidded around with two dishwashers who were clearly tickled that the boss stopped by AND that he knew them by name.

> When the two men crossed paths again, White mentioned to Yiankes that he knew he was in the Purdue hospitality program. "I hope you'll remember us after you graduate," White told him.

"I think sometimes in the hospitality business, there's what I call plastic hospitality, and then there's genuine hospitality, and it was always genuine with him, and that left a mark on me. That night was the first of literally thousands of times where I saw that Bruce had the ability to connect with people. And it was not for show or for anything other than he enjoyed encountering people and hearing their story."

When the two men crossed paths again, White mentioned to Yiankes that he knew he was in the Purdue hospitality program. "I hope you'll remember us after you graduate," White told him.

Yiankes appreciated the thought, but after receiving his degree, he headed immediately to New York, where he spent three years at HVS (Hospitality Valuation Services), a small consulting firm specializing in hotel appraisals and hotel market data. While at HVS, Yiankes handled more than 60 hotel appraisals and feasibility studies for developers, lenders, and institutions.

One day in early June 1990, out of the blue, Yiankes received a call from Bruce White. White wanted to know if he was going to attend an

---

[16] The Merrillville Holiday Inn was reflagged as a Radisson in 1990. Yiankes was a line cook when the property was still a Holiday Inn.

upcoming investment conference in New York City. When Yiankes said yes, the pair agreed to meet at the Waldorf Hotel for coffee. Dean White joined them.

"Bruce explained to me they were getting ready to open the first franchised Fairfield Inn by Marriott. The majority of my work at HVS was actually for Marriott. We had just appraised the first 50 Fairfield Inns that they had built to start the brand. So, I was really familiar with the brand. Bruce said he needed help in development and underwriting and doing the competitive market research, and that's exactly what I had done at HVS."

The fit was a good one for Yiankes and for White Lodging. White made him a job offer and Yiankes accepted, packed his bags, and headed back to Merrillville, Indiana, his home turf. For the next 30 years, he would help White build White Lodging from a handful of hotels to a collection of more than 150 properties.

Two years after bringing Deno Yiankes on board, White went looking for a new chief financial officer. He found what he was looking for in Larry Burnell. Or so Burnell thought.

"I took the day off from my job at a real estate development firm to interview for the job," recalled Burnell. "I told my wife I'd probably be home by lunchtime, and we could take the kids to the zoo in the afternoon. Well, I was still there hours later. I interviewed with Bruce. I interviewed with his father's CFO. I interviewed with the CFO I would be replacing. I took tests. Then I took more tests.

"At the end of the day, Bruce gave me a little review of my interview. 'Well, I think you can do the job, but I'm not sure you're a CFO. Would you accept vice president of accounting?' I replied, 'It depends. What does it entail?'"

White proved hard to pin down—especially about the position's salary—but promised to get back to Burnell in two weeks, after he returned from a trip to Spain. When Burnell didn't hear from White, he picked up the phone.

"I didn't say, 'Fish or cut bait' but that's the way I felt. I even drove down to Merrillville from Chicago, thinking he was going to make me an offer."

Instead, White asked more questions and told Burnell that moving to the Merrillville area was a condition of employment. Finally, White made an offer and Burnell accepted. The wait was worth it. Like Deno Yiankes, Burnell would end up spending the rest of his career at White Lodging, finding financing for deals and keeping track of the money flowing in and out of the company's coffers.

"I'm not a hospitality guy, I'm more of a finance accounting guy with a fair degree of tax knowledge," said Burnell. "For Bruce it was a good fit for that stage of White Lodging's growth. We had 16 hotels at the time.

"There was a certain genius to how he put the organization together," continued Burnell. "Most of us were first-generation college graduates, so I think there was a hunger there that Bruce tapped into."

> A devoted fan of management theories, White drew liberally from Stephen R. Covey's bestselling classic: The Seven Habits of Highly Effective People. His favorite Covey tenet? Number 2: "Begin with the end in mind."

Putting a solid financial team in place was a critical early step for White Lodging, but it was not the only priority. The company's *raison d'etre* was not real estate acquisition—even if it sometimes looked that way—its true mission was to provide hospitality. And not just any level of hospitality. White wanted his company to be known for excellence. He rarely missed an opportunity in the company newsletter, presentations, or speeches to underscore the importance of guest satisfaction.

"Remember, the most critical factor in determining our success is to attract and retain our guests," he wrote in an early issue of White Lodging's newsletter. "We must focus on making each guest a repeat guest. . . . Very simply our success or failure is determined during those moments we interact with our guests. Our guests leave with an impression of us. They fall into one of three distinct categories: plus, zero or minus. The only acceptable experience for our guests is a PLUS."

A devoted fan of management theories, White drew liberally from Stephen R. Covey's bestselling classic: "The Seven Habits of Highly Effective People." His favorite Covey tenet? Number 2: "Begin with the end in mind." White repeated the saying so often that anyone within his circle of executives and friends could rattle it off even if they had not read Covey's book. For White, the six simple words offered a model approach to work and life. It could be applied to finance, marketing, operations, training, even personal fitness—any area where problems needed to be solved or plans needed to be made.

> Ask yourself every day, "Am I being the person I want to be right now?"

Long before he picked up Covey's book, White had demonstrated a talent for planning events and managing other people. Skipping out of Sunday School in Crown Point as a kid had required skill in getting back to the church just in time to avoid detection by his parents. In third grade, White organized a citywide football league in Crown Point, complete with homemade stadium, a regular schedule, and scorekeeping.

"Our parents went out and bought us little kid football uniforms, not the same color or whatever, just little cheap stuff. . . . We built a football stadium in our side yard. We used swing sets as goalposts. And we built some very rudimentary bleachers using blocks and two-by-fours and two-by-sixes that we stole from local home building sites. . . . I found somebody in every grade school in Crown

> By the time he married Beth, White was applying rigorous planning concepts to his own life. He developed and used one-year, three-year, and five-year plans to make sure that he kept the big picture in mind.

Point and got them to organize a team. We formed a league. We named the field Woods Stadium, after my third-grade teacher Mrs. Woods. My team was the Hurling Tornadoes. . . . The guys that played, they all still talk about our football league."

By the time he married Beth, White was applying rigorous planning concepts to his own life. He developed and used one-year, three-year, and five-year plans to make sure that he kept the big picture in mind. The detailed plans reflected a few of Covey's other 'habits': "Be proactive." "Put first things first." "Sharpen the saw."—shorthand for a concept that White constantly promoted to his employees: continuous improvement. Another of his favorite expressions was "If you're not getting better, you're getting worse." To White's mind, the status quo—good or bad—was just a temporary stop on the long road to excellence.

"Bruce usually had his annual plan done before January 1," said Beth White. "I remember one time—we had been married a few years—he had written up a long list of his goals on pages and pages of yellow legal pads. He asked me my goals for the year. I said, 'Get pregnant by the time I'm 30.' He looked at me: 'That's it?!'"

"Everything is about life balance now, but back then it wasn't," continued Beth. "It was still the old-fashioned 'business first'. But Bruce was always thinking about me, and the kids, family, and friends. When he did his plan for the year, he always put together a list of the friends we should invite to do something or go somewhere that year."

Covey's "Begin with the end in mind" mantra was especially relevant in the realm of human resources. People—good or bad—would make or break White Lodging's success. Hiring the right individuals, training them to deliver top-notch service, and then retaining them was an endless quest in an industry notorious for annual employee turnover in the 80 to 90 percent range. If the desirable 'end' was customer satisfaction, then it made sense to 'begin' with good people—a point that White regularly hammered home to White Lodging managers in the CEO Message in White Lodging's newsletter. Rarely did an issue go to press that didn't include a reminder of the central role of humans in the company's success:

- "Surround yourself with great people. If you surround yourself with giants, you will become one yourself." (October 1991)
- "Treating people like volunteers works and works well . . . because in the final analysis, they are." (May 1993)
- "To become an extraordinary leader, we must continually seek to learn, teach and persuade. Leadership is 1% vision and 99% alignment." (December 1996)
- "People talk about the impact of technology on service, but in our business, it still comes down to people. (November 1997)
- "The most satisfying work for me has always been where I am working with a mix of people, whether they are guests or fellow associates. . . . People provide the life, the vitality, the conscience, and, yes, even the soul of the organization." (January 2001)

During White Lodging's start-up phase, White got by with a handful of staff at headquarters, supplemented by dozens of employees in the field who were taking care of the company's hotels. But White knew he needed to create a permanent structure within White Lodging to handle the inevitable increase in the payroll as the company grew.

"We had times when we were understaffed," said Deno Yiankes. "But for most of our growth years, we were generally staffed a year or two ahead of where we needed to be. Bruce's attitude was that he'd rather take a financial hit by putting someone on the payroll before we really needed them. Doing so would pay dividends by putting us in a better position to train them our way. So, I'd say we were always a little heavy in our management team by design."

In 1989, Bruce White hired John Januszko to build a human resources department for White Lodging.

"John worked for Consolidated Specialty Restaurants for several years before he came to us," said White. "I knew Sandy Levinson, who was John's boss. Sandy had been in the restaurant business since the 1960s and was a major franchisee of TGI Fridays."

When Levinson sold part of his business in 1989, White knew that Levinson's best executives were bound to be 'poached', so he asked him who White Lodging should go after. Levinson didn't hesitate: John Januszko.

> One of Januszko's earliest fans was Corinne White, age 5, who looked around John's unorthodox office and then buttonholed her father: "Daddy, how comes Mr. Januszko's office is so much more interesting than your office?

In addition to long experience in human resources, Januszko brought to White Lodging a memorable combination of humor, whimsy, and work ethic. His office was a kaleidoscope of seasonal decorations, memorabilia, eye-catching oddities, and conversation starters.

"I had a lot of stuff in that office," said Januszko, who retired in 2007. "A two-foot-high crow that perched on a filing cabinet. Heavy-duty cardboard fireplace at Christmas—loaded with real logs. Halloween stuff. A bag of chicken bones in my desk drawer to toss and 'read' when someone asked what I thought we should do about a problem."

One of Januszko's earliest fans was Corinne White, age 5, who

> Happiness equals something to do, someone to love and something to look forward to.

looked around John's unorthodox office and then buttonholed her father: "Daddy, how come Mr. Januszko's office is so much more interesting than yours?"

Januszko's day at White Lodging began at 5 a.m. and wrapped up at 7 p.m., after which he often took a colleague or two to play racquetball.

He never moved to the Merrillville area, preferring to head home to Illinois on Fridays. His weekly 'commute' required getting up at 1 a.m. on Mondays in order to drive more than two hours and pull into the White Lodging parking lot before dawn.

Januszko's arrival came just in time. A year after he joined White Lodging, the first Fairfield Inn by Marriott franchise was awarded to the company. From then on, growth would be the name of the game. And people would be a big part of that growth.

"John was a force, in a very positive, energizing way," said Bruce White. "He was beloved in our organization, absolutely beloved."

White might never have found Januszko if not for the fact that White Lodging had earlier dipped its toes into the world of restaurant franchising. In 1987, Dean White and a few partners purchased an ailing Howard Johnson's on Washington Street in Indianapolis. Bruce wasn't involved in the purchase, but he took on the job of figuring out how to make the best use of the property. Part of the challenge was the downtown area's sketchy atmosphere.

"It was more of a land play than a hotel play by my father," said White. "Marriott wasn't franchising yet—that was three years in the future. We knew immediately that the existing affiliation with Howard Johnson's was not going to let us maximize the value of the property. So, we went out to shop for new hotel flags (brands). But they either weren't available or the lack of quality of the property wouldn't support the flag we aspired to. But we thought we had a good location for a restaurant. So, I called up TGI Fridays because they were a strong brand nationally and were doing particularly well in Indianapolis."

White met with TGI Fridays' CEO, Dick Rivera, and executive vice president Frank Steed. Rivera and Steed green-lighted a franchise for the Washington Street property. The Whites transformed the old hotel into a Ramada Inn and added a TGI Fridays *inside* the hotel—a first for the restaurant franchise. The $8 million renovation virtually gutted the structure, replaced aging mechanical systems, added a pool, and carved out room for the TGI Fridays. The refreshed hotel and new restaurant opened in the summer of 1989 and "was immediately wildly successful," said White.

"In the first 12 months, I think we did about $4.5 million in sales. We ultimately did $6 million plus, which was huge for the Indianapolis market and huge for Fridays' franchise group."

The success of the Indianapolis Ramada-TGI Fridays became a big plus a few years later, after Marriott and White Lodging launched their relationship. Marriott approved conversion of the Washington Street property to a Courtyard by Marriott, further raising the property's profile.

> At a strategic planning meeting in Colorado, my team and I evaluated all of our forward-looking opportunities. We went into the meeting thinking that we were going to really grow in the TGI Fridays space.

As White got to know TGI Fridays' management, he liked what he saw and pondered the possibility of opening more restaurants. He and a handful of White Lodging associates went through TGI Fridays' much-admired training program.

"At one time, our plan was to grow with Fridays," said White. "We looked hard at buying the Atlanta market. And we looked at buying a couple of stores in the Chicago area. I had gone to the Harvard OPM (Owner/President Management) program and I'd learned how to do what I would call opportunity charts. At a strategic planning meeting in Colorado, my team and I evaluated all of our forward-looking opportunities. We went into the meeting thinking that we were going to really grow in the TGI Fridays space. But when we analyzed the financial models of our various ways forward, it became clear that growing through select-service hotels was the preferred route. So, at that meeting, we agreed 'No more TGI Fridays. We're going to focus on Fairfield Inns.'"

Among other things, White made good use of the TGI Fridays training manuals he brought home from a workshop. He handed them over to his new HR vice president John Januszko.

"At one point in time, I had a three-and-a-half-foot pile of TGI Fridays training programs on my desk!" said Januszko with a laugh.

"Our affiliation with TGI Fridays was transformational," said White. "I'll forever be indebted to those guys for the impact and the example and the assistance that they provided."

Another transformational moment for White came while on a trip to visit a fellow Marriott franchisee: Gary Tharaldson. Based in Fargo, North Dakota, Tharaldson started in the hotel business in 1982, just three years before White Lodging launched. His first few hotels were low-end Super 8 motels, but he soon jumped aboard the Marriott franchise train, along with White Lodging. In time he would build more than 400 hotels throughout the country and become North Dakota's sole billionaire. Tharaldson and White met at one of Marriott's earliest franchise gatherings and hit it off.

Mike Wells remembered White telling him about a trip that he and Deno Yiankes made to North Dakota to pick Tharaldson's brain. White was always game for learning from others, rather than reinventing the

The first franchised Fairfield Inn in Merrillville, Indiana.

wheel. The affable Tharaldson was happy to share his successful formula for building small hotels under the Marriott flag.

"White Lodging's real bread and butter early on was building Courtyards and Residence Inns," said Wells. "At first, they didn't really know what they were doing. So, they met with Gary, and Gary said, 'Here's how you do everything. Here's how you get the land. Here's how much you can pay. Here's how you get the permitting. Here's what you do. Here's what you need for food service.' He shared all of his secrets because he wanted to help Bruce. Down the line, Bruce was able to return the favor when Gary needed a hand."

Armed with Tharaldson's wisdom and his own hospitality experience, White and his team hit the ground running in the early 1990s, ready to build more hotels and score a few milestones along the way.

For White, White Lodging was the 'great idea' and taking it to the finish line would be his life's work and a labor of love.

"This year, our past becomes our future," he wrote, not long after White Lodging's first Fairfield Inn opened. "In other words, if we are successful in reaching our quality, financial, human resource, and strategic goals today, we will fulfill our growth objectives of tomorrow. Our future and yours [are] in your hands."

Or, if White had been in a musical mood, he might well have belted out the refrain from the band Timbuk 3's catchy 1986 release: "The Future's So Bright, I Gotta Wear Shades."

See "Rules of the Road: White Lodging at 10" on page 88 for the White Lodging basic principles of management, originally published in the company's monthly newsletter during their tenth anniversary.

RULES OF THE ROAD: White Lodging at 10

Originally published in White Lodging's monthly newsletter in June and July 1995, the year that the company celebrated its tenth anniversary.

Our quotes, philosophies and theories were first conceived in 1990. Very simple. The quotes have been proven to be a straightforward approach to teaching commonsense, management and good business decisions. They are used for solving existing problems and for preventing problems experienced in the past.

The following are some of the basic principles of management. Some of the philosophies deal with concerned managers interacting with their employees, while others deal with managers working together as a team toward a common goal. We have found that consistent use of these quotes and theories provide a common language for all of us to consistently communicate the how's, the why's, and the ways we do things in White Lodging.

- **The more you leave to chance, the less chance you have to see it happen.** Proper planning is essential to successfully accomplishing any given task; this is also supported by the quote: "Success is a Matter of Choice, not Chance." The hospitality business poses many challenges and roadblocks for the successful operator and we cannot afford to let our success be one of chance happening, but must provide programs that, when properly implemented, facilitate the type of success we are looking for.

- **Feedback (attention) is to people what fertilizer is to flowers.** It is the responsibility for each manager to establish goals and give consistent direction and feedback to our employees as to how they are doing and contributing to our success.

- **If you don't enjoy the climb, then given what it takes to get to the top ain't worth it.** Turning room hotel properties is an incredibly challenging task for even the best of managers. If one doesn't enjoy the challenges that come with the task at hand, then it isn't likely that they would be happy or successful in managing that type of opportunity.

- **Quality cannot be a program, it must be a way of doing business.** Quality is not a short-term button campaign or a quarterly promotion, but a way of life for all of those in WLS, as the ability to attract and retain business that is fundamentally essential to any success we can achieve.

RULES OF THE ROAD (continued)

- **Goals and objectives are achieved by departments, but they are earned by individuals.** You must pay attention and nurture those individuals that will make or break you: your staff.

- **Our mission is not that of a sprint, but better resembles a marathon.** We take on projects that have the opportunity for excellence and permanence, or we don't get involved at all. We enjoy short-term successes, but understand that a real success will be achieved by providing consistency over a period of time and that is how we evaluate ourselves.

- **A trained employee is a retained employee.** We can never expect to achieve our turnover objectives that are far below industry standards without a commitment to provide our employees with the best training in the hospitality industry.

- **The primary responsibility of any position is to serve the guest.** Inherent in any of our orientations or training programs should be the immediate understanding that each and every person's primary responsibility is to serve the guest and that should take precedence over any other activity.

- **Should the individual succeed, the team succeeds. If the team succeeds, then the individual succeeds.** This is a quote from Vince Lombardi and it states the obvious: "That, as an organization, we must understand in order for an organization to succeed, our individual employees and managers must be successful in their own responsibilities. Moreover, the individuals that make up our organization have to understand that they can only be successful if the organization is successful. So they should always be as cognizant of the organizational goals as they are of their own individual goals."

- **The most important thing we can all commit to do is to do what we say we will do.** We do not let our mouth and/or sales presentations write a check that our operation cannot cash. We are a results-driven organization, and pride ourselves on only committing to do what we are capable of doing.

- **You can shear a sheep every year, but you can only skin him once.** We are committed to building repeat business and "move heaven and earth" to make sure that a guest will become a repeat guest.

RULES OF THE ROAD (continued)

- **Our best strategy is only as good as our weakest execution.** Marketing plans and programs are great, but in the service business, execution by our front-line people determine whether or not a guest returns. Our focus should always be on consistent execution of our programs and philosophies.

- **It is not what you know, but what you show.** We recognize that we work with some of the finest franchise organizations available and many of us come from excellent hotel backgrounds, but it is what we deliver to the guest on a day-to-day basis that determines how well we are doing and bow we are evaluated.

- **Never give a second chance to make a first impression.** We must always be cognizant of how important it is to immediately make a favorable impression on the guest in such areas as property appearance and appearance of our employees at the front desk, etc.

- **Employees have both a line responsibility and a strategic responsibility.** As a growing organization, it is not enough for a manager just to take care of day-to-day activities and support positive guest experience, but must also communicate those strategic programs that support the growth of White Lodging.

- **Don't strive for perfection, you will never achieve excellence.** Our goals are very lofty in terms of how we evaluate our performance. Our reach should always exceed our grasp or we will never attain the type of recognition from our guests and piers that we expect.

- **Babies and promises have a lot in common, easy to make but hard to deliver.** We must only commit to do that which we are committed to do.

CHAPTER 6

Just Warming Up

> *John Januszko, Larry Burnell and Deno Yiankes—they were the core. All smart guys, great guys, but Bruce really empowered them. I think Deno would tell you, we would have walked over the top of a mountain or through a wall for Bruce. He just made us believe we could do it.*
>
> Steve Poe
> Friend + Business Partner

In 1995, White Lodging celebrated its tenth anniversary. From its start as a scrappy offshoot of Whiteco Industries, White Lodging was now a full-fledged—and fully independent—business. Key executives had been hired. The ranks of support staff now included people like Jan Grabow, John Szczepanski and Roger Aufieri, who would all stay on board for decades. Mike Williams was ever ready to pull off a property opening or fix a problem. A corporate structure was in place. The relationship with Marriott was thriving. The company had established a network of bankers and other financial institutions who trusted White Lodging. Awards were rolling in for individual properties and for the company's leadership in the industry. By April 1996, White Lodging could boast that the company was now managing *one million room nights* annually.

For many businesses, such tangible signs of success would have been an invitation to slow down, relax and bask in the glow of their accomplishments. White and his team had other ideas. They were just warming up. The days of converting distressed properties were disappearing in the rear-view mirror. From now on, new ground-up construction would be the ticket for most White Lodging hotels.

"Some of the first sites we bought for new construction were owned by Marriott," said Deno Yiankes. "They had bought property with the

> For many businesses, such tangible signs of success would have been an invitation to slow down, relax and bask in the glow of their accomplishments. White and his team had other ideas. They were just warming up.

intention of building their own hotels on them. But when Marriott slowed its development pipeline in the early 1990s, they decided to liquidate the sites. We got them at a steep discount. The only condition was that we couldn't buy the site and then build a Hilton on it. We had to build a Marriott select-service hotel."

Among the sites purchased directly from Marriott were three locations in Florida and a property close to the Indianapolis airport. Several sites in Austin and San Antonio, Texas were also acquired by White Lodging on its own. The company kicked into development mode and opened eleven new hotels in 1996, up from two in 1995. The following year brought another eleven openings—heady progress for a company that was only 12 years old.

With only two exceptions—a Sleep Inn and a Hampton Inn—White Lodging's first forty properties were all Marriott-branded. Both organizations were clearly benefiting from White Lodging's eagerness to grow.

"I call it our 'head down period,' where for 10 or 12 years we were just really focused on finding opportunities, grinding out new hotels, and staying laser focused on getting those hotels up and running," said Deno Yiankes. "We were really learning as we went. We built good hotels, but it was rough around the edges. As we got better and better, we could look back at earlier projects and say honestly, 'We didn't know what we didn't know.' But Marriott was happy, and we were fortunate to win a tremendous amount of recognition from them."

Marriott, in fact, was sufficiently happy to ask what it could do to help White Lodging grow.

"We didn't have much money, so I suggested that they guarantee our debt," said Bruce White. "So, we started building all of our properties 100 percent financed. And we paid Marriott a certain amount of basis points. We wouldn't have been able to do that without the support of Bill Marriott and Bill Shaw. So, instead of building one or two properties a year, we ramped up to building 10 or more."

As White Lodging's development team turned out new select-service properties, White and his team began to think more strategically about the future. Where should White Lodging build next? Which markets around the country held the most promise? And what did the company need to do to be able to quickly snag multiple desirable locations in any target market?

Picking markets was a matter of research and a bit of luck. Deno Yiankes' experience assessing hotel properties and markets while at HVS was a big asset as White considered where next to plant White Lodging's flag. The development team looked at a potential market's demographics, economy, politics, infrastructure and other ingredients that together would paint a picture of a community's next 15 to 20 years. Based on those factors, White Lodging could decide where to focus.

"If you pick the right town in the right proximate area where the growth is going to be," explained Larry Burnell, "if you can foresee the future, then it works out famously for the next generation."

Austin, Texas was a textbook example of White Lodging's strategic approach. The company was familiar with the city, having converted a bankrupted 198-room Ramada Inn to a Courtyard by Marriott in 1993.

"We called it The Tower of Power because it was several stories high," said White. "And we had incredible success there, even though at the time Austin was on its butt. But the

> The company's success in any city required climbing a steep learning curve. Every community has its own way of doing things. Real estate laws and local regulations could vary widely, requiring a deft touch in winning support from the local bureaucracy.

University of Texas at Austin was there. IBM had a research facility there. You could see that high tech was getting started. The city had a growing music scene. And Texas in general was poised to grow. So, our gut told us that Austin would be a good bet, but we couldn't do anything without the financial numbers to support our belief. At the end of the day, we had to show numbers to whoever might be financing it. But we could see that Marriott was grossly underrepresented in Austin and the potential was there."

White Lodging's calculated gamble in Austin paid off royally. Between 1993 and 2025, the company converted or built more than 30 hotels in or near the city.

White Lodging's success in Austin and in identifying other promising markets might seem like a case of simple sleuthing. But the company's success in any city required climbing a steep learning curve. Every community has its own way of doing things. Real estate laws and local regulations could vary widely, requiring a deft touch in winning support from the local bureaucracy. Not everyone in every community welcomed the kind of development that the hotel industry brought with it. Markets could also differ dramatically in terms of building costs. Figuring out the right ballpark budget was important to control cost overruns and secure financing. Getting the numbers 'right'—or at least close to right—could mean the difference between making a great investment or pouring money down the drain.

> **In the beginning it was the Bruce-Larry-Deno Team. Bankers would ask us how we worked. I would say, 'Well, Deno is a reasonably optimistic guy. He says the glass is half full.' Bruce is like 'You mean those six glasses of overflowing water?' And I would say, 'What glass? I don't see a glass.' That sums up our personalities.**
>
> **Larry Burnell**
> Strategic Advisor, Board Member

"Deno was the data guy and he would keep White Lodging's wheels out of the ditch," said Steve Poe. "Bruce would sometimes listen to Deno's numbers and say, 'That's great data, but data is in the past and we're going into the future. You can look at all the appraisals in the world, but they don't forecast.' Deno would start his response with 'Well, respectfully, Bruce. . . .' Which meant that he didn't agree with Bruce. We would laugh. They complemented each other very well. They trusted each other."

Fortunately for White Lodging and its assorted project partners, White had prioritized getting to know his fellow franchisees. When Marriott created franchisee advisory councils for its select-service brands, White jumped on board. Among other things, the councils could provide real-life feedback to Marriott about what was working—or not working—in the field.

"Marriott headquarters was like a second office for me," said White. "I was there constantly. Marriott's team listened to us. At one point, the franchisees redesigned the architectural models for all of the select-service brands."

"The advisory councils were a tremendous resource for us," said Deno Yiankes, who also was a fixture at Marriott's headquarters. "In the hospitality business we all shared data. We benchmarked information, and we had a handshake deal that it would never be used in the wrong manner to try to hurt a competitor. It was used to try to make us *all* better and share knowledge and make one plus one equal three. That helped us tremendously. We would share benchmarks on costs. We didn't know if we were building for the right costs. We would share operating performance, how the hotels were running. A lot of the data that's available today wasn't available back then in the early and mid-1990s, so sharing information was important for all of us."

Understanding data and real-life numbers was particularly important to White. Liam Brown of Marriott recalled a conversation early on with White in which he was trying to nudge him into embracing the Residence Inn brand more enthusiastically.

"Residence Inn was a category that had a little bit of a different model in terms of sales," said Brown. "I remember being at a three- or four-day sales class where Bruce told me, 'Courtyards and Fairfields, I understand that if you build it, they will come. I'm not so sure about Residence Inn, how do you make that work?'"

Brown encouraged White to take a closer look at the Residence Inn sales framework. He did. Once White thoroughly grasped how the extended-stay franchise model functioned financially, he was all in.

White's hesitancy—albeit brief—was a bit of an anomaly. From his earliest days on South Park onward, he was renowned for pushing the envelope and following his own instincts when he was confident that his ideas improved the status quo. He wanted things to be right, not merely 'good enough.' The sermon about excellence that White's junior high school basketball coach had preached again and again did

> **❝ Bruce was always an innovator. We innovated early on with some of our properties by modifying the prototype a little bit if we thought it would enhance things for the guests. We would move something like a small wall by two feet if it created better flow for the guest. ❞**
>
> **Deno Yiankes**
> Strategic Advisor, Board Member

> No one cares how much, before they know how much you care.

not go to waste. To no one's surprise, White was usually involved in the choice of carpets, lights and furniture in many of White Lodging's properties. Improving the guest experience was his north star.

"I think a lot of people don't realize how hands-on Bruce was," said Steve Poe. "He had practically grown up in the hotel industry, thanks to his dad's Holiday Inn. Our first hotel deal together was a Residence Inn in Austin in 1998. I found the land for it near Parmer and I-35. Then we agonized. Should we stick with the standard 88-room model or try to squeeze in 100 rooms? Bruce agonized. Larry Burnell agonized. Deno too. We ended up building an 88-room hotel with room to expand. Looking back, it's hard to believe that we worried about the difference.

"Bruce was involved at every stage," continued Poe. "He understood how things worked. He could streamline the whole operation. For example, I know nothing about designing a kitchen. But he could look at plans and say, 'No, we're not doing that. Or this. That's not the way to do it.'"

"Bruce was absolutely, positively a visionary and an innovator," said John Januszko. "He could look at a piece of ground, he could visualize the hotel there. He could, if he tried hard enough, check into that hotel that he envisioned and spend the night there."

If White didn't agree with something in Marriott's official brand templates, he did not hesitate to tweak something if he felt there was a better solution. Efficiency was important, but the guest's comfort was paramount. In his March 1995 CEO Message, he underscored the reality that *guests* are White Lodging's lifeblood:

"We must not allow our associates to forget that the guest, in the final analysis, pays the bill for every bit of work done by everyone in WLS. Each associate, by doing his or her job well, has the opportunity to give the guest a good value for his money. If he doesn't do a good job, he gives the guest poor value. . . . You don't have to meet the guest face-to-face to please or displease them. A poorly typed letter, a piece of equipment that doesn't work, a mistake in billing—things like these can make a guest lose confidence in our ability to serve them."

By 2000, White and his team had opened a total of 63 hotels, almost all of them affiliated with Marriott. White Lodging had planted its flag in multiple markets around the country. The company's hotels could be found in six Indiana cities, from Merrillville to Valparaiso, South Bend to Goshen, Fort Wayne to Indianapolis. Other properties were in Florida, Colorado, Tennessee, Michigan, Utah, and Kentucky.

As proud as White was to watch a new hotel rise from the ground, he was equally proud of the awards bestowed on the company's properties, staff and corporate headquarters. Even before he launched White Lodging in 1985, White had learned the value of recognition—not for himself, but for the people around him who worked hard and often didn't hear "Attaboys!" or much praise for quietly doing their jobs. Whether the awards came from a corporate partner like Marriott or were internal White Lodging awards, he wanted associates to know that they were appreciated.

John Szczepanski, who joined White's team to help develop White Lodging's corporate culture, was assigned the task of kick-starting an internal recognition program.

> **"I guess I looked a little nervous, because Bruce explained the importance of what he was asking me to do. 'John, do you know how many people we have working here? How many do you think get recognition?'"**
>
> John Szczepanski
> White Lodging Executive (Retired)

"Bruce came to see me and said, 'John, I want you to get an associate awards banquet set up. I want you to start a 10-year club for anybody that's been here ten years or more. I want you to set up an annual dinner for them. And I also want you to set up a five-year luncheon.'

"I guess I looked a little nervous, because Bruce explained the importance of what he was asking me to do. 'John, do you know how many people we have working here? How many do you think get recognition?' He wanted me to make sure that the local newspapers ran a story anytime something significant happened. 'You know why?' he asked me. 'Because the only other time that most people might have their names in the newspaper is in the obituary section.' He turned around and walked out."

Szczepanski got the message and set to work following through on White's request. One of the first events he organized was a luncheon for employees who had been with the company for five years. Just as the luncheon was getting underway, White came through to shake hands with the banquet staff and look over the arrangements. He called Szczepanski into the kitchen to the place where tall carts called stackers held the plated entrées, ready for serving.

"I'll never forget it," said Szczepanski. "He goes to one of stackers and takes the lid off one of the plates. 'What size filet is this?' he asked me. 'Six ounces,' I replied. He asked, 'Do you know what size filet they serve VIPs?' I honestly didn't know. 'Well, it's eight ounces. The next time we serve filets at an event like this, they'd better be eight ounces.' He dropped the top back on the plate and walked away. I never made that mistake again! But the important part of the story is that he cared enough to go into the kitchen to check. How many company owners would do that?"

White's disappointed reaction to the undersized filets reflected his long-held belief that people should all be treated with respect, whether they're a Fortune 500 CEO or a part-time dishwasher. Growing up in the Region had taught him never to underestimate or disrespect someone simply because of the job they held. On South Park, neighbors had jobs that ranged from steel mill worker to telephone company executive. The lesson was reinforced when his father Dean sent him out on the road in the summer with a crew of men who installed White Advertising signs for a living. The young White had learned to look past their gruff exteriors, respect their work ethic, and get along with people whose lives were entirely different from his own. Right up to the end of his own life, he would never lose his habit of connecting on whatever level put another person at ease.

"Bruce truly believed in the Golden Rule," said Purdue friend Lacy Johnson. "Not only did he treat people the way he wanted to be treated he wanted you to feel comfortable doing the same."

Sometimes the way to show respect was a simple matter of kindness and common sense. White made sure that the full-time housekeepers at White Lodging properties had three sets of uniforms, not the standard two. The decision might sound like a small one, but to staff who must find time to wash their uniforms, the gesture was a sign that the boss was looking out for them. If he found that a property was not supplying three uniforms, the general manager had some explaining to do.

"Bruce wanted people to be treated fairly," said Szczepanski. "He wanted them to be taken care of."

Despite having more than 60 hotels to look after—and many more in the pipeline—White did his best to make sure that his work life did not take a big bite out of his time with family. By 2000, he and Beth were parenting three bright and engaging children: Corinne, Conner, and Otis.

Beth handled most of the basic day-to-day parenting tasks, but Bruce came in a close second. Both had fond memories of growing up in classic two-parent households where life unfolded to the dependable rhythm of school, homework, sports, and family time. Beth's upbringing in quiet Mount Vernon, Indiana, was, in her words, idyllic. Bruce's childhood on South Park was filled with pranks and boyish hijinks, but also stability and routine. The couple wanted their three kids to experience a childhood like their own.

With that in mind, the Whites decided to move from Valparaiso, Indiana, where they had lived since 1990, to Edwards, Colorado. Staying in "Valpo" would have required their young trio to navigate the social challenges of being the grandchildren of a billionaire. Dean White had sold his billboard business to Chancellor Media in 1998 for $960 million. (He held on to several other smaller businesses.) The sale boosted Dean to the Forbes list of ultra-wealthy Americans. Dean and Barbara White were far from showy people, but their financial stature and name recognition made it difficult to be a "White" living in northwest Indiana without dealing with unwanted attention and assumptions.

> Bruce sometimes arranged for his executives or financial partners to come out to Edwards to enjoy a mix of skiing and business. Newbies to the daunting prospect of skiing with White learned to take his trademark downhill yodeling and hellbent-for-leather speed in stride.

Colorado was a good fit for Bruce, Beth, and their three children. Bruce could run White Lodging from almost anywhere, as long as he

A family photo: Beth and Bruce White with their children, (left to right) Otis, Corinne, and Conner.

had access to phone, Internet, and reliable express delivery service. He traveled so frequently that he was accustomed to operating from a de facto mobile office. The kids, who were all under the age of 10 at the time of the move, were happy to enjoy the mountains, attend the local charter school, and make new friends. Skiing became a family focal point. A steady stream of family and friends visited the Whites to enjoy the slopes and sit by a fire at night to catch up on personal news. Bruce sometimes arranged for his executives or financial partners to come out to Edwards to enjoy a mix of skiing and business. Newbies to the daunting prospect of skiing with White learned to take his trademark downhill yodeling and hellbent-for-leather speed in stride: "That's just Bruce being Bruce!"

No one enjoyed White's playful side more than his three children. The blue Econoline van of his youth was long gone, but White was still a kid and mischief-maker at heart. When his kids were young, he tapped out the first few notes of the Power Rangers TV theme song on the car horn when he headed off to work in the morning. As the kids grew up, he did his best to instill his love of classic rock in each of them.

"He was definitely a CEO at heart," said Otis, the youngest, laughing. "When it came to the car radio, he ruled. Nobody in the backseat had any say over what station was on. He told us that when we were old enough to drive, then we could pick the station. But, of course, he still pulled seniority.

"Dad had a great singing voice," continued Otis. "So, he would sometimes sing songs that none of us recognized. He also made-up songs on the fly. His knowledge of music was encyclopedic."

"I remember being a kid and singing, "Bye-bye, Miss American Pie" at dinner parties, and my dad getting everyone to sing it, even all the kids," said older son Conner White.

From his days booking acts at the Holiday Star, White had met all the major bands of the day, including Crosby, Stills, Nash & Young, the Marshall Tucker Band, the Eagles, and the Doobie Brothers (the infamous "Doe-bee Bros"). But he also dipped into outlaw country, blues, and more obscure genres. The Purdue fight song was a favorite; his kids often heard him singing it around the house. Classic rock, however, remained White's sweet spot.

"Dad and I shared a passion for classic rock," said daughter Corinne. "We were both huge fans of Neil Young. Once we actually flew to Winnipeg—Young's hometown—to see him in concert. It was pretty epic. I have a great memory of listening to Peter Frampton's "Do You Feel Like I Do"—which I think runs 11 minutes—while Dad insisted on driving around the neighborhood rather than pull into the driveway. He was rocking out to it while my brothers and I were thinking 'Can we just go home, you crazy person?!'"

> *When the kids were young, every morning before school, Bruce or Beth would have all three recite a simple mantra: "Be a leader. Be a learner. Be a friend."*

As much as White delighted in goofing around with his kids, he treasured even more his role in helping them grow up and find their places in the world. He and Beth wanted their children to recognize the privileges they enjoyed and understand that those privileges did not exempt them from hard work, setting goals, helping others, and pulling their own weight in the world. When the kids were young, every morning before school, Bruce or Beth would have all three recite a simple mantra: "Be a leader. Be a learner, Be a friend."

"It was one of those things that you don't realize your parents are nurturing in you until you're older," said Conner White. "So, although we repeated it every day, it took time to sink in. Now that I'm an adult, I'm grateful and I plan to do the same thing for my own kids."

One of the special privileges that the White children enjoyed growing up was in the "be a learner" category: world travel. The ability to introduce their three kids to other cultures and exotic landscapes was an opportunity that Beth and Bruce did not want to miss. Beth had not traveled much in her youth, but Bruce had vacationed out West with his family when he was a kid—experiences that had opened the

Enjoying family travel: Bruce with Conner, Corinne, and Beth in the middle row, and, in front, Otis.

world to him. Hitchhiking up and down the West Coast in college with his Purdue buddy Steve Poe had also given him a permanent case of wanderlust.

Planning family trips was one of White's passions. Beth learned to quietly back out of the room if she found her husband occupied with his GeoSafari Globe and directories of airports around the world.

"He would figure out where he wanted to go, and then calculate each leg of the trip based on where the airports were and whether the runways were long enough for us to land. He would be in 'the zone', making calculations, and I knew to come back later."

"We traveled all the time," said Otis White. "The trips were always very educational. I had been to fifty different countries before I turned 10. Everything was planned out. The plane would land and we would be met by a tour guide who whisked us away to sightsee."

White always brought work with him, but when he could take a break, he joined the family, often taking them on casual walks through the local hotels and restaurants. The impromptu tours were never the focal point of the family's travels but, a hotelier to the bone, Bruce couldn't resist checking out how hospitality was offered in other countries.

In the meantime, White Lodging continued its successful strategy of saturating promising U.S. markets with select-service hotels. Where possible, the company secured multiple building sites in an up-and-coming city and filled them with the different select-service tiers. A Courtyard here. A SpringHill Suites or Fairfield Inn down the street. A Residence Inn around the corner. Another Courtyard near the airport. Being able to offer a variety of price points and amenities in a single community guaranteed White Lodging a steady influx of guests.

> **"I went to a party where I was chatting up a beautiful girl who asked me if I had joined a fraternity yet. When I said no, she said she would have her boyfriend call me. Bruce White was the boyfriend. I got the message!"**
>
> Mike Wells
> Friend + Business Partner

The approach was clearly a winning formula. White Lodging had nailed the process of building small hotels, mainly on the periphery of large cities where airports and suburban office parks promised a reliable number of "heads in beds" most nights. The company could easily

> Even a blind squirrel finds a nut now and then.

keep doing what it was doing for years, as long as nothing drastic happened to put a damper on business travel or family vacations.

But Fate had other plans for White. Mike Wells, a Purdue fraternity brother, called out of the blue one day in the late 1990s with an intriguing proposition. The two men had been casual friends since Wells's sophomore year.

"My freshman year at Purdue, I didn't have any interest in pledging to a fraternity," said Wells. "I was just trying to survive. But the next year I went to a party where I was chatting up a beautiful girl who asked me if I had joined a fraternity yet. When I said no, she said she would have her boyfriend call me. Bruce White was the boyfriend. I got the message!"

Wells also got the promised phone call, and in short order Bruce sponsored him for Beta House. He was 'in.' The two young men couldn't have been more different. Wells was a serious student who eventually was awarded the Iron Key, one of Purdue's most coveted honors. In the meantime, White was cutting classes and playing hoops at Co-Rec with Lacy Johnson, Steve Poe and anyone else who could dribble and shoot. The Beta House bond, however, was a strong one and the two men remained on each other's radar screen after graduating and going their separate ways.

Unlike White, who had little interest in politics, Wells felt a strong pull to get involved with Indiana's state government. After graduating from Purdue with a degree in interdisciplinary engineering, he took another degree from Indiana University's Robert H. McKinney School of Law. While practicing law in Indianapolis, he joined a long-term, slow-moving effort to transform the state capital into a major convention city.

Wells understood the challenges. He recalled staying at the old Howard Johnson on Washington Street in the late 1970s while he was still a student at Purdue, a decade before Dean White bought the property and breathed new life into it. Wells's impression of the core of Indianapolis was far from positive.

"There wasn't much of a downtown in the 1970s," said Wells. "I saw a guy get mugged just across the street from my hotel. I grew up in rural farm town, so I was pretty dubious about the city."

In 1987, Dean White and partners bought the rundown Washington Street property and poured $8 million into a complete overhaul. The newly refurbished hotel gave the Whites the same kind of toehold in Indianapolis that the Tower of Power supplied White Lodging in Austin, Texas. Having at least one property in a city provided a useful ear to the ground in case the market proved worth exploring further.

Seven years passed before White Lodging took another look at Indianapolis. In October 1994, the company opened a Fairfield Inn close to the airport. Two months later, it was joined by a Residence Inn. In 1996—when White Lodging was revving up its development pipeline—the company opened three more hotels in the Indianapolis metro area, including a Courtyard at the Capitol and the Residence Inn Downtown.

At the time, Bruce White was keeping an eye on Indianapolis, but he wasn't looking to be a major player in the transformation of the city into a convention hub. White Lodging was busy in Austin and other markets that held promise. But when Mike Wells called to pitch Bruce and Dean White on the possibility of building a convention-worthy, full-service Marriott, the Whites were game for hearing the details. Wells was happy to oblige. He rolled out the plan for the downtown overhaul.

"We had a convention center, but it was small," said Wells. "The city had gotten some federal money and started to demolish older buildings in the downtown area."

The next step was construction of several large office towers in the 1980s. Market Tower and BMO Plaza opened in 1988. 300 North Meridien opened in 1989. The SalesForce tower went up in 1990. There was a lull in construction in the 1990s, during an economic downturn, then a couple of large name-brand hotels were added to the mix.

What Indianapolis needed next, said Wells, was another major expansion of the

> *Wells knew that White Lodging specialized in select-service properties of 100 or so rooms, but it didn't strike him as out of reach for the company to stretch and build a much bigger hotel, particularly if it happened with Marriott's backing and blessing.*

convention center. The original meeting facility on South Capitol Avenue opened in 1972, was expanded in 1984, and again in 1993. Ideally, under the new plan to reinvigorate downtown, another large-scale, full-service hotel should be built adjacent to an updated and much bigger convention center.

Wells knew that White Lodging specialized in select-service properties of 100 or so rooms, but it didn't strike him as out of reach for the company to stretch and build a much bigger hotel, particularly if it happened with Marriott's backing and blessing.

White was intrigued. He was also ready for a new challenge. Like his mentor Bill Marriott, Bruce loved big hotels. His early experiences with his dad's Holiday Inn (later Radisson) and with Hyatt in California had given him a taste for the hustle and bustle of big banquets, live entertainment and lavish decor. The select-service hotel space was certainly rewarding, but the small-scale properties did not buzz with the excitement of a large hotel.

"Bruce made a lot of his beginning fortune in limited-service properties, but I think what burned inside of him was the idea that you're not a really true hotelier unless you own a full-service hotel," said Larry Burnell. "He never said that to me, but I really believe that."

Naturally, there was more to the Indianapolis convention center story than simply building a hotel. The sticky wicket was the extraordinarily tight deadline. Wells explained to White that Indianapolis was in the running to land the Republican National Convention in 2000. Representatives from the Republican National Committee (RNC) had already visited Indianapolis and liked what they saw. But they also pointed out one major weakness: the lack of a hotel large enough to serve as the RNC headquarters during the convention. To win the RNC contract, the city needed to show that it could build a big headquarters hotel in time for the convention. The clock was ticking.

Wells connected White with Indianapolis Mayor Steve Goldsmith for a preliminary conversation about the project. The city had not yet selected a site for the big hotel near the convention center, so Wells convinced Goldsmith to move the existing convention bureau and use that piece of land for the hotel. The location problem was now solved, but the tight deadline was still a big issue. After hearing more details, White said he'd take a pass. Wells was disappointed but accepted White's decision and set about finding another solution to the problem. He rounded up a few investors, but then he decided to try White again to see if White Lodging would be interested in managing the property after it was built. This time White said yes and joined in planning meetings for the hotel. Then, to Wells' surprise, White told him that he and his father wanted to be investors after all. Wells welcomed the news. The Whites' willingness to take part-ownership would guarantee project financing.

> **"In typical Bruce fashion, he said, 'I hear you, but what's the path to allowing us to do this?'"** recalled Deno Yiankes. "The first three times, Marriott said, 'There is no path.' But the fourth time, they said 'Well, let's see' and then we were able to do it."

Just when it looked like things were falling into place, Wells got a call from Mayor Goldsmith. The Republican National Committee representatives were coming back to town in a few days and wanted to see progress.

"Progress?!" said a panicked Wells to Goldsmith. "You've got to be kidding! We don't even have complete plans yet!"

Nothing if not resourceful, Wells came up with an ingenious temporary solution.

"I told the Mayor's office to have the convention bureau block off the parking lot so no one could park there the next Wednesday. I said, 'I'll arrange to get a backhoe there and we'll start tearing up the asphalt.' So, on Wednesday, a guy with a backhoe goes out and starts ripping up asphalt. And the limo comes by, a convoy of all these RNC people, accompanied by the Mayor. Goldsmith pointed out where the backhoe was working and said, 'That's the site for the new hotel.' And the RNC people nodded and said, 'Great. Looks good.'"

The next major hurdle involved Marriott. As a rule, the company did not franchise its full-service hotels. Reasons ranged from wanting to retain the management fees for large properties to nervousness about allowing a franchisee to try its hand at operating a hotel that was easily five times larger and far more complex than any Courtyard or Fairfield Inn.

When Marriott inevitably said no, White didn't give up.

"In typical Bruce fashion, he said, 'I hear you, but what's the path to allowing us to do this?'" recalled Deno Yiankes. "The first three times, Marriott said, 'There is no path.' But the fourth time, they said 'Well, let's see' and then we were able to do it."

Working in White's favor were two major plusses. First, he had an impeccable track record of operating more than sixty Marriott hotels. No one could quarrel with White Lodging's ability to run a hotel and win accolades from guests. Second, White Lodging was, in fact, already managing a full-service Marriott, albeit a smaller-than-usual property. In May 1997, White Lodging had opened a 157-room full-service Marriott in Boulder, Colorado.

"I had gotten a call from Steve Joyce, who was head of franchising at Marriott at the time," recalled White. "He had been contacted by a man who owned a piece of property in a strip mall in Boulder and wanted to build a Marriott. Steve said that Marriott had no interest in building such a small full-service property, but he thought we might be interested in checking out the opportunity.

"So, I went out to Boulder, talked to the guy, and I could see that it was a great location," continued White. "I went back to Steve and told him the Boulder location could be a great hotel and promised that I would make it work financially."

Initially, White got what he called "huge resistance" to the Boulder project from others in Marriott, because Marriott simply did not 'do' full-service properties of fewer than 300 to 350 rooms. But Steve Joyce went to bat for White and convinced Marriott to let White Lodging work its magic. According to Mike Williams, who opened the Boulder hotel for White Lodging in 1997, the Colorado property hit the ball out of the park right away and won "Hotel of the Year."

After listening to similar arguments in favor of letting White Lodging tackle the huge Indianapolis convention hotel, Marriott greenlighted the project. The fact that the Whites were financing 50 percent of the convention hotel also boosted Marriott's confidence. The Whites had skin in the game and would pull out the stops to make the property a big success. Ground was broken on August 10, 1999. White and his team dove in headfirst and hands-on. Every detail had to be right. White wanted to show that—as ever—Marriott's faith in White Lodging's abilities was amply justified. The exercise echoed his experience twenty years earlier designing the Holiday Star Plaza theater out of a book.

"We made every single decision on that hotel," said Mike Wells. "The carpet. The tile. The wallpaper. We spent hours and hours poring over every detail. We were afraid we were going to bankrupt ourselves."

With Marriott's encouragement, White hired Dave Sibley as general manager of the convention hotel. Sibley was a senior manager at Marriott who brought 17 years of experience to the new Indianapolis Marriott Downtown. Many of the new hotel staff also came from other Marriott properties.

Some hiccups toward the end pushed out the opening date by two months, but on April 26, 2001, the $103 million, 19-story hotel opened with great fanfare. Marriott International's Chairman Bill Marriott attended the festivities.

The RNC had long ago crossed Indianapolis off its list of contenders for the 2000 convention, but it no longer mattered. The new hotel and expanded convention center were a big success. The opening of the Indianapolis Marriott Downtown kicked off a brand-new chapter for Bruce White and White Lodging. The project proved definitively that White and his company possessed the expertise and ambition to build and operate ANY hotel property, including a complex convention hotel.

Just five months after the star-spangled opening of the Indianapolis Marriott Downtown, the party—and the world—came to an abrupt halt.

The date was September 11, 2001.

CHAPTER 7

The White Lodging Way

> *"The future may be more turbulent than ever, presenting us with many challenges that may seem daunting, but White Lodging will not change ... our vision, culture, or our plans for the future."*
>
> Bruce W. White
> Message from the CEO
> September 2001

September 11, 2001. Everyone remembers where they were that morning. In a car, driving to work. Riding a school bus. Scrolling through email at the corner coffee shop. Exchanging 'Good mornings' with colleagues in the break room.

"I was at a Residence Inn franchise board meeting in New England on the morning of September 11," said Bruce White. "The hotel's banquet houseman came into the meeting room and said to us, 'I think you really ought to come out and see what's going on.'

"We weren't happy about interrupting our work to watch a television broadcast, but the houseman politely repeated his statement. So, we all got up and went into the next room."

On the large television screen was live footage of the second World Trade Center burning and collapsing. In under two hours, four hijacked passenger airliners had crashed into New York's World Trade Center, the Pentagon near Washington, D.C., and a field outside of Pittsburgh, Pennsylvania. The world watched in horror and disbelief as both of Manhattan's iconic 110-floor Twin Towers collapsed, killing thousands of people, including scores of first responders who were trapped in the inferno. Buried in the rubble was a 22-story, 825-room Marriott.

"Obviously, that was the end of our board meeting," said White. "I'll never forget that. I couldn't do anything other than go back to my room, turn on CNN, and get further depressed. And I was stuck. All air traffic was shut down. We had a company plane in the air that was heading to Florida, if I recall correctly. Later, the guys on that trip told me that when the pilots got the emergency order from the Federal Aviation Administration, they were given two minutes to land. The pilots called out, 'Hold onto your seat belts!' And the plane just—boom!—landed."

> "September 11 was a fist in the face for anybody in hospitality," said White. "It was a fist in the face for the entire country. We just had to manage our way through it."

The immediate aftermath of the 9/11 terrorist attacks was chaotic. Many people who were hundreds or thousands of miles from home at the time of the attacks rented cars and drove home. Commercial flights began a tentative return to normal on September 13 but welcomed far fewer passengers. The short-term fallout from the attacks was predictable: Millions of people canceled trips. In the first full week after flights resumed, passenger numbers fell by nearly 45 percent, to 5 million from 9 million in the week before September 11. Airports and airlines scrambled to institute new security rules. Congress issued $15 billion in grants and loan guarantees to keep the airlines flying.

Although the airline and insurance industries took the biggest hits, hotels and travel agencies around the world also felt the acute financial pain of processing millions of cancellations in the days and weeks after the attacks. According to a 2003 report, the U.S. hotel industry suffered an estimated $700 million loss in revenue during the *first four days alone* following the surprise attacks. The luxury hotel segment was most heavily impacted, but room occupancy numbers dropped in every segment, including select-service.

"September 11 was a fist in the face for anybody in hospitality," said Bruce White. "It was a fist in the face for the entire country. We just had to manage our way through it."

In White Lodging's September 2001 newsletter, White expressed his anger over the terrorist attacks and the unwelcome reality that "our crazy world [is] forever changed. . . . These events will make a disappointing year even worse." Then he struck a comforting note: "Short-term, our priorities may change out of necessity, but longer term, the view remains the same. . . . While recent events are truly a tragedy beyond comprehension for those directly involved and an issue of tremendous complexity and cost for our country to deal with, it is only a matter of inconvenience for WLS; we will deal with our cancellations and re-engineer to our expected lower levels of business. . . . Sometimes it takes a catastrophic event to give us a wake-up call of all the wonderful things we enjoy in everyday life that can too easily be taken for granted."

Unlike many of its industry peers, White Lodging did not lay off hundreds of people as a cost-cutting measure post-9/11. Instead, a hiring freeze was instituted, positions were eliminated by attrition, and expenses were trimmed wherever practicable. All vice presidents and high-level executives had their salaries frozen until further notice. White took care to point out that being a privately owned business meant that White Lodging was not held hostage by Wall Street's demands for drastic cost-cutting. The company had the flexibility to be nimble in good times and bad. White himself was the ultimate buck-stops-here.

"Decisions could be made quickly," said Steve Poe. "If we were competing for a piece of land, for example, we could tell landowners that we really had only one decision-maker: Bruce White."

White was confident that prudent financial management would steer the company through economic rough patches, including 9/11. After all, White Lodging had started its life by rescuing bankrupt hotel properties that had failed to plan for tough times. White and his financial wizards Deno Yiankes and Larry Burnell had evaluated dozens of poorly managed hotels and knew how little it took for a property to lose its luster . . . and soon, its profit margin and investors. They were not going to let White Lodging make the same mistakes . . . terrorists or not.

The hospitality industry began a slow recovery in January 2002, but progress was uneven and hard to predict. One welcome bright spot for White Lodging, according to Larry Burnell, was the fact that the brand-new Indianapolis Marriott Downtown—by far the company's largest property—was in a Midwestern city that was easy to drive to. After an initial drop in reservations immediately after the attacks, convention business in Indianapolis overall suffered less damage than in some of the other major convention hubs around the country.

White Lodging's management team was featured on the cover of Hotel Business magazine in April 2007—(left to right) Deno Yiankes, Larry Burnell, Bruce White, and Dave Sibley.

White was grateful for any positive news, but 9/11 and its aftermath underscored how quickly and easily a major disaster could upend plans or aggravate existing problems. In the months before the terrorist attacks, White Lodging had been dealing with internal challenges of its own. At issue was the fallout of the fast-paced growth of the company's portfolio of properties between 1996 and 2000—from 21 properties to 63. The growth was gratifying, but tripling the number of hotels in five years was sorely testing the young company's infrastructure.

"For an organization that was small and growing as fast as we were, you have to go faster than people think," said White. "Everybody's going to think it's chaos, because there is a lot of chaos involved. But when the opportunity is there and you have everybody else competing with you for the same opportunity, you just have to move faster than other people."

"Founders put innate pressure on themselves and on people that are around them," said Tim Ozark, a member of White's Young Presidents Organization (YPO) forum. "They look for two major qualities: trust and performance. And if they don't get that, you're not going to be around very long. They set a very fast pace. They expect you to keep up. . . . They do that because when they're starting off, they're wearing multiple hats. They don't have the luxury of having committees or boards or others that help support them."

The company's internal growing pains were further complicated by external forces. A downturn in manufacturing in the U.S. in 2000 rippled through the economy as companies cut orders for supplies and laid off employees. The high-tech dot.com bubble of the 1990s burst in March 2001, hitting financial markets hard and adding to the general economic recession. The boom times of 1991–2000 were coming to an end. September 11 only added to the anxiety.

"We are now facing a weakened economy that has had a negative impact on our major demand generators and eroded our bottom lines," wrote White in May 2001. "I would love to turn back the clock and relive those growth years, but let's get out of denial and deal with the hand we are currently dealt. The past few years have been a great party . . . one that seemed like it would never end. . . . I view a downturn as a time for WLS to build for the future. This is not a time to panic, but to focus and increase White Lodging's value in the eyes of our owners, associates, and guests. WLS accrued much of its growth during good times, and we will solidify our value and reputation during times that may not be so good."

During its start-up phase in the late 1980s, White Lodging's high guest satisfaction scores at its properties had helped to establish the small company's reputation and win the confidence of an industry giant like Marriott. If White Lodging wanted to continue to grow, those standards needed to remain high or, if possible, go even higher. But lately, instead of improving or holding steady, performance at White Lodging's properties appeared—at least to White—to be slipping.

> "While people may be the problem, they are also always the solution."
>
> Bruce W. White

"I would be remiss if I did not admit that I have an uneasiness that often keeps me awake at night," White wrote in April 2001. "We still have a lack of internal consistency in our Fairfield and Courtyard properties. . . . Are we growing too fast? Are we victims of believing our own press clippings? Is our leadership really committed to the WLS vision? I know the problem always seems like people . . . lack of quality leaders, lack of quality associates, etc. While people may be the problem, they are also always the solution."

One of the big challenges for hospitality companies large and small is employee turnover. Hospitality is a 'high touch' business, one that depends on delivering not only the tangibles—a clean room, thoughtful amenities, smooth check-ins and check-outs—but also the intangibles of the staff's attitude, energy, and friendliness. A hotel with gorgeous rooms but a restless or unhappy staff might do well for a time. But eventually, when the shiny newness wears off, the costs of constant turnover and so-so guest reviews will take a toll.

The U.S. hotel industry's employee turnover rate typically hovers between eighty and ninety percent annually. The cost of replacing staff is measured not only by the number of empty positions and the expense of training new recruits, but by the negative impact on guests and customer service. The industry's revolving door problem was too big and widespread ever to be solved, but White felt it could be made less of a problem—at least at White Lodging—by deploying the right tools and the right management. If he could reduce associate turnover at the company by even a few percentage points, it would be a win-win for the associates and the company.

Creating a professional workplace was the first step. In hiring John Januszko in 1989, White laid the groundwork for an expertly run human resources department. Januszko brought not only deep HR experience from his 10 years working with Sandy Levinson, but he also had the ability (and humor) to navigate the chaos that went with the company's growth spurt in the late 1990s. His famously idiosyncratic office provided a lighthearted headquarters for White Lodging's effort to create an inviting workplace. Januszko's office was an oasis of quirky calm in the rough-and-tumble world of a start-up.

> We train until we get it right and then keep training until we can't do it wrong.

Januszko led the charge in helping White Lodging invest in serious training programs, establish a set of standards and procedures that all employees could embrace, and create a culture that would make implementing those procedures day-in and day-out a matter of pride. In time, these efforts combined would become the bedrock of the company's *modus operandi*: "The White Lodging Way."

"Personnel and human resources are two separate issues," said Januszko, explaining his definition of human resources. "*Personnel* is name, rank, and serial number in a file cabinet. *Human resources* is how we treat our folks. What is our moral compass? What is right and what is not right? How do we want to do business? And how quickly do we want get phone calls returned? How do we want to help our people and not just simply blow them off? Trust was the only practice we had, and if we failed on that score, then in my mind, we were useless and our department should be disbanded."

Januszko's colleague John Szczepanski, who joined White's team before White Lodging was launched, believed that "hiring John Januszko and Larry Burnell did two important things for Bruce: Freed him up from worrying about who was taking care of the people and who was taking care of the finances."

Soon after coming aboard in 1989, Januszko discovered one of his boss's favorite pastimes: reading . . . voraciously. True to his favorite Covey caveat—"Begin with the end in mind"—White plunged into a steady stream of books about management theories, customer service, training, and more, always on the lookout for ideas worth trying at White Lodging. His office bookshelves were crammed with binders and books. In the latter category, subjects covered every aspect of business

OPEN BOOK: Bruce White's Reading List

Bruce White was a lifelong learner and voracious reader. The shelves in his Merrillville office are stacked with books on a wide range of topics, from basketball and bourbon to entrepreneurship, marketing, real estate, customer service and management theories. Mixed in for good measure are dozens of binders filled with employee training materials, White Lodging business plans, and a prized set of vintage Marriott operating manuals.

A few business classics that White kept handy:

Open Secrets of Success: The Gary Tharaldson Story, Patrick McCloskey (2018)

The Seven Habits of Highly Effective People: Powerful Lessons in Personal Change, Stephen R. Covey (1989, multiple reprints)

The Spirit to Serve: Marriott's Way, J. W. Marriott, Jr. and Kathi Ann Brown (1997)

Positively Outrageous Service: How to Delight and Astound Your Customers and Win Them for Life, T. Scott Gross, Andrew Szabo, and Michael Hoffman (2016)

Rhythm: How to Achieve Breakthrough Execution and Accelerate Growth, Patrick Thean (2014)

The Effective Executive: The Definitive Guide to Getting the Right Things Done, Peter F. Drucker (2014)

Without Reservations: How a Family Root Beer Stand Grew into a Global Hotel Company, J. W. Marriott, Jr. and Kathi Ann Brown (2014)

A Passion for Excellence: The Leadership Difference, Tom Peters and Nancy Austin (1989, multiple reprints)

The Luxury Strategy: Break the Rules of Marketing to Build Luxury Brands, Jean-Noel Kapferer and Vincent Bastien (2009)

Managing in Turbulent Times, Peter F. Drucker (1994)

Moments of Truth: New Strategies for Today's Customer-Driven Economy, Jan Carlzon (1989)

American Icon: Alan Mulally and the Fight to Save Ford Motor Company, Bryce G. Hoffman (2012)

Competitive Advantage Through People: Unleashing the Power of the Work Force, Jeffrey Pfeffer (1994) organization, plus a sizeable number of biographies by or about successful entrepreneurs and companies.

John Szczepanski recalled being on Bruce's recipient list for a book about the Japanese auto industry's phenomenal success in the 1980s. It was the first of many tomes that would land on his desk at the Star Plaza Radisson—Szczepanski's early headquarters—accompanied by White's unspoken invitation to absorb every tidbit that might be useful.

Others, like John Januszko, tried to get ahead of the curve.

"Bruce's assistant Elsa Bruining used to tell us what books were on his desk," said Januszko, grinning. "We'd all run out and get copies so we would have a heads-up about what new trend or idea he was probably going to want to try. We tried to stay a quarter-step ahead of him!"

White described himself as "obsessed" with learning as much as he could about other companies' best practices: "You can see it in my library. My executive education courses. My networking. My seeking out other people who know a lot more than I do.... It got to the point where I was reading too much and was overwhelming my direct reports. People were begging me not to read another book. And, by the way, they were right."

In addition to what he picked up in books, White gleaned general business advice from his peers in the Young Presidents Organization (YPO). No one else in his YPO forum was in hospitality, but all were grappling with fundamental issues common to business start-ups. One of the best things about White's forum—nicknamed The Jugglers—was the strictly-observed rule: What happens in YPO, stays in YPO. Members could ask any kind of question about how to handle sticky or sensitive issues in business, family, wealth management or life, knowing that it would be kept confidential. The forum also helped members think through the mechanics of running and growing a business.

> "Bruce was a lifelong learner, like no one else I've ever encountered in my life," said Deno Yiankes. "Hands down."

"Many new entrepreneurs miss coming up with a strategy," said Tim Ozark, one of White's YPO forum members. "When you're starting a business, you're running so fast and hard, and you're facing problems for the first time, and you don't have a deep bench to which you can hand off those problems, you don't have time necessarily to focus on strategy. YPO gave us a place to think and talk about it."

"Anytime Bruce came back from one of his YPO meetings, we would be prepared for an onslaught of new ideas," said John Januszko, chuckling.

One of the challenges for Januszko, Szczepanski, and the rest of the team was White's relentless itch to take new concepts for a test-drive.

"Unless you actually worked for Bruce or spent a lot of time with him, he could be—simultaneously—simple and a very difficult man to describe," said Januszko. "His wants were simple, but his thought processes, his ideas, his innovativeness, his challenges were always coming at you. You didn't know which ones to focus on first. He was an idea generator; we were the team to execute the ideas. Fortunately, I had a tremendous group of people working in human resources with me."

Before launching White Lodging in 1985, White had been exposed to models—good and bad—for operating a hotel business. Two years with Hyatt in California after graduating from Purdue had introduced him to the ways a successful hotel company trains its employees. That hands-on knowledge came in handy when his father Dean was struggling to make a go of the Merrillville Holiday Inn in the late 1970s, and asked Bruce to come home and "fix" it. Bruce agreed to help and quickly implemented basic procedures and systems that he had learned at Hyatt. A lack of standardized processes, combined with the wrong people for the job, could hamper or break a business, especially one that depended heavily on pleasing the public. It was a fundamental truth that he would keep in mind as he built his own company.

> Kamen was the expert who told Bruce and Dean White in no uncertain terms that they were too alike to work together. In so doing, Kamen became the unofficial midwife for the birth of White Lodging soon thereafter in 1985.

"Hire right" was one of White's top workplace priorities. If White Lodging wanted to keep its employee turnover rate below the industry average, the first step was to do all that was humanly possible to pick the best people for the job. White wanted new recruits to the small-but-growing ranks of the corporate team to be "Kamenized"—undergo a battery of tests conducted by Dr. Herbert S. Kamen, an industrial psychologist in the Chicago area. Kamen was the expert who told Bruce and Dean White in no uncertain terms that they were too alike to work together. In so doing, Kamen became the unofficial midwife for the birth of White Lodging soon thereafter in 1985.

John Januszko "inherited" Dr. Kamen when he joined White Lodging in 1989. Kamen vetted candidates for key jobs at headquarters and certain general manager positions in the field. He followed up with reports detailing his impressions.

"Kamen understood our company and he understood Bruce," said Januszko. "He understood what we were looking for, the kinds of skills needed for each position. I hate the word 'testing' but after a day of it, he could give us a pretty good idea about whether someone was the right candidate. He was really accurate. We passed on some people that upfront looked like they were a good fit, but they didn't do well with Kamen. He wasn't cheap! I used to say that we paid for his yacht on Lake Michigan, the *USS White Lodging*."

Setting up a first-rate training program at White Lodging was also high on White's list of assignments for the human resources department. Good training programs would accomplish two important goals: teach staff what they needed to know to do their jobs well and, second, give White Lodging employees a way to upgrade their skills and move into more challenging positions and higher pay. Both goals were important, but the second one had the potential to help reduce turnover. If an associate could see a clear path to advancement in the company, they might be less likely to leave.

"We begged, borrowed, and stole anything we could from everybody," said Januszko, laughing. "That's the only way we could have done it!"

"TGI Fridays had this wonderful service culture," said Bruce White. "We learned so much about how to hire the right people, the importance of quality training, and the right way to do training. Their standards were very high and how they communicated and reinforced and measured those standards was great. Their real focus was on execution. So, we applied those to the hotel industry as well."

White did not believe in reinventing the wheel. He loved being first in most endeavors, but if someone else had already perfected a process or other useful tool, his attitude was, borrow freely and with gratitude. His trip to North Dakota to pick the brain of fellow Marriott franchisee Gary Tharaldson was a prime example. Tharaldson shared his considerable knowledge with White at a time when White Lodging was still new to select-service, a generous gesture for which White was forever grateful.

Conner White, Bruce's older son, observed: "When my dad wanted to learn how to do something, he would look around and say, 'Hey, who does this best at the moment? Let's first learn from them and then we can go from there.' His approach was to master the fundamentals and build a foundation of knowledge. Then you can tweak it to fit with your own values and your own organization."

> In White's eyes, the guest was always the ultimate gauge of White Lodging's success—indeed, any hospitality company's success. If posh Ritz-Carlton could lose sight of what its guests experienced, what was to stop White Lodging from doing the same?

White and his team sought out models for White Lodging's processes, training, and more. Disney was a company that White admired for its culture. John Januszko headed to a couple of workshops at Disney World in Florida.

"I was impressed with the fact that, if you were going to work there as an associate, you actually had to know the names of the Seven Dwarves," said Januszko. "And you had to know a lot of the history of the various Disney characters, because if you get stopped in the park by somebody, and you have the Disney uniform or badge on, guests expect you to know that. Where's Dumbo? Where's Goofy? Where's so-and-so? You'd better know that. And the company would test you on your knowledge."

Another source of wisdom was Ritz-Carlton, a hotel brand long associated with luxury and top-flight service. In 1992, Ritz-Carlton won the prestigious Malcolm Baldrige National Quality Award[17] in the Service category. The next summer, White took several White Lodging executives to California to hear a presentation by the company's president and chief operating officer, Horst Schulze.[18]

John Januszko was one of the White Lodging team members who traveled from Indiana to the West Coast for Schulze's presentation: "Part of the deal in winning the Baldrige was that Ritz-Carlton had to open their doors and do training sessions for people that wanted to come in and find out how in the world they did what they did to win the Baldrige. So, we took them up on that and went out there. Bruce, myself, John Szczepanski, and a couple of other people went."

> Treating people like volunteers works and works well... because in the final analysis . . . they are.

In August 1993, White shared a memorable story that Ritz-Carlton's president had told the audience at the training session:

"[Schulze] was asked what prompted Ritz-Carlton to pursue a goal as ambitious as the Malcolm Baldrige Award, and he told the story that the Ritz-Carlton had previously been recognized by *Meetings and Conventions* magazine and several other prestigious institutions as the number one hotel chain; they had a banquet to celebrate their success. At the banquet, they dined on the finest foods and drank the finest of champagne as they toasted the many successes they had been recognized for.

"Horst got to the office the next day and found four escalated guest complaints on his desk from the previous day, and he realized that while they may be recognized for the finest levels of service in the hotel industry, they were all too frequently failing in the guests' eyes and he had to find a better way.

"The top management of the Ritz-Carlton conducted a self-evaluation and graded themselves a 9+ compared to their competitors, but a four on a scale of ten as to where they needed to be in their guests' eyes," continued White. "It was then they decided to pursue the Baldrige and commit themselves to a total quality management process with consistency of their services, productivity and efficiency of their operations."

---

[17]Ritz-Carlton won the Baldrige Award in 1992, and a second time, in 1999.
[18]Marriott International later acquired Ritz-Carlton in two transactions: 1995 and 1998.

White did not put White Lodging through the formal rigors of competing for the Baldrige, but he was delighted to absorb the lessons in quality from Ritz-Carlton's efforts. In White's eyes, the guest was always the ultimate gauge of White Lodging's success—indeed, any hospitality company's success. If posh Ritz-Carlton could lose sight of what its guests experienced, what was to stop White Lodging from doing the same? Schulze's story was a reminder that even a revered brand could fall into Success Syndrome—believing its press clippings—if a company took its past reputation for granted. White worried that White Lodging's successful growth might lead to a similar blind spot among associates. He often used his CEO Message to express his worries about whether White Lodging was keeping its eye on the ball. He had been in business long enough to know that the road to success was littered with defunct companies that had started off strong and ended up losing their way.

"Bruce would get frustrated," said John Szczepanski. "You can't blame him. Here's his dream and he wanted to realize it. He wanted the company's general managers to adopt a mentality that 'You own this building, that you're managing. You own it. Make your decisions like you own it. Not make your decisions like you think I want it.'"

The White Lodging wallet-friendly Passport to Excellence—now known as a Pledge Card—reinforces the company's vision, values, and approach to guest satisfaction.

Besides absorbing Schulze's insights into top-tier guest service, White Lodging adopted one specific idea from the luxury brand. Ritz-Carlton gave each of its employees a small wallet-friendly card on which were printed the company's service values. The card served as an ever-present reminder of the standards to which employees were expected to hold themselves. The card idea resonated with White.

"Bruce wanted to find out what might be useful to White Lodging from all different sources," said John Szczepanski. "It was like a treasure hunt. He would pick out the two or three items that had value to him, and then make something out of it."

"We called our card the Passport to Excellence," said John Januszko. "The first one was a little trifold card that had our basics printed on it. There were 21 basics or 22 basics, depending upon which associates we were targeting. So, if you were in maintenance, for example, you had a card that was slightly different from the one the front office people had. Because the jobs required different critical success factors."

Over time, the lists would change—sometimes a little too often for associates to commit to memory the specific wording. But overall, the concept of keeping the company's key values handy for regular reference became a permanent fixture of White Lodging's culture, thanks to Ritz-Carlton.

"I am probably one of the least creative people you could ever meet," White wrote in March 2000. (A self-deprecating claim that many people would contest.) "I do consider myself a methodical gatherer and organizer. I am always trying to collect ideas from others that can improve WLS. I have enormous files of notes and articles that I regularly refer to and then shape them in a way that makes sense for WLS application. That is why we can look at successful people and/or organizations and learn from them."

❖ ❖ ❖ ❖ ❖

Through the years, White Lodging developed training programs designed to help every associate master their jobs. White wanted the company's employees to become the kind of lifelong learner he was—always curious, always eager to tackle a new subject. Not everyone

> The company launched its signature multi-day "Flight School" in 1991. For more than thirty years, the program has helped thousands of White Lodging associates prepare for management roles.

shared his zeal for learning, but White did his best to provide not only a model, but tools.

Certain training programs were tailored for associates entering management positions, where knowing how to lead, inspire, and keep tabs on daily operations was critical. The longest-running program is White Lodging's signature multi-day Flight School, launched in the early 1990s. For more than thirty years, the Flight School program has helped thousands of White Lodging associates prepare for management roles. The inaugural Flight School was a makeshift arrangement, complete with theatrical costumes as a backdrop.

"The third floor of the old Star Plaza Theater was where we would meet," recalled John Januszko. "That was where they stored all the extra costumes and props. We put screens up to block that out. That was the only room we had available, so we would set up tables and whatever else we needed. I always felt sorry for the F&B people from the hotel next door, because they had to lug coffee and everything up three flights of stairs. There were no elevators that went up to the third floor."

White wrote frequently and passionately about the importance of training. In January 1997, amid White Lodging's biggest growth spurt to date, he devoted his monthly column to "Developing Star Performers," in which he underscored the value of training to reach the company's long-term goals:

> "Everyone would readily agree it is imperative that a forward-looking growth company attract talented managers, develop them quickly and keep them effectively employed. Very few companies do what is necessary to achieve this. Lack of poor hiring and training along with poor standards are the primary causes of poor performance.
>
> "We say that, as a management company, people are our most important asset, but what do we do to indicate we treat people as important as we do profits? Do we watch our people development as

closely as our P&L? Do we have a people development "budget" as we have an operating budget?

"We have the best training available and the commitment to implement these tools to the fullest extent. It is our goal to develop the most effective management team in the industry, and we are prepared to offer whatever support is necessary to support this objective.

"Every year our talent pool will get deeper and better because we are constantly building critical mass on the premise; we never have enough great people. We hire for leadership, not position. That way, when opportunities arise, we don't have to create a hole in one part of our company to fill an opening in another."

> Future growth would rest heavily on White Lodging's day-in-day-out processes and culture. And those processes and culture, in turn, depended on the attitude of the company's managers and associates.

As the company's properties evolved, more training programs blossomed, tailored to specific roles and areas of the company's operations, from safety and maintenance to brand immersion and onboarding new associates. In 1996, SOAR—Simply Obsessed with Associate Retention—was added, along with the Leadership Development Series (LDS), which opened the door for non-management-level associates to train for management positions. In addition to its core training and leadership development curriculum, White Lodging now includes LinkedIn's 22,000 courses available to associates 24/7.

Setting and maintaining superior standards was another critical area in which Bruce White wanted to see White Lodging excel. Setting standards isn't necessarily difficult, but living up to them can be.

"Founders are an unusual but an extremely demanding type to work for," said Tim Ozark. "I think Bruce was that way. He set a really high standard, but that standard was his own standard. So, it wasn't false. And I appreciated that about him."

Unlike training for specific mechanical tasks—how to clean a room, set a table properly, slice a cake, mix a martini—absorbing and upholding high standards requires a combination of aptitude and attitude. You can be diligent about picking up the phone before the third ring, but if you bark into receiver or exude boredom, your efficiency will be eclipsed by your bad manners. Conversely, a cheery smile and great attitude alone can't fix a running toilet or find a guest's missing dry-cleaning.

Returning from a meeting at the JW Marriott Desert Ridge Resort near Phoenix, Arizona, in May 2003, White summed up what he considered the perfect balance between taking care of a property and taking care of guests—and doing both at a very high level: "The resort is spectacular, only exceeded by the quality of the associates and their eagerness to exceed even the most demanding guest's expectations. I was very impressed that the local management team has a profound understanding of the need not to rely on the physical impressiveness of the property to succeed, but to make sure the backbone of the property's success is in the attitude and orientation towards service by the associate team."

> In March 1992, White unveiled a new Vision Statement, the last sentence of which gave all associates a clear message about the company's standards:
>
> "White Lodging Services will be the preferred management company for those owners who desire to maximize the value of their investment by supporting our commitment to market segment leadership. We will only commit to excellence and permanence, or not commit at all."

Long before that trip to Arizona, White kick-started the process of creating similarly high standards for White Lodging. He and his executive team hammered out a few fundamentals: a vision statement, a mission statement for the staff at headquarters, and the start of a full-time campaign to develop, communicate, enforce and reinforce the company's service aspirations. The words and procedures would be tweaked now and then for the next three decades, but never veer far from the original message and values.

In November 1990, White reported on progress in creating a few of the basic tools the company needed.

"We . . . finished our Mission Statement that focused on the ability to attract and retain business and have been working hard to fulfill these objectives. Also completed is the WLS Long Term Plan, and we are in the process of implementing Best Practices, Certifications Programs,

Management Training Programs, as well as manpower development and career pathing for our managers."

The launch of a company newsletter in 1989 supplied White with a monthly pulpit for expounding on the standards he wanted everyone at White Lodging to embrace. Every issue touched on training and standards. Sometimes White used personal stories to engage readers; other times, he shined a direct spotlight on performance and reminded associates that guests have the final say on questions of quality.

"Remember, the most critical factor in determining our success is to attract and retain our guests," White wrote in February 1990. "We must focus on making each guest a repeat guest. To do this, we must create an experience for all those that use our service. Very simply our success or failure is determined during those moments we interact with our guests. Our guests leave with an impression of us. They fall into one of three destined categories: plus, zero or minus. The only acceptable experience for our guests is a PLUS."

"Guest service is not confined to front line personnel," White wrote nine years later. "Guest service must be a way of life . . . our culture and a way of doing things. It begins at the top and is reflected in our processes and measurements. It must permeate the entire organization, in every hotel and every department. We must care enough to hold ourselves accountable. We must

THE MANAGEMENT PHILOSOPHIES that White Lodging implemented through the years usually came with catchy names to make them easy to remember. An undated memo in the company's archive lists 15 theories that had staying power and contributed to the overall philosophy known today as "The White Lodging Way."

- Plus, Zero, Minus Theory
- Back Dock Theory
- Four Walls Theory
- Success Syndrome Theory
- Ownership Theory
- Ten Thousand Beer Can Theory
- Bubble Theory
- Don't Know, Don't Care, Can't Do Theory
- Sinking Boat Theory
- Stadium Theory
- Walking Your Talk
- Top Gun Theory
- Pie Theory
- Moment of Truth Theory
- First and Ten Theory

evaluate our efforts, not by our standards, but how our guest senses it. After all, if we are going to invest in training, the ultimate judge of its effectiveness is the guest, isn't it?"

"Bruce spoke our language," said Liam Brown of Marriott International. "He hit on what was important. No matter how bad the economic environment is or how good it is, if you don't get the **guest piece** right, it's very hard to get anything else right."

Together with setting high standards, the company needed to help associates keep those standards top of mind. White believed in the power of standardized procedures, accountability, and benchmarking. In his own life, he created annual plans and checklists to help him stay on top of personal and professional goals. He knew how easy it is to let things fall through the cracks without a system for follow-up and follow-through.

> "Dad always preached shift to shift excellence," said Otis White, Bruce's younger son. "Those were things that Conner and I always heard as we were growing in our management positions. You need to be focused on executing every shift perfectly every day."

"Implementation means consistent execution and development of the right habits," White wrote in December 1993. "Once we have the right habits, we have character. And with the right character, we control our destiny."

The Passport to Excellence, modeled on Ritz-Carlton's card, was one method for helping the company's associates master White Lodging's values. Other methods included the pre-shift meeting, where associates gather before their shift to be briefed on important issues and get revved up.

"Dad always preached shift to shift excellence," said Otis White, Bruce's younger son. "Those were things that Conner and I always heard as we were growing in our management positions. You need to be focused on executing every shift perfectly every day. That is what will lead to sustained success. You can't just be putting out fires. If you're running every shift perfectly, it will lead to a successful operation. But you have to be focused on the processes, you have to be focused on doing everything right, you have to correct in the moment, and that will lead to success."

White Lodging also implemented an assortment of catchily named theories or 'philosophies' that were intended to be readily remembered and easily implemented. Examples included First and Ten, Four Walls, Three Promises, Ten Commitments, Five Keys to Success, Balanced Scorecard, and, of course, the Seven Habits from one of White's favorite books: Stephen Covey's classic *The Seven Habits of Highly Effective People*.

The Balanced Scorecard was a concept White took straight out of one of his management how-to books: "There's a book titled, *The Balanced Scorecard*, authored by Robert S. Kaplan and David P. Norton. It's a pretty simple concept. You just decide which are the most critical areas of success for your business and you create measurements; you don't focus on one thing. It facilitates you taking a broader look at your business than just its profitability. So, you start focusing on lead as opposed to lag indicators. We always wanted to build a company that was long-term and would have sustainable growth. So, we put together our balanced scorecard and it had a large impact on how we evaluated people. We incorporated it into incentive compensation."

Other early initiatives included VAM: Vision Accountable Management, which teaches managers to constantly check their actions and decisions for alignment with the company's vision statement. The Hotel Improvement Plan—nicknamed HIP—launched in January 1994 and supplies every White Lodging property with a toolkit of how-tos and how-oftens for every aspect of a property's physical plant.

> "The White Lodging Way, to Dad, was just: 'This is how you operate a hotel.' For him, it was second nature."
>
> Otis White
> Son

"The HIP or Hotel Improvement Program is more for the maintenance department than it is for the front desk department," said John Januszko. How often do you check this piece of equipment? How do you clean a room? If you follow the HIP book, then you're doing all the right things for your property."

"The White Lodging Way is basically our set of standardized processes for hotel operations," said Otis White. "It's a combination of things. It's checklists, it's leading from the wall, it's your daily pre-shifts. It's the structure that no matter what hotel you're operating, if you're focused on shift-to-shift excellence, you can succeed. It's just a way to consolidate it all and put a bow on it. The White Lodging Way, to Dad, was just 'This is how you operate a hotel.' For him, it was second nature."

Starting from White Lodging's earliest days, White wanted to emulate the service culture he saw at successful companies.

Culture is not easy to duplicate, however. It rests in large part on emotional buy-in by the employees of an organization. If the culture feels fake or is at odds with other signals that employees receive from their managers, the purpose is defeated.

By hiring the right people, setting high standards, developing company-wide processes and procedures, and supplying the tools to benchmark progress on every front, White Lodging put into place the building blocks for the future. It was up to White and the company's managers to set the tone, "walk the walk," and earn associate buy-in every day.

> **"I always wanted to give people more to do than they thought they were capable of doing."**
>
> Bruce W. White

The formula worked.

"A lot of White Lodging general managers have been around a long, long time," said Liam Brown of Marriott International. "General managers are relatively easy to poach, so you want to be a preferred employer, you want people to *want* to come work for you. Some folks in our industry sometimes don't get that, but I think Bruce certainly got it. White Lodging was and is a great place to work—great culture, great opportunities to grow and develop."

White himself was the walking-talking embodiment of the company's culture. Like Bill Marriott, he loved walking through hotels, checking out the latest and greatest in decor and amenities, and—above all—visiting with staff. His ability to remember names and find something in common with every person he talked to was legendary inside and outside of White Lodging.

When Deno Yiankes was working as a line cook at the Star Plaza Radisson in the late 1980s, he recalled seeing White come through the hotel any number of times.

Bruce White with students from Purdue University's hospitality school, which is named after White Lodging.

"My first impression of Bruce was that he was 'on the go.' I never saw him sitting in a chair. If I had twenty encounters with him, all twenty were him walking around the hotel. He was always on the floor, never sitting in his office. . . . Bruce just had the ability to connect with people. And it was not for show or for anything other than he enjoyed encountering people and hearing their stories.

"Bruce would rather have been late to a very important meeting with the CEO of a bank and ask for forgiveness than cut short a conversation with an associate at a property," continued Yiankes. "The pleasure you would see in these individuals' eyes was amazing when 'Bruno Blanco' took time to sit there, talk with them, ask them how their day's going."

"I went with Bruce to see the Fairfield Inn in Austin," said Steve Poe. "It's a small hotel, probably 100 rooms. Bruce did his thing: picked up trash in the parking lot, greeted the manager, and then went into the back to talk with the housekeeping staff, most of whom spoke only Spanish. The whole hotel probably had all of ten employees. Bruce did his best to speak Spanish to them. And he recalled their names. That was a big deal for them. 'Mr. White's coming and he still remembered my name!"

"I used to kid him about finding and picking up a gum wrapper or cigarette butt on his way into the hotel," continued Poe. "I told him he probably planted it! But the truth was that it sent a message: 'This place is important to me. I'll pick up the trash. I notice these things. You should too. I'm not going to tell you to pick it up; I'm going to *teach* you by example."

When the three White children were growing up, it was a given that their father would take them along to check out hotels. The trio saw him talk to everyone from the front desk to the loading dock. White's upbringing as a friendly and proud Region Rat was on full display.

"I've always thought that one of my dad's greatest strengths was his knowledge of geography," said Otis White. "He was so well traveled that he could meet a housekeeper, ask her where she was from, and say, 'Right outside of X? I've been there!' Faces would just light up. . . . We saw from an early age that Dad thought every person was the same. Everybody should be treated with respect. Everybody should be given an opportunity. That was very much a part of who he was."

As White Lodging continued to win awards, and receive good press, White enjoyed it all, but was never entirely satisfied. He often quoted J. W. Marriott, Sr.: "Success is never final." Some of the restlessness was rooted in White's highly competitive nature. Whether on the basketball court, ski slopes or at an annual awards ceremony, he loved winning.

"There was no prouder moment for Bruce than when one of our general managers was getting an award for a hotel," said Mike Williams, who opened many hotels for White through the years. "He would be right at the base of the stage to hug him or her and give a high five. He was like a kid in a candy store. That was the competitiveness coming out in him."

In White's mind, there was always something that could be done better. One of his constant worries about the company was the possibility of White Lodging contracting a case of Success Syndrome. Continuous improvement was a way of life for him. He wanted it to be a way of life for White Lodging's associates.

"The goalposts are always going to be moving, always," White said in a 2022 interview. "And I'm unabashed about that. I make no apology. If you're not getting better, you're getting worse. And my attitude is, if you get frustrated by the idea of continuing to focus and working to get better, then go find a different organization that wants to be mediocre. Because we know that to be a company that lasts forever, we have to be a leader. Otherwise, we'll end up getting bought by somebody else.

"You've got to stay on message, and you've got to be consistent with your expectations," White continued. "I don't care what business you're in, that's just the ABCs of effective leadership or management. I always wanted to give people more to do than they thought they were capable of doing."

> "*The goalposts are always going to be moving, always, And I'm unabashed about that. I make no apology. If you're not getting better, you're getting worse. And my attitude is, if you get frustrated by the idea of continuing to focus and working to get better, then go find a different organization that wants to be mediocre.*"
>
> Bruce W. White

"Bruce really believed in stretching people," said Mike Williams. "He had no problem putting you in a role that you weren't ready for."

"One of Bruce's big issues was consistency, consistency, consistency," said John Januszko. "He would say, 'I don't want five of our properties to be platinum level properties and five properties to be red level properties. I'd rather everybody be green—which is basically neutral—than have this discrepancy with up and down, up and down, up and down. I want consistency, Januszko, get me consistency.'"

"Bruce didn't fully understand at times why everyone didn't share his passion for continuous improvement," said Deno Yiankes. "It was just in his DNA. That's just the way he was wired.'"

◆◆◆◆◆

White's 'wiring' included not letting the 9/11 terrorist attacks derail White Lodging's trajectory. White and his development team continued to build hotels. Some projects had already been committed to before the 2001 terrorist attacks, but others were new opportunities. Like many Americans, White was determined not to let the terrorists 'win' by altering course. He had told White Lodging's associates immediately after 9/11: "WLS will not change . . . our vision, culture, or our plans for the future."

He had worked every day since then keeping that vow. But even someone as far-sighted as Bruce White didn't see that the stars would soon align to change White Lodging's fortunes . . . and his own.

"We were in great markets like Austin, Denver, Indianapolis, Chicago, where we would build a Courtyard or a Fairfield Inn or a Residence Inn, often in the suburbs," said Deno Yiankes. "But we had an appetite to do more. So, it made sense to complement what we had already built with other brands. Why? Because we weren't the only ones building Marriott brand hotels; other franchisees were doing the same thing. So, for example, maybe we wanted to build a Courtyard somewhere, but that brand was already claimed by someone else, maybe a developer already had a Courtyard approved. Or maybe we had already built enough Courtyards in that area. So, we might build a Hilton Garden instead. It was a natural evolution to establish relationships with other hotel companies."

"Our philosophy from the beginning was to go into markets with great long-term growth potential," said White. "We wanted to be multi-brand, multi-segment in that market. In other words, we just don't want to own one hotel and try to keep that little corner to ourselves. We want to be the largest hotel owner or the second largest hotel owner in that marketplace."

"Part of the strategy that Bruce and his management team figured out is that you want to be in a city in which there's a good business climate," said Tim Ozark, a YPO peer. "It's growing, it's got recognizable educational institutions that bring young people there and contribute graduates to the workforce, and its lifestyle makes it a desirable place to live. That's the right market."

Marriott remained a preferred brand partner, particularly now that White Lodging had amply demonstrated its capabilities with the 2001 opening of the 600+ room Indianapolis Marriott Downtown. White was eager to explore opportunities to build another full-service Marriott. He didn't have long to wait. White's fraternity brother Steve Poe had been itching to build a convention hotel in Louisville, Kentucky along the lines of the Indianapolis Downtown Marriott. Poe brought Kentucky's Governor Paul E. Patton to Indianapolis to tour the property. The governor liked what he saw and in December 2002, local Louisville leaders held a "site dedication" for a 616-room Marriott hotel near the convention center. An official groundbreaking ceremony took place on May 25, 2003, after the city succeeded in putting together the last parcels of land needed for the hotel to proceed. The new hotel would replace an old block of adult entertainment stores (long known locally as "the porno district") and contribute to the city's efforts to spruce up its downtown and attract national conventions.

Twenty-two months later, the 17-story Marriott Louisville Downtown officially opened on March 28, 2005, across the street from the expanded Kentucky International Convention Center. When the $110 million property threw open its doors, the hotel won Marriott's "Opening of the Year Award"—the same honor that the Indianapolis Downtown Marriott earned in 2001. Once again, Bill Marriott flew in from Washington, D.C. for the opening.

> "Now this is a 17-story building, so when the fire alarm goes off, it automatically calls five different fire companies," said Poe, smiling ruefully at the memory. "Not only that, but it shuts down the elevators."

Six weeks later, the 131st Kentucky Derby brought thousands of race fans to Louisville—a perfect opportunity to show off the new hotel. As a thank you for their support, Poe and White invited several Marriott executives to enjoy the Derby weekend. All went

The Marriott Louisville Downtown won Marriott's "Opening of the Year Award" when it opened in 2005.

swimmingly until Saturday morning—race day. The hotel was sold out and the only meeting room available for the group's private brunch was small and not ideal for setting up and serving food for sixteen people.

"So, we blocked off the pedway leading to the convention center, because there were no conventions in town and it wouldn't be needed," said Poe. "Staff set up the food stations there, because they wouldn't take up space in the small room. So, we're drinking mimosas and enjoying our food and suddenly the fire alarm goes off."

The omelet station was sitting directly under one of the smoke alarms.

"Now this is a 17-story building, so when the fire alarm goes off, it automatically calls five different fire companies," said Poe, smiling ruefully at the memory. "Not only that, but it shuts down the elevators. All the strobe lights are going off. A loudspeaker is booming out 'Evacuate! Evacuate! Evacuate!' So, you have hundreds of people hurrying down the stairwells. There are all these women down in the lobby in their house coats, their hair pulled back because they're still getting ready to go to the track. Nobody's happy. It's a fun story to tell today. It was *not* a fun story at the time!"

Brunch snafu aside, the addition of the Louisville convention hotel to White Lodging's portfolio finished what the Indianapolis Marriott Downtown had started: establishing the company's credentials for constructing and managing large and complex hotels. White Lodging was no longer typecast as a builder and manager of select-service properties only. The company would continue to build hotels in the 100-to-200 room range, but many of its future properties—large and small—would be markedly more stylish and upscale than the relatively simple select-service templates that marked the company's first fifteen years.

As White Lodging entered its third decade, the company continued to polish its skills in analyzing markets. Not every bet paid off. Memphis, Tennessee, proved to be a disappointing market. According to Deno Yiankes, the city was simply too difficult and expensive to reach to provide the level of traffic a new hotel needed to flourish. Fortunately, the company built only one 63-room Fairfield Inn, in 1995, before realizing that its energies would be better spent elsewhere.

Phoenix, Arizona was another market that didn't pan out, according to Yiankes.

"We had never built anything in that area, so I spoke to a very well-respected consultant that I've known for years," said Yiankes. "He warned Bruce and me that you have to be careful with hotels there because the weather is comfortable only four months of the year; the rest of the time, no one wants to come there. It's too hot. So, to survive, you must either drop your rates by 50 percent or more or accept that the hotel will run only 30 to 40 percent occupancy during the off months. He explained that unless you're a resort, it's tough to make select-service work in Phoenix.

> For someone as well-traveled as White, giving the cold shoulder to overseas markets might seem odd. But he had sound reasons for turning down opportunities to expand abroad.

"Well, we went ahead anyway and built four beautiful hotels, including a Courtyard, thinking it would run at 75 percent occupancy," said Yiankes. "Wrong! We did okay, but never came close to what we had anticipated. Eventually we sold all four properties. Maybe we suffered from a little bit of Success Syndrome. But we learned from the experience. As a result, we became that much more thorough in our market analyses going forward."

One enormous market that Bruce White had no interest in was international. For someone as well-traveled as White, giving the cold shoulder to overseas markets might seem odd. But he had sound reasons for turning down opportunities to expand abroad.

"I had the chance to go to China, I forget the year, but I could have done sixteen hotels in a joint partnership with the Chinese government," said White. "I love adventure, I love travel, I've been to 110 countries, so the idea of the adventure was great. But there's no better place to do business than the United States. The rule of law, the growth in the economy, our market knowledge, our understanding of the consumer in the United States. So, despite inheriting an adventurous soul from my father, at the end of the day, reason had to rule. And so, my answer was always no."

Craig White, Bruce's youngest brother, recalled their father's efforts to interest White in doing business in China: "He was really trying to sell Bruce on the idea that through his business connections he could maybe open some hotels in China. And Bruce told him, 'Hey, Dad, I appreciate this, but we have such a great thing going here, we know our strategy, we know our focus. And there are so many opportunities here in the United States that there's no need to take the risk.'"

> Living on a ranch has taught me that money is like cow manure, put it in one place it stinks but spread it around and it makes things grow!

Tim Ozark, one of White's YPO peers, credited White with having the discipline not to get pulled into something that sounded sexy on the surface: "Bruce's passion, besides his love of the operational aspects of a hotel, was developing hotels. He really loved building new properties, but I think he looked at the risk of building in China and felt it was greater than the returns that he could get. I walked through hotels with him all over the world. It didn't matter if we were in Cairo or Kathmandu, he wanted to see local hotels. He would talk to the general manager, look around, and when we'd get back to the United States, he would always say, 'Glad I dodged that bullet!'"

Although White routinely turned down opportunities to build hotels overseas, he couldn't resist traveling the globe himself, usually hauling along friends and family on once-in-a-lifetime adventures. Beth and the three White children were old hands at traveling with 'Bruno Blanco', but others were new to the thrill of hopping aboard the family's jet and heading to exotic places. In keeping with White's love of planning, every trip was wall-to-wall fun for those lucky enough to step on board.

"I went on dozens of trips with Bruce," said Mike Wells. "We went to South America, we went to the Pacific. I've been to London with Bruce and Beth a number of times, plus Italy and Spain. He traveled everywhere. And he was always willing to share what he had. He wanted people to enjoy the trips and he expected nothing in return. He just wanted to be with his friends."

Tim Ozark accompanied White and White's cousin Terry Bird on one memorable around-the-world jaunt: "We watched the movie 'Lawrence of Arabia', just to get in the mood, because we were going to Egypt. Bruce would spend time before the trip researching and finding local tour guides. When we were in the Valley of the Kings late one afternoon, we were guided by a woman who had a dual Ph.D. in hieroglyphics and archeology. She was so interesting, Bruce tried to talk her into joining us for dinner."

The guide explained politely that she needed to go home to give her husband his after-work bath. White recorded her reason for turning down the dinner invitation and sent the video clip immediately to Beth, who likely just shook her head and laughed.

One around-the-world adventure with fraternity brothers Steve Poe and Mike Wells and YPO pal Tim Ozark was particularly unforgettable . . . and totally on-brand for Bruce White.

"Bruce had a penchant for going to unique places," said Poe. "So, on this trip, we were supposed to fly from Argentina to the Falkland Islands. If you recall, England took the Falklands back from Argentina in 1982. The dictator in Argentina had tried to take over the Falklands to distract from all the woes going on at home, inflation and such. So, there was a huge British air base on the island. Our pilots filed the flight plan. We were going to stay there just a day, to see the penguin colonies."

> "The government guy came back and said no again," said Poe. "So, our pilot says, 'Well, what happens if I do it anyway?' And the man replied matter-of-factly: 'We'll shoot you down.'"

To the pilots' surprise—and White's—the flight plan was rejected. The ostensible reason was that no commercial air traffic from Argentina was allowed to travel to the Falklands. The pilots then explained that the planned flight was private, and the stay would be short.

"The government guy came back and said no again," said Poe. "So, our pilot says, 'Well, what happens if I do it anyway?' And the man replied matter-of-factly: 'We'll shoot you down.'"

Not willing to give up, the group decided to fly from Buenos Aires, Argentina to Montevideo, Uruguay and then onward to the Falklands. Doing so added time to the trip but the change to the itinerary took care of any worries about being harassed or—worse—by the Argentinian military.

"By the time we finally head to the Falklands, it's getting late," said Poe, relishing the retelling. "So, the pilots radio ahead to let them know that we're running behind, and the British military guy on the other end says, 'Well, we're shutting down for the night.' They literally turn off the base's runway lights at night. So, Bruce goes up to the cockpit and says, 'Ask him if they have a bar there.' The response is yes. Bruce replies, 'Tell them that we're buying for everybody, as long as the bar is open.' Bingo, the lights stay on and we're allowed to land. We had the greatest time playing darts, drinking beer late into the night with British Royal Marines."

The next day, after seeing the penguins, the group skipped Uruguay and flew directly back to Argentina, where they were greeted by military officials holding machine guns.

"They took our pilots away and put them in a separate room," said Poe. "Then, if I'm remembering correctly, they made us all sign a statement swearing that the Falklands were part of Argentina, not England. After two hours, they let us go. They simply wanted to make their point."

Back at home, in Colorado, the White family was ready for a change of scenery. Or, more precisely, one member of the family was: Corinne. The oldest child and the family's bookworm, she decided in eighth grade that she was ready for a bigger academic challenge than the local schools around Edwards could supply.

"Without telling anyone, she filled out applications for boarding school," said Otis White, Corinne's youngest brother. "She had a habit of doing that. Once, when she was in middle school, she filled out an application for a reality TV show without telling anyone. And then we got a call from the studio that we'd been accepted. The show concept was to trade our mom to another family for two weeks. Corinne has always had a gift for good writing and storytelling.

"Without our parents' knowledge, she sent in applications to several schools," continued Otis. "One day my parents got a call from, I think it was Deerfield Academy, and they said, 'Hey, Corinne is basically through the admissions process, we just need to do the final interview and then we can make our decision from there.' My parents were mystified: 'What are you guys talking about?!' The school rattled off Corinne's name and address. My parents said, 'Yes, that's our daughter.' The school tells them she applied and basically has been admitted. So, that sparked a family conversation: 'Do we really want our kids to go off to boarding school?' I think our parents were concerned because they thought that if Corinne went to a boarding school, most likely Conner and I would follow the trend. And it just didn't really feel like us, as a family."

Bruce and Beth held a family meeting with the trio and asked if they would be game for moving to Chicago. White could work from anywhere, but Chicago would put him closer to White Lodging headquarters if he needed to attend meetings. Corinne would be able to fulfill her ambition to attend an academically challenging school. All three children gave their enthusiastic thumbs up and the family moved to the Windy City. The kids enrolled at the Latin School and settled into urban living.

> Bruce had grown up on a street in Crown Point where kids ran in and out of each other's houses at all hours. Beth and Bruce's household operated on the same principle, much to the benefit of kids whose homes weren't as stable as the Whites'.

One of the bright spots of keeping the family all in one place was the effect on the circle of friends the White kids collected through the years. Whether in Valparaiso, Edwards or Chicago, classmates of Corinne, Conner, and Otis knew they were always welcome in the White household. Bruce had grown up on a street in Crown Point where kids ran in and out of each other's houses at all hours. Beth and Bruce's household operated on the same principle, much to the benefit of kids whose homes weren't as stable as the Whites'.

"When I was growing up, our home was the home base for all of us and our friends," said Conner White. "Always. We constantly had friends sleeping over; we'd always eat at the breakfast table the next morning. My dad had a way of finding the kid that wasn't so confident and kind of building him up. And whoever was the cockiest, he had a way of playfully bringing them down. I think it created this environment where people just loved being around him. I think if there were things that disappointed him, it was arrogance, vanity, hopelessness and giving up."

Chicago brought White new business opportunities and a new high-profile partner: Al Friedman. Friedman had been in Chicago real estate since 1970, when the then-21-year-old inherited the derelict Capitol Hotel at 417 Clark Street from his father, Julius Friedman. Throughout the next five decades, Friedman slowly transformed much of Chicago's blighted River North district block by block, earning him the unofficial title of Mayor of River North. Friedman courted artists, chefs and other creatives to be his tenants in old buildings that had seen better days. Occasionally he accepted artwork in lieu of rent, just to keep the creative vibe going while he bought up blocks of neglected properties. Under Friedman's guidance, grand old historic buildings along the Chicago River were given new life as commercial or residential spaces. Restaurants and art galleries opened. By the time the Whites moved into the neighborhood, River North had become one of the most desirable areas in the city. Friedman owned 12 full blocks and five million square feet of space.

> The mind is like a parachute... it works better when it is open!

In 2002, Friedman put together a deal to build a Marriott in downtown Chicago, but the hotel operator he had partnered with wasn't able to follow through. Without an operator on the project, Friedman was stuck. Marriott suggested that he connect with Bruce White. The initial meeting between the two men verged on comical.

"Bruce says, 'You got to come to this meeting with me.'," said Larry Burnell, White Lodging's chief financial officer at the time. "So, we go to Friedman's office. Bruce has this old camel-colored overcoat on. He couldn't find where to hang it, so he started to roll it up in a ball to stick in a corner. That's Bruce. Al walks in. He's got the $4,000 suit on. He's Hollywood handsome. His hair is perfect. He sees Bruce rolling up the camel coat and goes 'No! No!' and yells to his secretary, 'Get his coat!'"

Fortunately, the clash of sartorial styles had no effect on a promising business relationship. Friedman had an option on land for the hotel and plenty of city government connections; White had the operating expertise and a stellar track record with Marriott. The two agreed to pair up. Friedman Properties and White Lodging would own the hotel together; White Lodging would manage it. The next few months were spent trying to nail down the terms of a very complicated land deal. When the last of the real estate obstacles were swept away, construction of the 24-story hotel began.

In November 2003, White Lodging's first Chicago property—a 306-room Courtyard—opened at 155 East Ontario Street, near the city's Magnificent Mile. Unlike Marriott's earliest Courtyards, this one was unabashedly upscale, boasting a Chicago-themed Art Deco decor, plenty of granite, an indoor swimming pool, expansive gym, and fabulous views of the city. The hotel was within walking distance of dozens of Chicago landmarks and fine restaurants—quite a change from White Lodging's first suburban Courtyards.

> The idea of joining two brands in a single property was the brainchild of White, who was always on the lookout for ways to innovate. The company's first dual-branded property opened in downtown Austin, Texas in 2006: a Residence Inn and Courtyard in one building.

Friedman Properties and White Lodging teamed up to build another Marriott hotel in River North in 2008, one that offered Chicago visitors the novelty of two-hotels-in-one: SpringHill Suites and Residence Inn. Guests enter the 29-story structure through the lower lobby at street level on Dearborn Street and go up one flight to a common registration area. From there, guests head to one of two banks of elevators, depending on which brand they reserved. The only guest-facing services the two brands share in the building are a swimming pool, exercise room, whirlpool, and guest laundry room.

The idea of joining two brands in a single property was the brainchild of White, who was always on the lookout for ways to innovate. The company's first dual-branded property opened in downtown Austin, Texas in 2006: a Residence Inn and Courtyard in one building. The Residence Inn portion contained 179 rooms; Courtyard offered 270. In an echo of the campaign five years earlier to convince Marriott that White Lodging could manage the huge Indianapolis Downtown Marriott, White had to persuade Marriott to let him combine two brands in a single building.

"The separate brands hated the idea," said Mike Wells. "But Bruce used his influence with Marriott to ramrod it through. It wasn't easy. He

The Courtyard & Residence Inn Austin Downtown was the first dual-branded hotel in the country and opened in 2006.

basically had to say that if Marriott wouldn't let him do it, he would try another brand, like Hilton."

In 2013, White Lodging and Friedman Properties put together a combination of *three* brands by *three* different companies into a 19-story "triplex" in River North. The Clark Street location blended a Hyatt Place, a Fairfield Inn by Marriott and an Aloft (a Starwood brand at the time) in one property.

"As a developer, it's attractive to have a more concentrated footprint with multiple brands to attract a wider range of customers at the same location," said Chris Anderson, chief commercial officer for White Lodging, in a 2017 article in *Meetings and Conventions*. "As an operator, it affords us the opportunity to maintain the individual brand experience customers expect. It's also attractive for our associates, because it provides them the opportunity to see how different brands operate without having to change companies, commutes or even buildings."

White's willingness to be an industry pioneer launched a national trend. By 2018, several hundred dual- and triple-branded hotels had been built across the United States by the major hotel companies. Hundreds more were in the pipeline.

"Today, all the brands encourage it because it cuts the cost of having two pools, two exercise rooms, two delivery areas, and the like," said Mike Wells. "It's the only way to economically put hotels together today. And Bruce was a real leader in that."

"We're already moving in the direction of full-service, upper-scale dual brands," said Chris Anderson in the 2017 article, "and I am certain you will see dual brands at the highest segment levels."

Anderson was soon proved right. One of White Lodging's most interesting combinations of brands was the Distil/Moxy complex in downtown Louisville, Kentucky. Steve Poe was instrumental in making the deal happen in his hometown.

"Distil is a very high-end boutique hotel," said Poe. "Bruce said, 'We don't want over 200 rooms. We want it to be exclusive.' But we had enough space to build 300 rooms. So, we built a hundred Moxy rooms as part of the complex. You can't tell that the Moxy and the Distil are even in the same building. The exterior entrances are separate and around the corner from each other. But all the back of the house stuff is shared: one loading dock, one laundry, all those types of things."

Distil, now part of Marriott's Autograph collection, showcases Louisville's role in the history of distilling bourbon. The hotel occupies the site of the old T. S. Brown & Sons barreling warehouse. For White Lodging, the project was a bewitching opportunity to integrate local flavor—literally—into a hotel design.

"Ninety-eight percent of the world's bourbon is made in Kentucky," said Poe. "So, in Louisville, we created the Urban Bourbon Trail. Not far from our hotel there are 12 different distillers. I'm talking about the big guys: Old Forester, Maker's Mark, Jim Beam, Michter's, Rabbit Hole,

> "Louisville has the highest concentration of cast iron facades west of Soho, on our Main Street. Back in the 1800s, cast iron facades were a sign of prosperity. So, we saved the cast iron facades and integrated them into the hotel."
>
> Steve Poe
> Friend + Business Partner

and more. All of them have facilities up and down Main Street where you can go taste their bourbon. Their main distilleries are all outside of Louisville and guests can take tours to those.

"It took me five years to buy the land for Distil/Moxy," continued Poe. "It's on Louisville's historic Main Street. Louisville was a very rich city in the 1800s and it thought it was going to be the New York of the West. Frederick Law Olmsted designed our park system. We had the railroad, but we also had the Ohio River and the Falls. So, every boat in the 1800s that went up and down the Ohio River had to go through our canal to avoid the Falls. We charged them a toll and we sold them whiskey and tobacco and probably some other illicit things.

"At 7:33 p.m. every night, we ring a bell at Distil and raise a toast. Every guest gets a 'prescription' for bourbon when they register, guaranteeing that if Prohibition mysteriously kicks in while they're there, they'll still get their alcohol. The 7:33 p.m. time is a sly reference to 1933—military time is 19:33. That's the year Prohibition was officially repealed."

As White Lodging's projects became increasingly upscale and larger, the question of restaurants arose. Select-service hotels—White's early focus—require only a minimum of meal service, usually a buffet breakfast and a small snack selection near the front desk that guests can

At 7:33 p.m. every night (19:33 in military time) Hotel Distil hosts a 'toast to the repeal of Prohibition' in its lobby. Prohibition was repealed in the year 1933.

access on their own. As hotels increase in scale, guests sometimes want to dine on the property and not go to the effort of heading elsewhere.

White was no stranger to hotel restaurants. His hospitality career began with the one-night stint as a busboy and dishwasher at his father's Holiday Inn in Merrillville in 1969. When he later managed that same hotel (under the Radisson flag) in the 1980s, he learned the ins and outs of operating multiple dining and banquet rooms. But those restaurants were not upscale . . . and didn't pretend to be. Most of the cuisine was good but basic, nothing that would cause a restaurant reviewer to swoon.

"There was a time period of about twenty years when people didn't really go to restaurants that were in a hotel," said Deno Yiankes. "Thankfully, that has changed quite a bit, thanks to the incredible uptick we've seen in quality of operations and branding."

The pendulum was swinging back in favor of hotel restaurants when White Lodging opened the Indianapolis Marriott Downtown, next to the Convention Center, in 2001. A convention-scale hotel was expected to provide a range of dining options. White worked hard to ensure that the hotel's restaurants offered more than standard fare, but it wasn't easy. As always, White wanted to do the job right, not simply score a passing grade. In November 2002 he raised more questions than he answered about whether White Lodging should invest in the F&B space more aggressively.

"Our growth into full-service hotels certainly provides all of us, individually and collectively, both opportunities and challenges," wrote White. "One of the biggest challenges in food and beverage is: How do we make it an 'added value' part of our business for guests, associates and owners alike? Are the products and services good enough? Have we created the culture, passion and career-pathing opportunities that create commitment by our people? Can we drive sales and profits to justify the investment by our owners?"

"I can remember when Bruce was unhappy with the way our hotel restaurants were doing," said Steve Poe, a frequent partner in White's projects. "He even said 'We're not building any more hotel restaurants. No one wants to eat in a hotel restaurant. The only time they eat in hotel restaurants is because they don't have another option.'"

"One of Bruce's big, big, big challenges was the F&B piece," commented John Januszko, who joined White Lodging in 1989. "It was an albatross around White Lodging's neck. . . . Then, when we teamed up with Richard Melman's Lettuce Entertain You group, we got the experience we needed to open restaurants. We had people on loan from Melman to come in and help us open up some of our first big hotel restaurants."

Richard Melman's Lettuce Entertain You Enterprises, Inc. started in Chicago in 1971 when Melman and Jerry A. Orzoff founded R. J. Grunt's in Lincoln Park. The restaurant was a hit. Melman became one of real estate magnate Al Friedman's principal go-tos for creating restaurants in the city's evolving River North district. By 1988, Melman had 27 restaurants; that number jumped to 68 by 2006. One consultant dubbed him the Steven Spielberg of Chicago's restaurant scene. In 2008, Lettuce Entertain You set up the Hub 51 restaurant on the ground floor of the new Friedman-White SpringHill Suites-Residence Inn collaboration on Dearborn Street—one of Melman's earliest associations with White Lodging.

> "I think Bruce's relationship with Rich Melman changed his life," said Mike Williams, who started working for White in 1982. "I know it changed our company's life."

"I think Bruce's relationship with Rich Melman changed his life," said Mike Williams, who started working for White in 1982. "I know it changed our company's life."

White wanted to have great dining places, restaurants that locals wanted to go to in addition to hotel guests, restaurants that were hard to get into.

To make that happen, a bit of innovation was called for. Instead of building a restaurant hidden inside the hotel, White decided to take a different approach and build restaurants that just happened to be attached to a hotel.

"That changed Bruce's whole mindset," said Steve Poe. "He made sure that each of our upscale restaurants had its own entrance, its own identity, its own brand. And it had to be designed so that it would become a place where locals would want to dine."

> How you do anything is how you do everything.

Typical of White, he dove into high-end F&B with gusto, soaking up knowledge from Melman as fast as he could. White's older son Conner saw his father's love of challenges kick in.

"After Dad met Rich Melman, he became so motivated to get on their level, or at least as close as he could get within food and beverage and restaurants," said Conner White. "Something that my father always told us when we were growing up was that his greatest wish for us was that we'd find something we love to do but weren't good at. He was most proud of us when he saw us striving for something and working hard at something that we weren't naturally good at. For him, restaurants were the challenge. It was if he had reached a mountaintop on the hotel side, and he found this whole side of the business that he wasn't good at, and he wanted so badly to get better and have fun doing it."

No one who knew White was surprised that he was as hands-on in restaurant design as he was in hotel plans. Mike Wells sat in on many planning meetings with White.

"Bruce would say, 'This design for the restaurant is terrible,'" said Wells. "'The chairs have to be closer together. The light has to be down on the top of the table. The music has to be right. Food has to be crave-able, and it has to be reproducible every single time for those four things.' It wasn't a secret formula, of course, but he really made it work. Steve Poe and I didn't see it, but Bruce had the vision. And now our F&B is fabulous in all of our hotels."

White Lodging's restaurants received a major boost in 2016, when White hired Jean-Luc Barone to be vice president of food and beverage. Born and raised in Toulon, France, Barone's interest in all things culinary took him to Vancouver, Canada, where he earned a bachelor's degree in hospitality management. Before joining White Lodging, he spent 16 years with Starwood in various roles, including vice president of global food and beverage. Barone's arrival cemented White Lodging's commitment to create high-end restaurants, bars, and rooftops that are trendsetting destinations both for locals and for hotel guests. The

The sparkling test kitchen at White Lodging's Merrillville headquarters is the epicenter of the company's culinary research and development.

sparkling test kitchen at White Lodging's Merrillville headquarters is the epicenter of the company's culinary research and development. In 2018, White promoted Barone to Chief Operating Officer. When White tapped Barone to become CEO of White Lodging in January 2022, his elevation was another sign that fine dining is a permanent part of the company's repertoire.

In the years since White dove into high-end F&B, White Lodging has created more than 60 restaurants, indoor bars, and rooftop lounges around the country. The decor and menus are one-of-a-kind. A few restaurants are named for White family members: Corinne, Conner's Kitchen, Dean's Italian Steakhouse.

White's passion for fine wine took root in the early 2000s when he decided to enhance the restaurants in White Lodging's hotels. While learning everything he could about wine production, White started collecting vintages, installed a wine cellar at home and studiously applied his knowledge to White Lodging's wine offerings.

"Bruce really didn't get into the wine thing until he started in full-service hotels," said Steve Poe. "When they had to pick the wines out for the restaurants, he wanted to understand the business. It went

> Friends no longer batted an eyelash when White pulled out a can of Campbell's soup or jar of peanut butter and a spoon on international jaunts.

from that to a passion. We could go anywhere, and he could look at a wine list and give you the history of just about every vintage on the list."

Developing a deep knowledge of premium wine and *haute cuisine* did not change White's own idiosyncratic eating habits. He was an unapologetic disciple of the 'food as fuel' school of dining. White was famous among friends and family for preferring a hamburger to a gourmet meal. He would head straight for the closest McDonald's when visiting foreign cities. Friends no longer batted an eyelash when White pulled out a can of Campbell's soup or a jar of peanut butter and a spoon on international jaunts.

Ron Hawkins, ranch manager at Brush Creek in Wyoming, recalled a trip to Japan where Bruce, Beth and he were set to dine at one of the top Japanese restaurants in Tokyo: "We found out that we were going to have to sit at one of those low tables to have our dinner. We had already had a traditional tea that day, sitting on the floor. Bruce looked at the low dinner table and said, 'I can't do this. I've got to go.' I said, 'I'll go with you.' So, we bailed out. People wait months to get into this place. Bruce said, 'Ron, come back to the hotel with me. We're eating Italian tonight!'"

Tim Ozark told a similar tale: "We were staying at a hotel in Kathmandu. We looked at the menu and Bruce's cousin Terry Bird and I ordered, I think it was chicken or maybe it was duck. When they brought it out, it really looked like a stale old pigeon. We each took a bite. Terry and I looked at each other. Not too good. That's when Bruce pulled out his crackers, peanut butter, and his chunky soup. He said, 'Boys, how much are you willing to pay for a bite of this?'"

As White Lodging shifted its focus to premium-level hotels, White made room on his agenda to build his biggest hotel yet: the JW Marriott in Indianapolis, across the street from Victory Field, a minor league baseball stadium. Indianapolis had decided to ramp up its tourism and convention business and opened a new international airport in 2008.

The city invited White Lodging to bid on building a second convention hotel, this one bigger than the first. The company responded to the Request for Proposal (RFP) and was selected for the job. More his father's hotel than his, White still put White Lodging's muscle behind the project to ensure that Dean's 1,000-room *piece de resistance* was as perfect as possible.

Ground was broken for the JW Marriott on March 24, 2008. In June, Mike Wells's REI Real Estate—which was overseeing construction—dug up the ruins of several old brick buildings. Indianapolis dates back to 1821, so such finds were not uncommon during excavations. Old Sanborn insurance maps suggested that the hotel site had once been home in the late 1880s to a drugstore, feed store, furniture store, restaurant and warehouses. Those structures disappeared in a series of block razings in the early 20th century, leaving behind traces of basements and foundations. Although the original businesses on the block were long gone, the colossal new hotel in a sense paid silent homage to the area's commercial heritage.

Not long after construction began on the JW Marriott, a major financial meltdown threatened to derail the nation's economy. Signs of trouble appeared in 2007 when losses on mortgage-related financial assets began to strain global financial markets. Initially, the decline in overall economic activity was modest but steepened in the fall of 2008. U.S. gross domestic product fell by 4.3 percent, kicking off the deepest recession since World War II. The eighteen-month downturn was also the longest, giving rise to the nickname the Great Recession. The nation's unemployment rate more than doubled, from less than 5 percent to 10 percent. Once again, White Lodging carefully navigated the downturn, heartily sorry to see the hospitality industry tighten its belt so soon after the long-awaited recovery from 9/11. Because Dean White had deep pockets and was a primary investor in the new JW Marriott, the project was able

> *In a 2014 lecture to Purdue University hospitality students, White commented that from a purely pragmatic viewpoint, the company would have been wise to pass up the Indianapolis JW Marriott—at the time, the largest in the world.*

to proceed with fewer financial hiccups than might otherwise have been the case during the Great Recession.

In a 2014 lecture to Purdue University hospitality students, White commented that from a purely pragmatic viewpoint, the company would have been wise to pass up the Indianapolis JW Marriott—at the time, the largest Marriott hotel in the world. But more compelling considerations eclipsed practicality.

"From an entrepreneurial viewpoint, where you really have a passion for what you're doing, what you're doing really means a lot to you," he told students. "This project made our company. We outperformed everyone's expectations. It's completely enhanced the profile of our company. . . . We thought that this would have a halo for our entire organization and open up larger opportunities for us and would be a real litmus test in terms of our credibility, and all those things fortunately proved to be true."

The JW Marriott Indianapolis opened to great fanfare on February 4, 2011, a decade after the unveiling of its 600-room predecessor, the Indianapolis Marriott Downtown. The new crescent-shaped hotel was

Opened iin February 2011, the new crescent-shaped hotel was the crown jewel of the $450 million seven-acre Marriott IndyPlace development adjacent to the convention center.

the crown jewel of the $450 million seven-acre Marriott IndyPlace development adjacent to the convention center. The cluster of five Marriott hotels offered more than 2,200 rooms to convention-goers and tourists. The 1,000-room property was the largest of 45 JW Marriott hotels around the globe at that time. The shimmering blue curtain wall façade required 7,300 glass panels. Each panel measured four feet by ten feet and weighed approximately 800 pounds. If laid end-to-end, the glass panels would stretch nearly 14 miles. When completed in early 2011, the 34-story flagship hotel was one of the most visible landmarks in Indianapolis—and still is. Many people considered the hotel Dean White's tribute to the state where he had made his fortune and resided for more than fifty years.

> *RLJ's first private equity real estate fund scooped up a number of hotels, including the Hilton Garden Inn on Chicago's Magnificent Mile. White Lodging came aboard soon thereafter to manage the property.*

White Lodging's ability to keep building new hotels during the Great Recession might have been impossible if not for a home-run deal a few years earlier. In 2002, White Lodging assumed management of a Hilton Garden Inn in Chicago, owned by RLJ Companies, a Maryland-based holding company owned by Robert L. Johnson, founder of cable channel Black Entertainment Television (BET). Johnson founded BET in 1980, after a career in Washington, D.C. that included television and politics. Viacom acquired BET in 2001 for a reported $3.2 billion, making Johnson the country's first black billionaire. Johnson immediately created RLJ Companies and assembled a high-dollar portfolio that ranged from hotel real estate investment to automobile dealerships, sports and entertainment, and financial services. RLJ's first private equity real estate fund scooped up a number of hotels, including the Hilton Garden Inn on Chicago's Magnificent Mile. White Lodging came aboard to manage the property.

Three years later, the hospitality and real estate markets had finally put the 9/11 doldrums behind them and were on the upswing. Interest rates had dropped. White and his team pondered the positive news. White Lodging was in solid financial shape. Many of its hotels were less than ten years old. Other than the concentration of hotels in Austin,

> Success should not be measured by the position one has achieved in life but the obstacles overcome.

the company's portfolio was also geographically diverse: Illinois, Michigan, Indiana, Texas, Florida, Colorado, Kentucky.

"The question was 'Should we refinance, or should we sell?'" said Larry Burnell. "Most of our properties were Marriott-affiliated, which put a premium cachet on our portfolio."

The post-9/11 economic recovery had spawned a surge of capital formation, some of it in the form of Real Estate Investment Trusts or REITs. Invented in the early 1960s, REITs were designed to allow investors to invest in large, diversified portfolios of income-producing real estate, through the purchase and sale of liquid securities. Low interest rates and rising room rates in 2005 inspired REITs like Bob Johnson's RLJ fund to hunt for investment-grade hotel properties.

White decided to explore the possibility of selling White Lodging's real estate while the market was hot. Getting the existing hotel real estate off the company's books would supply the financial liquidity needed to dive into a whole new phase of building.

In May 2005, RLJ Lodging Trust's president and CEO Tom Baltimore attended the Kentucky Derby in Louisville at the invitation of White and "that's when it started," said Larry Burnell. White Lodging was acquainted with Johnson's real estate team, which included Baltimore, who previously had been with Marriott, Host Marriott, and Hilton. Baltimore became the point person for discussions. RLJ expressed interest in White Lodging's portfolio; White Lodging weighed the pros and cons. One sticking point: the two parties weren't on the same page on a potential price tag.

"We hired an investment banker broker: Mark Elliott, of Hodges Ward Elliott," said White. "It was just a strategic decision. We knew the market was very active and we thought we could get a favorable valuation."

In October 2005, White told Crain's *Chicago Business* that the properties in White Lodging's portfolio would fetch more than $1.6 billion. The company took care to make clear that the management company itself was not for sale, just the real estate it had developed and owned with a variety of partners. Among the rumored potential buyers were Equity Inns, Goldman Sachs & Co., and Hicks Muse Tate & Furst. The article made no mention of RLJ.

The following month, RLJ and White Lodging quietly came to an agreement. For $1.7 billion, White would sell RLJ 100 hotels in two transactions: 87 hotels in the first group; the remaining 13, then under construction, would transfer later. The deal was announced internally at White Lodging in November, but not made public until February 2006. The deal closed in June.

"At the end of the day, RLJ was an easy decision for us, because the other group that was interested was a pure institutional private equity Wall Street group," said Deno Yiankes. "Relationships were a huge thing to Bruce. We already had a relationship with Tom Baltimore. Bruce had met with Bob Johnson and gotten comfortable that they were going to perform. So we put the deal together."

"The closing was incredibly tough," said Larry Burnell. "But the best part is that we sold the real estate and kept the management contracts. The contracts were for 20 years, plus two 10-year renewal options. And they were non-cancelable."

"We paid off our debt, which was a little over a billion dollars, so it gave us the capital to continue to grow our company at an accelerated rate," White explained to students at the 2014 Purdue lecture. "It allowed us for the first time to monetize the value of those 100 management agreements and that gave us the ability to really look and have a strategic plan with real teeth in it. So, 2006 was really the turning point in White Lodging."

"If Bruce had refinanced instead of selling, we would have had real estate risk," said Burnell. "Under the RLJ deal, by keeping the management contracts, he still had his management office, he still could keep his team together, which was important for creating the next generation of built hotels and managed hotels. Some of us had money in the

> **"I think a lot of people know Bruce White today and think of him as the guy that built these big mega hotels,"** said Steve Poe. **"I was there with the Bruce White that actually built this company, who was happy to build an 88-room property."**

earlier deals, so he offered us bonuses for staying at least five more years. Bruce was incredibly generous with everyone in the organization when the deal closed."

When the RLJ transaction was announced publicly in February 2006, White Lodging simultaneously unveiled a reorganization of the operating side of the company along geographic lines. Two divisions—one Eastern and one Western—were created, to be led by senior vice presidents of operations. In each division, regional vice presidents would oversee smaller segments. The two divisions were to be supported by a vice president of food and beverage, vice president of sales and marketing, regional director of recruitment and training and a director of revenue management.

There would be more tweaks in coming years, but most of the changes and restructuring from this point out were geared generally toward supporting and boosting White Lodging's public profile as a proven premium hotel developer and manager.

> "We cracked a billion dollars in managed sales in 2013 and we'll exceed $1.5 billion in 2017," said Yiankes. "Frankly, it's very consistent growth but we happen to be in an accelerated period and some of that is driven by this notion of getting more heavily weighted in the urban and major lifestyle hotels."

"We now have the platform and national prominence to fill the growing void for institutions that want high quality brands for their hotels without the large bureaucratic brands managing them," wrote Dave Sibley in November 2005 when announcing the RLJ deal internally. "Our goal is to communicate an identity and to create awareness to the industry and institutional hotel ownership community of leadership, reliability and trust. We can be trusted to maximize the value of each and every asset we manage by adding value through the development, asset management and operation of the hotel. . . . We want to be 'top of mind" for those seeking a significant growth relationship whether it is an owner or a potential leadership recruit. Leadership, reliability and trust will become synonymous with White Lodging."

When the RLJ deal closed in June 2006, White Lodging wrapped up one winning streak and immediately began a new one. Some things would remain the same: 'The White Lodging Way,' devotion to training, stretch goals, building out select markets, the focus on customer experiences, sticking to "best in class" brands. Other things were new or would expand: more focus on urban lifestyle hotels—one-of-a-kind properties, complete with rooftop bars, high-end restaurants, and a modern, edgy feel that would appeal to younger travelers.

Although the 2008 Great Recession—and later, the devastating 2020 pandemic—would impact White Lodging's short-term plans, White's long-term vision for his company remained, as ever, upbeat and ambitious. In 2013, the company achieved $1 billion in annual sales; in 2017, the number was $1.5 billion.

One unexpected revelation emerged in the years after the 2006 RLJ transaction: White realized that he did not enjoy being a third-party manager of properties over which he had little or no say about maintenance or upgrades. Without an ownership stake in a property, White Lodging was limited in what it could do to persuade hotel owners to invest in the things that White knew mattered. At risk was White Lodging's reputation for top-notch management services. If a hotel looked shoddy or out-of-date, management—not the owner—would be the one fielding complaints or watching occupancy numbers fall. In the future, the company would make sure that its third-party management contracts allowed White Lodging to do what it does best . . . for the owners and investors, the properties, the guests, and the associates.

> "Good times and good memories are what we really sell," White had written in May 1990, in one of his earliest CEO Messages. "Just remember: quality doesn't cost, it pays."
>
> Almost forty years later, he believed as fervently as ever that quality was the ticket to success.

"Good times and good memories are what we really sell," White had written in May 1990, in one of his earliest CEO Messages. "Just remember: quality doesn't cost, it pays." More than thirty years later, he believed as fervently as ever that quality was the ticket to success.

White Lodging unveiled a corporate rebranding in February 2017. Chris Anderson—author of "I'm Not Buying It: How to Turn Skeptical Millennials into Loyal Customers" (2015)—was the force behind the rebranding campaign. Anderson brought years of experience with Marriott and Marcus Hotels & Resorts when he joined White Lodging

Bruce White featured on the cover of Hotel Business in March 2011.

in January 2015. The rebranding included a new logo, fresh website, jazzier photography, multimedia content, and a brand anthem video.

"We are an innovative company, but in the past, quite frankly, we just haven't told that story," Anderson explained to *Hotel Business* when the campaign was rolled out. "We didn't really do a good job telling the world who we were, and so part of our rebranding is to let people know we're hip and innovative, as well as being really great at operating hotels."

A year in the making, the campaign reintroduced White Lodging to the world with the tag line "Success Knows No Boundaries," a phrase designed to resonate with investors, franchisors, and White Lodging associates. The catchy slogan neatly summed up Bruce White's 'continuous improvement' philosophy for a new generation.

Another tag line of the campaign was "Passion Works Here." White wanted associates at White Lodging to feel the same excitement that he had experienced fifty years earlier when he discovered that hospitality—making others happy—was his life's purpose, his joy, and his true north.

> White wanted associates at White Lodging to feel the same excitement that he had experienced fifty years earlier when he realized that hospitality—making others happy—was his life's purpose, his joy, and his true north.

"I don't know anyone that was made for the hospitality world more than Bruce," said Deno Yiankes. "All of us experienced it on the personal side, his hospitality. It was genuine. It was real. There was no script."

Chris Anderson explained the origin of the "Passion Works Here" tag line to *Hotel Business:*

"Millennials want to work someplace where they can bring their passion to work and bringing that passion actually helps them be successful. What we're doing, from a grassroots standpoint, is we're having all of the associates tell their stories, and as they tell their stories, it might be an Instagram post that fuels up through our website. Everyone can tell what is it about what they do that they really love and we want them to bring that to light and we want them to know we support that to bring their passion to life. When people do that, they're happy, and when people are happy, it makes for great guest service, and great guest service means the guest will come back. It's just a great formula."

In the waning days of 2017, White Lodging sold 82 suburban management contracts to Interstate Hotels, a move that took care of much of White's concern about maintaining White Lodging's standards and reputation. It also reflected a profound and permanent shift in the company's focus. After the 2017 transaction, the company's portfolio included 87 premium hotels, 30 restaurants/bars and 26 brands, including Marriott International, Hilton Worldwide, Hyatt Global, and InterContinental Hotel Group. The company had 18 projects on the fast track, many of which reflected White's desire to take White Lodging to the next level. From now on, he wanted his company to be known for its imaginative approach to creating spaces that would surprise and delight everyone who came through the doors.

In 2022, White Lodging completed its pivot to "premium brand, urban and experiential" properties by selling its remaining suburban hotels and management contracts. The sales to Hersha Hospitality and ZMC marked the beginning of another new phase for the company—this one devoted to showcasing and supporting 'hospitalitarians'—White Lodging's word for associates who are passionate about providing guests with "good times and good memories" by supplying exceptional service and experiences. The company's portfolio was smaller now but filled with choice properties. And more hotels were in the pipeline. Convention hotel management expertise remained a major selling point, but White was finally the kind of hotelier he wanted to be: building or managing stylish hotels and restaurants that offered guests unforgettable one-of-a-kind moments.

In 2022, White Lodging changed its tagline to A Company of Hospitalitarians.

Among the dozens of beautiful properties managed by White Lodging was one special place that had laid claim to White's heart at first sight. Since childhood, the boy from South Park had heard the American West calling his name. Half a century later, White answered that call when he fell in love with a chunk of land nestled at the foot of rugged Medicine Bow-Routt National Forest in Carbon County, Wyoming.

The place was an old rundown ranch named Brush Creek.

CHAPTER 9

Landscape of the Heart

> *Bruce and Beth decided that Brush Creek is something that needs to be shared. And that's big-hearted. He could have made his own quiet little spot in the world to go and get away from the hustle and the bustle. But instead, he invited everyone to come and share this place.*
>
> Ron Hawkins
> Ranch Manager, Brush Creek Ranch

The small jet taxied to a stop on the tarmac of Shively Field, the tiny municipal airport at Saratoga, Wyoming. While ground crew secured the plane, Bruce White and his young son Otis disembarked, stretched their legs and walked toward the airport's operations building. There they were greeted by a local real estate broker who politely ushered the pair to a waiting car. The driver pulled out of the airport parking lot onto Route 130—Saratoga's main drag—and turned south, away from town. To the left, on the east side of the highway, the North Platte River meandered through a broad flat valley between the Sierra Madre and Snowy Ranges. A few miles into the drive, Route 130 swung abruptly from south to east, crossing the river, passing through the small community of Ryan Park and tracing the southern perimeter of Medicine Bow-Routt National Forest.

Father and son gazed out the car windows at the rugged landscape while the broker described the properties he wanted to show them.

Months earlier, Beth White had commented to her husband that they had done almost nothing to celebrate the $1.7 billion RLJ deal after it closed in June 2006.

"I'm not a believer in closing dinners or celebrations of financial transactions, because I've always thought that the work is ahead of you," explained White in a 2022 interview. "Celebrating the transaction itself is premature because you never know if a transaction works out or not until years down the road. So, I've been accused of being a fuddy-duddy in that regard because everybody else in the world has these elaborate closing dinners and celebrations. But literally, Beth and I, we didn't celebrate, nor did I celebrate with my management team in any meaningful way."

In lieu of hosting a fancy event, the couple went away for a quiet weekend at the posh Amanyara Resort in the Turks and Caicos.

"At dinner one night, Beth commented that the RLJ transaction had created some personal liquidity that we had never had," said White. "She asked: 'Have you ever dreamed of something, now that you have some money?'"

White did have ideas, but they had long been relegated to the back burner. Until the RLJ deal closed in 2006, the Whites had always put profits right back into White Lodging. New cars were a rarity; the family's early homes were nice but not palatial. The biggest splurges were the trips that the family took, sometimes with friends. Even when the family began to enjoy the financial fruits of White's labor, he had limited himself mainly to traveling, collecting a handful of vintage sports cars, and indulging his budding passion for wine.

This time, in answer to Beth's question, White had a ready response: "Well, I've always dreamed of owning property out in Wyoming."

Beth encouraged her husband to go for it. Why not?

"My dream was prompted by a childhood trip to the Grand Tetons with Indian Guides," said White. "It was a father-son camping trip. I thought the Tetons were magnificent. That trip kindled a real passion for the West. But being a South Park Avenue kid, I never dreamed that I'd have the resources to consider buying some recreational property out there."

Now that the kid from South Park had "resources," he was ready to make his childhood dream come true. Beth and Bruce told their three kids that they would begin looking for property in the West, but it might

For Bruce's 50th birthday, Beth surprised Bruce with a gift of a 1959 Corvette identical to one once owned by his father.

take two years or more to find just the right spot. They were in no hurry. The idea was to find an ideal place to serve as a family vacation retreat when they wanted to get away from the bustle of Chicago.

"My brothers and I were surprised," said Corinne White Troise, White's daughter. "I think I was a senior in high school when Dad told us he wanted to buy a ranch out West. I basically said, 'Sounds good! Have fun!'"

White being White, he developed a checklist of criteria before heading out.

"We wanted to be part of an authentic ranching community," said White. "We didn't want to be near a major ski resort. We had already lived in Edwards, Colorado. We had to be within 45 minutes of an airport we could fly into because we knew we'd often be coming out for relatively short periods of time. We wanted great recreational opportunities, which meant we had to have water, particularly a river for fishing and wildlife for hunting. We wanted it to be very private and we wanted it to be beautiful, of course."

To add a bit of fun to the hunt, White took his younger son Otis along to look at properties.

> "Otis, of course, thought that hopping on ATVs, buzzing around all these ranch properties and then going out and having dinners in small town cafes was a lot of fun. I did too."
>
> Bruce W. White

heavily forested Medicine Bow and Sierra Madre mountains. An 1890 article in the same newspaper gushed over the pristine beauty of the area around Brush Creek, as well as its economic value: "The place is beautifully located in a valley way up in the mountains over 10,000 feet above sea level, is well watered and well-timbered...."

According to an archived 2007 website of Brush Creek Ranch (pre-White ownership), plus a 2015 article in *American Cowboy*, the property passed through various hands until around 1925, when Edgar Uihlein of Chicago purchased it. A member of the Schlitz brewery dynasty, Uihlein bought more ranches nearby to bring Brush Creek's acreage up to more than 6,000. Cattle at Brush Creek bore a distinctive "U" brand. The blacksmith shop and barn on the ranch were purportedly added by the Uihleins, and the property's lodge was tripled in size to 20 rooms. In the 1930s, the *Chicago Tribune* occasionally mentioned Uihlein family members spending weeks or months at Brush Creek Ranch with friends and family.

During the Great Depression, federal Civilian Conservation Corps (CCC) workers built and lived in a camp in nearby Ryan Park. During World War II, Italian and German prisoners of war were housed at Ryan Park in the old CCC buildings, and possibly on Brush Creek Ranch as well. The POWs cut and transported logs and are credited with building Brush Creek's large rock garden. During the 1930s and 1940s, the Ranch raised prized Herefords that commanded top prices. In 1948, Edgar Uihlein sold the Ranch and 250 head of registered Herefords for $250,000 to Don Anderson and James Dalton of Eaton, Colorado. Brush Creek Ranch changed hands more than once after Anderson and Dalton, but subsequent owners, including the local Caldwell family, maintained the Ranch's reputation as a top breeder of Herefords. In the early 1990s, the property was advertised in national magazines as a rustic 'guest ranch' for city dwellers who wanted to ride horses, hike in Medicine Bow National Forest, fish in the North Platte, and enjoy a taste of the old American West.

> Many people would have torn down the buildings and started anew. But in White's eyes, the utilitarian buildings and creaky old house were part and parcel of the ranch's magic, rather than an eyesore.

When Bruce and Otis White saw Brush Creek Ranch a few years later, the dude ranch business was closed, and the old 20-room homestead and outbuildings needed serious attention. Many people would have torn down the buildings and started anew. But in White's eyes, the utilitarian buildings and creaky old house were part and parcel of the ranch's magic, rather than an eyesore. He was fascinated by Brush Creek's history and wanted to preserve it. Tapping the same power that he used to imagine the design and layout of White Lodging's hotels, he could envision sprucing up the main house and shoring up as many well-worn outbuildings as could be salvaged.

"Brush Creek had been held in a conservatorship for the family that owned it," said White. "It hadn't been very well maintained, so it didn't show particularly well. But you could see the beauty, it had everything we wanted. And Saratoga is a great ranching community, very authentic. Great people. There was also the advantage of having the Old Baldy Club in town, which is an old-line golf and fishing club that has been around for more than fifty years."

"I think the town of Saratoga was a big part of Dad's decision," said Otis White. "He grew up on a street that had a real sense of community. Saratoga is still a small town. Everybody knows everybody else. If you go into Duke's Bar and Grill, you see people from all the different ranches hanging out."

White was captivated by the prospect of buying Brush Creek. When he told YPO pal Tim Ozark about his plans, Ozark was astonished.

"Bruce called me and said, 'I think I'm going to buy this ranch in Wyoming. Great rock outcroppings, incredible views. The buildings are really pretty old and decrepit. But I'll try to save those. I'm thinking of buying it and developing something out there for Beth, the kids, and myself. What do you think?'

"I replied, 'Are you out of your mind?! How are you ever going to get Beth to go to Wyoming?' Without missing a beat Bruce replied: 'Easy! Puppies! Who can say no to puppies?' And sure enough, he bought the ranch and a bunch of puppies. And the rest, as they say, is history."

After the sale closed in December 2008, the adventure began. Cleaning up was the first task. Cattle had walked through the empty

> White was not going to be a pretend rancher—"all hat, no cattle." He wanted to be a genuine steward of the land, the water, the wildlife, the history and the heritage of Brush Creek Ranch.

house and deposited cow patties. Broken glass crunched underfoot. Some of the wood used in the buildings had seen much better days.

The land and water also needed help. The 6,000-acre ranch had been overgrazed by cattle owned by ranchers leasing a portion of the land. Fences were broken or missing. Brush Creek—the main waterway after which the Ranch was named—needed rehabilitation by an expert. Many of the irrigation ditches and canals would require repairs.

White's first step was totally in character: he went looking for the best ranch manager he could find. He had chosen Brush Creek in part because it had been a working ranch for more than 100 years. White had no intention of being a pretend rancher—"all hat, no cattle." He wanted to be a genuine steward of the land, the water, the wildlife,

Bruce with one of their dogs.

the history and the heritage of Brush Creek Ranch. Cattle, horses, and even bison would once again be part of the Ranch's landscape.

Knowing that his real estate broker was plugged into the local grapevine, White asked him to recommend a ranch manager, even before the purchase formally closed. The broker thought he knew the perfect person: Ron Hawkins.

Born and raised in Colorado, Hawkins had been ranching his entire life—except for a stint in military service. He and his wife had lived in Wyoming for 35 years. A no-nonsense, independent character straight out of the hit Netflix series "Yellowstone," Hawkins was quite content overseeing the three ranches he was leasing on the other side of Medicine Bow, near Centennial.

"I had not had a boss or an employer for several years in my life, and I wasn't sure I wanted one again," said Hawkins. "But it didn't take Bruce very long to kind of win me over. Now, of course, I did go home and Google him, to find out just who this Bruce White was."

When Hawkins agreed to work for the Whites, he asked White what his greatest expectation of him would be. Knowing that he was bound to share Brush Creek with friends and family, White replied, "Treat my guests well and just ensure they have a great time." Hawkins responded: "Okay."

"Then Bruce turned around just as quick as can be and said, 'What's your greatest expectation of me?' And I said, 'Well, my expectation would be that you keep this ranch land intact, that it stays whole and it stays a ranch, that we keep it as beautiful as it was the day that you drove onto it.' And he agreed. We shook hands, and that was the start of it."

Bruce White (left) with Ron Hawkins, ranch manager.

Soon the two men were spending hours together bumping across the landscape in a pick-up truck, investigating and exploring every inch of the property. Ever the student, White asked a million questions and soaked up the information that Hawkins supplied. White wanted to understand irrigation, water quality, fences, cattle, horses, anything and everything that had to do with bringing Brush Creek up to date and preparing it to be a working ranch again.

"We would be nowhere if Ron didn't manage the land for us," said Mike Williams. "We didn't know how to make a road. We didn't know how to do irrigation. We didn't know that a thistle plant will ruin your whole pasture. I had no idea!"

> **"** We've always said our original mission at Brush Creek was to Educate, Enhance, and Enjoy," said White. "We try to educate our guests on not only the history of the Ranch and the ranching community, but also environmental education. That's because we look at ourselves as stewards of the Ranch, not owners. **"**

"We've always said our original mission at Brush Creek was to Educate, Enhance, and Enjoy," said White. "We try to educate our guests on not only the history of the Ranch and the ranching community, but also environmental education. That's because

Chapter 9 ◆ Landscape of the Heart

we look at ourselves as stewards of the Ranch, not owners. And we've certainly done a lot of work to enhance the ecology of the ranch through stream restoration, watershed management, noxious weed reduction, rotational grazing. I mean, I could go on and on and on!"

One of the first lessons that Bruce White learned from Hawkins was gate etiquette.

> "I'm watching in the rearview mirror. Bruce closes the gate and he chains it. Then he looks at me, looks at the truck, looks down at the gate, looks back at the truck, and realizes that he has just locked himself in on the wrong side of the gate."
>
> Ron Hawkins
> Bush Creek Ranch

"If you're not doing the driving, you're sitting in the passenger seat," said Hawkins. "Which means you're the guy that gets out and gets the gate. So, we're driving around and we come to a gate. Bruce says, "My job to get it! My job to get it!" And he hopped out. Well, I pulled through the gate and stopped. I'm watching in the rearview mirror. Bruce closes the gate and he chains it. Then he looks at me, looks at the truck, looks down at the gate, looks back at the truck, and realizes that he has just locked himself in on the wrong side of the gate.

"So he fixes the gate, gets on the right side of it, then comes and gets in the truck. Now, I ain't going to say nothin'. But I got tickled and I started giggling about it a little bit. And Bruce said, 'You saw that, didn't you? You saw that?' He said, 'That's the dumbest I've ever felt in my entire life.' I said, 'Bruce, other people have done that.' He said, 'Have you ever done it, Ron?' I said, 'Not that I can recall.' He said, 'You're not making me feel any better!'"

One of the biggest tasks facing Hawkins and the Whites was rehabilitation of Brush Creek Ranch's waters. White wanted the rivers and streams to be restored to good health. The timber-cutting industry a century earlier had rerouted Brush Creek to make it easier to transport thousands of wooden railroad ties down and out of the mountains. The Sterrett brothers—the ranch's original homesteaders—were probably among those who used the creek to transport logs.

"The river had been abused since the beginning of time," said Hawkins. "The railroad tie guys would float their ties down there. So, they wanted to channel the river and just get their logs down."

"We have three to three-and-a-half miles of Brush Creek passing through the ranch," said Mike Williams. "It had completely busted out of its banks because of all the beaver dams. We had to go through thirty years of beaver dams and blow them up. We had old photos of the course the creek used to follow, and we restored it to the best of our ability. Also, every irrigation ditch on the ranch was in bad shape, so Ron had to rebuild all of those too."

> People respond to motives and objectives . . . they simply tolerate orders and directions.

While Hawkins dealt with water issues and fencing, White took a closer look at the existing buildings on the property. He wanted to restore whatever could be salvaged. By February 2009, only two months after finalizing the purchase of Brush Creek, repairs and construction began. The first renovations focused on fixing up six cabins and the bunkhouse, creating a Recreation Center, installing a chuck wagon, and repairing the old homestead well enough to accommodate Bruce, Beth, their kids and anyone they invited to see the place.

That first summer 'anyone' included more than three dozen Latin School classmates of Corinne, Conner, and Otis.

"I was a junior in high school," said Conner White. "I remember my parents telling me that they had bought the Ranch. I couldn't wrap my head around exactly what that meant, but then they told me that we were going to host our high school class for basketball camp and for us all to work out there. At the time, I was horrified! I remember just thinking, 'Why can't we just be normal? I just want to stay in Chicago and hang out with my friends and maybe have a job. Why do we always have to be doing something crazy?'"

"I was wrong, by the way," continued Conner. "People talk about that summer being the best summer of their lives. One of the coolest parts was that they took away our phones, so we only were able to be on our phones once a week during a dedicated hour, to call family. So, it was a chance to truly disconnect. The iPhone was out and people were always on their phones. So, I think it was a big culture shock for everyone, but we were all together and had a great time."

The Whites hired Dan and Kassie Houlihan—both 1997 graduates of the Latin School—to run the camp. Dan Houlihan taught at Latin, so he was a familiar face to the students who came to Brush Creek that summer. He was also a gifted drill sergeant.

"The kids had to be on the job at 7:00 a.m.," said Bruce White. "So, they had to have breakfast before then. We didn't have an indoor place for eating, so meals were outdoors at the chuck wagon. Their rooms had to be kept in good shape. That summer was a kind of outdoor leadership program. In their free time, they could go out and camp, hike, learn how to saddle a horse, ride a mountain bike."

Otis White recalled that his basketball team would play in the morning and then work; Conner's basketball team would work in the morning and early afternoon, and then have their turn on the basketball court. The Rec Center was one of the first buildings to be finished before the kids poured in from Chicago.

> "We painted or stained a LOT of fences," recalled Corinne White Troise, the Whites' daughter. "My first ever job at Brush Creek was cleaning out the old hayloft. A friend and I swept or threw out dead mice and who knows what else."

"We're an Indiana family, so of course, we prioritized getting the sports facility done!" said Otis White.

The summer camp was co-ed, but the young women opted for lifting weights,

Family photo on the ranch: (left to right) Conner, Corinne, Bruce, Beth, and Otis.

running, and generally working out instead of playing basketball. The female contingent worked at their assigned chores just as hard as their male counterparts.

"We painted or stained a LOT of fences," recalled Corinne White Troise, the Whites' daughter. "My first ever job at Brush Creek was cleaning out the old hayloft. A friend and I swept or threw out dead mice and who knows what else. And I learned how heavy hay bales are!"

The young men dug post holes, installed fencing, and moved large rocks where needed to help Ron Hawkins with the irrigation canal restoration.

The summer of 2009 also brought more construction and repairs to buildings. The sound of hammers, saws, and power tools filled the air for hours and days on end. The Trailhead Lodge, Saloon, blacksmith shop, chicken coop, and Jo's Cowgirl Cabin all emerged from the dust, noise, and grime.

By June work had progressed enough that the Whites issued an invitation to their extended family and the families of the Latin School campmates to celebrate the July 4th holiday at Brush Creek Ranch.

In the meantime, the Whites put their heads together to determine who would be a good choice to become the overall manager of Brush Creek. Ron Hawkins was already in the perfect role, managing the restoration of the land and readying it for livestock.

It didn't take long for the couple to narrow the list to one of White's earliest employees: Mike Williams. His tenure with White dated to 1982, before White Lodging had been formally organized. Williams had opened many hotels for White Lodging through the years. He knew by heart the ins and outs of running a property, large or small. Granted, a ranch wasn't the same as a hotel, but Williams had always been ready and able to leap into whatever assignment White gave him. To boot, White knew that Williams was toying with the idea of retiring from White Lodging. So, he called Williams into his office late in the day while on a trip back to Merrillville. White small-talked more than usual and Williams thought for sure that he was about to hear a "thank you for your service" speech and be handed the proverbial gold watch.

"Instead, Bruce started to tell me about how he and Beth had bought a ranch," said Williams. "I'm thinking of something along the lines of a small farm in rural Indiana. But then he tells me it's in Wyoming. And it's more than 6,000 acres. He goes on to tell me that he and Beth agreed at dinner the previous evening that it would be too much for Bruce to manage a ranch on top of White Lodging. So, he says, "We landed on you." I said, "Landed on me for what?" And Bruce goes, "We'd like you to go out and run the Ranch."

> **"When we had all the kids' parents out to visit, and we saw how much they enjoyed it, that's when the wheels started turning in Bruce's head."**
>
> Beth White

Williams was stunned. White continued: 'Why don't you give it a shot? Just go out and see it.' I said, 'Why would you choose me?' He goes, 'Well, you grew up in the country, right?' I said, 'Yes.' He says, 'You had horses, right?' I said, 'Yeah, we had four or five at a time.' 'You had cattle, right?' I said, 'Yeah, we had one or two black Angus that ended up at the butcher shop.' He goes, 'You'd be perfect at this.'"

Williams flew out to Wyoming to check out his potential new home. He liked what he saw. In August 2009, Williams was named Executive Vice President and Chief Operating Officer of Brush Creek Ranch. White wanted Williams to hustle and get settled in because a bewitching idea had taken hold of him during the summer basketball camp.

"When we had all the kids' parents out to visit, and we saw how much they enjoyed it, that's when the wheels started turning in Bruce's head," said Beth White.

"I guess my hospitality gene took over," said White.[20] "So, we said, 'Well, why don't we open up the Ranch?' Brush Creek had been a guest ranch before it fell into disrepair. We rehabbed the cabins, which we largely did to retain the historic nature of the Ranch. Then we started having people stay in them. One thing led to the other and we said, why don't we open to the public and see what happens?

"We're dedicated to maintaining open spaces in the West and have a conservation easement that precludes additional development on any

---

[20]Possibly the understatement of the century.

of our ranch properties," continued White. "We also wanted to make the Ranch economically sustainable. We knew we couldn't do that as a traditional cattle ranch, raising only livestock. That business is tough to make any money in. So, we opened it up as a high-end dude ranch."

The childhood dream that had spurred White's search for a simple family retreat began to take on a life of its own. Plans for more building restorations and new construction were in the works. By the time Williams and his belongings arrived from Indiana, construction of the main lodge on Brush Creek was underway.

"The lodge was only supposed to be 8,000 square feet, eight rooms," said Williams. "They thought that would be just enough room to do their family stuff. One thing led to another, and when I got there, they had already blown the hole in the ground. And the lodge had grown to be 33,000 square feet on the blueprints."

The Lodge at Brush Creek Ranch.

Once White started playing with ideas for the Ranch, the high-end hotel developer side of him was bound to take over. Sure enough, in January 2010, White added more acreage by buying the old TZ Ranch when it became available. Now home to Brush Creek's private Magee Homestead, the 7,500-acre TZ Ranch purchase more than doubled the size of the White family's holdings.

A year after the acquisition, restoration of the old cowhand cabins at Magee Homestead began. The painstaking process meant disassembling the logs, numbering, cleaning, and refinishing them, before carefully reassembling the cabins. New foundations, plumbing and electrical systems were added, and heated floors were installed. Eventually historic cabins at Brush Creek were similarly restored for use by Ranch guests, complemented by a few newly built cabins. A later upgrade of the Magee Homestead included installation of a pool, pavilion, and firepit.

After Williams arrived, the plan was to get the Ranch ready for a 'soft opening' to outside guests. A spa was added, and the property was officially branded The Lodge & Spa at Brush Creek.

Jan Grabow—White's longtime right-hand assistant—took on the task of developing Brush Creek's brand identity and marketing strategy. The main target were families and groups that wanted to experience authentic Western culture, but who would also appreciate the luxe ambiance and amenities that White envisioned.

One of the Whites' chief wishes was to entice Ranch guests to be outside, active, and engaged with Brush Creek's unique offerings. None of the guest rooms or cabins has a television. There's no golf course or swimming pool.[21] The Ranch's landscape was meant to be the star of the show. Aware that many Brush Creek guests might have no experience with horses, fishing, shooting a gun or hiking, the Ranch's summertime outdoor sports employees were trained to offer lessons or instructions.

The first paying guests arrived in September 2010. By December 2012, Brush Creek Ranch had logged $2.5 million in annual sales. A year later, the number was $4 million. In June 2014, the ranch received its first Conde Nast Award: #2 resort in the world and #1 in the U.S. In fewer than five years, a rundown ranch had been transformed into one of the top resorts in the world. In 2015, annual sales topped $8.5 million. Brush Creek became known as a 'destination wedding' venue, discreetly hosting the nuptials of celebrities who wanted beautiful Western landscape and total privacy for their ceremonies and receptions. One of Corinne White Troise's jobs at Brush Creek Ranch after college was organizing tours for wedding planners and others who were interested in holding upscale group events at the Ranch.

> Instead of "Begin with the end in mind"—his oft-repeated rule of thumb—Brush Creek provided White with a blank canvas many magnitudes larger than the footprint of even his largest full-service hotels.

"I would invite 10 to 15 top wedding planners out and have them just all come together and experience the Ranch, in the hope that they would

---

[21]One exception: The Magee Homestead has a small pool for the exclusive use of guests staying there.

then recommend us to their clients," said Troise. "Wedding planners, travel agents, and some corporate event planners. A lot of our business is word of mouth: Someone will call and say 'I was a guest at a wedding at Brush Creek five years ago, and now I'm engaged.'"

> You're only successful when your guests and associates think you are.

Brush Creek's swift evolution under the Whites was a rare exception to White's usual approach to a project. Instead of "Begin with the end in mind"—his oft-repeated rule of thumb—Brush Creek provided White with a blank canvas many magnitudes larger than the footprint of even his largest full-service hotels. The biggest space he had to work with on large-scale hotel projects was a full city block. At the Ranch, he had thousands of acres. If he chose, White could keep adding to Brush Creek for years.

And so, he did.

In June 2014, White purchased the historic "A-Cross Ranch,' known locally as the Sanger Ranch, for $29 million. Working with the Wyoming Stock Growers Land Trust, all 10,158 acres of Sanger were put under conservation easement in 2018, joining the other tracts owned by the Whites. The conservation easements rule out further development.

Sanger ancestor Elijah Moore is credited with homesteading on the property in the 1860s. In the mid-1930s, Moore's great-grandson Charles J. Sanger and his bride Millie Popovich-Enberg Sanger put down roots on the property and built a small homestead on the banks of French Creek. Charles Sanger had majored in Agriculture at the University of Wyoming; he was an officer of the school's Ag Club and a member of the Rifle Team. In 1960, following their divorce, Millie Sanger and her son Chuck purchased adjoining French Creek Ranch—a former 'dude ranch'—and set up a small camp for girls. By the time the Whites purchased the property in 2014, the A-Cross/Sanger Ranch had grown to more than 10,000 acres.

The Sanger family home on the banks of French Creek was in rough shape, but intact. Bruce and Beth planned to renovate the small house for their own use. But the old house burned down just two months after the Sanger Ranch purchase closed, when debris in the chimney caught fire. The silver lining? The riverside site was perfect, with or without the historic homestead. The Whites built a much larger home on the spot, one that would lend itself to the kind of entertaining that the couple loved to offer family and friends. They named the new place River House, not just for its location on French Creek, but because the restaurant in Indiana where the couple had had their first date decades earlier was named River House.

Farther down the road beyond the Whites' house is the updated French Creek Sportsmen's Club, a private fishing and hunting club that is now part of Brush Creek Ranch's offerings.

"Brush Creek has world-class recreational possibilities for the fishermen, for the hiker, for the biker, for somebody who's a passionate upland bird hunter like me, or hunting game," said White. "But the sports were being somewhat overshadowed by Brush Creek Ranch as a leisure destination. So, the sportsmen who came to us in the early years of the Ranch gave us some advice: If we were going to be taken seriously in the fishing and hunting space, we needed to have part of our facility that really focused on their needs. So, we restored a historic fishing camp on French Creek, which if I were to be candid is probably my favorite spot out of all the wonderful spots on the Ranch."

The French Creek Sportsmen's Club pays homage to a predecessor: the Sanger Fishing Club, a members-only organization of 28 fishermen founded in 1993. The club's annual lease with the Sanger family began in 1993 to the tune of $20,000. Most of the members were from Greeley, Colorado, a three-hour drive from the Sangers' ranch. Under club rules, each member could sign up for a particular fishing hole along French Creek or the Platte River, first-come-first-served: Cement Hole, French Creek Hole, Pine Tree Hole, Harry's Hole, The Upper Cedars, the Lower Cedars, Cliff Hole, etc. Kids and grandkids under the age of 14 were welcome at no extra charge. One of the original members of the club—William D. Farr—said in 2000 that he had been fishing in

> Sometimes White waited years until the time was right to put in an offer, but the wait was worth it. Today, the collection of ranches that comprise Brush Creek total 30,000 acres, including 20 miles of private riverfront.

the area for 70 years. Today, French Creek draws serious anglers and hunters to one of the quieter sections of the Ranch.

In time, White would purchase a few other smaller properties close to Brush Creek Ranch, including Green Mountain, and the Hillyard and Boykin ranches. Sometimes White waited years until the time was right to put in an offer, but the wait was worth it. Today, the collection of ranches that comprise Brush Creek totals more than 30,000 acres, including 20 miles of private riverfront.

"Some people buy a ranch and they're talking about the Back 40, not 30,000 acres in Wyoming," commented Mitch Daniels, former Indiana Governor and former president of Purdue. "But Bruce didn't do anything on a small scale."

The Ranch was not all work and no play for White. Almost from his first day on the job, Ron Hawkins introduced White to outdoor activities he had rarely or never tried.

"When I first came on board, I was giving Bruce trail rides," said Hawkins. "I was taking him fishing. We'd go and shoot guns. He was doing things that were way outside of what he had done before. Bruce had never gone hunting, but he turned into a pretty avid bird hunter. He

Bruce and Beth found a passion for English driven hunts and regularly introduced friends to the sport, which is offered at Brush Creek Ranch.

shot bigger game, including elk. So, he became a hunter. So did Beth. She shared his drive to learn new things."

When the couple were at the Ranch, they hiked all over the property and up steep trails into Medicine Bow-Routt National Forest. The pair also could often be seen zipping around the Ranch on their mountain bikes.

"Bruce was a big bike rider, but he was also a big bike crasher," said Mike Williams, laughing. "He'd injure himself pretty damn hard, every season. He'd go over the handlebars. It was ridiculous. He'd get black eyes, and we would just look at him: 'Bruce, you got in another accident, huh?'"

When not hiking or biking, Beth often rode horses while Bruce dive-bombed here and there on an ATV. White particularly enjoyed taking 'city slicker' friends on wild rides around the Ranch. Josh Hale, president and CEO of Big Shoulders, one of the Whites' principal philanthropic interests, can laugh now at two episodes that at the time scared the daylights out of him.

Bruce and Beth out riding in a Razor ATV in Wyoming.

"Bruce's family got him one of those Razor ATVs," said Hale. "I was visiting Brush Creek, and he said, 'Josh, you've got to go out with me in this thing. It's unbelievable.' I had never been in one. So, we're cruising around the Ranch and then Bruce stops. 'All right, you drive now.' I said, 'I don't know what I'm doing!' Bruce replied, 'This thing can go over water. It floats . . . a bit . . . but you've got to keep it moving.'"

Hale gulped.

"So, Bruce says, 'We're going to go across the river. Just remember that you've got to keep your foot on the gas and gun it. If you stop, we're going to get swamped.' So, one part of me is thinking, 'OK, that's what I'm supposed to do—foot on the gas, foot on the gas.' The other part of me is thinking, 'I'm going to go into the river, and this thing is going to sink. I'm going to die out here in Wyoming!'"

Hale tried to follow White's directions, but as they were approaching the river, he froze. Just as they reached the riverbank, White took control.

"Suddenly Bruce's foot came across, he jammed it on top of my foot, and he gunned it. We went flying across the water. My head went back and I'm flying. I hear Bruce shouting over the noise: 'I told you to keep your foot on the gas!'"

Another episode on the same trip likewise left Hale wide-eyed.

"We were still on the Razor, up on top of a ridge. Bruce was driving. He spotted a mountain lion in the distance. He was so excited. He told me that seeing a mountain lion is really rare. 'We've got to go see him!' So, Bruce speeds up, trying to catch it. I'm thinking 'Why are we driving toward the mountain lion?? Shouldn't we be going the other way?!' Fortunately, it disappeared, and we never saw it again.

"Then it was my time at the wheel," continued Hale. "So, we're cruising along and we come around a large rock formation and there are two buffaloes. These are BIG animals. Bruce said, 'Just sit here for a minute.' I said, 'What do I do if they start charging us?' 'Well, you hit that gas pedal and boogie down Broadway!'"

"One of them started snorting and pounding the ground. I'm thinking, 'This is *not* going to be good.'"

Hale smashed the gas pedal to the floor. The Razor leaped and took off: "We're boogieing down Broadway, Bruce!"

> **"When we built the horse arena, there were rumors that Brush Creek was going to be the training facility for the Chicago Bears,"** said Beth White. **"And then there's the rumor about putting in a golf course, which has never been in our plans. That one never goes away."**

Despite the visible signs of progress on Brush Creek Ranch in just a few years, not everything White wanted to do was quick or easy. The Whites owned Brush Creek privately, but White Lodging was doing the managing. The Ranch's new higher profile raised a few eyebrows around Saratoga. Dude ranches were nothing new in the area, but Brush Creek was in a class by itself. The local rumor mill sometimes churned up scuttlebutt that was downright comical.

"When we built the horse arena, there were rumors that Brush Creek was going to be the training facility for the Chicago Bears," said Beth White. "And then there's the rumor about putting in a golf course, which has never been in our plans. That one never goes away."

Learning the ins and outs of working with local Carbon County commissioners was critical. Fortunately, both White and Williams were affable, friendly, did not put on airs, and had decades of experience dealing with city and state governments. Ranch manager Ron Hawkins was a big help too. He was a longtime local not a 'come-here' from outside the community. Hawkins was plugged into the area's grapevine, knew the characters, and understood contentious issues like water and mineral rights, fencing, conservation easements, and public access roads crossing private property. He also knew that an outsider's words or attitude could unwittingly rankle residents and make straightforward matters needlessly complicated. Conversely, being neighborly paid dividends.

"We would always keep Bruce involved on anything that affected property around us. Whenever we had an issue, he would say, 'Mike, I don't want to have a neighbor mad at me. Figure it out.' When we have to appear before the Board or deal with a neighbor who is upset about something, I always keep uppermost in mind that it's not my reputation that's on the line, it's Bruce and Beth's reputation."

When the Whites bought Green Mountain in May 2019, locals were concerned about the environmental impact. The plan called for creating a private ski mountain on the 620-acre parcel for Brush Creek guests. Access to the secluded area requires a four-mile drive on a snowcat.

"Neighbors thought we were going to ruin the ecosystem up there," said Williams. "We had to go before the County Commissioners three or four times until everyone was satisfied."

Acquiring Green Mountain boosted Brush Creek Ranch's ability to stay open in the winter. But every conceivable aspect of the proposed ski operation required County approval, from installing yurts or "warming huts" for guests, to developing an emergency response plan and guaranteeing that ski runs would be groomed by machine. The number of skiers was limited to fewer than 30. The ski area could be used only during daylight hours. Guests were to be shuttled between Brush Creek Ranch

The Whites bought Green Mountain for private skiing for their Brush Creek guests.

and Green Mountain, a 25-minute trip one way. The plan was given "temporary" approval by the County on December 17, 2019. The mountain opened for business three days later.

Meanwhile, White's imagination was still cooking up ideas for Brush Creek—ideas that involved wine, food, greenhouses, a distillery, a brewery, a top-tier dining room, plus beautiful decor and furnishings to create the right Western ambiance. White also decided to add a herd of Japanese Wagyu Beef cattle to Brush Creek. Out of the swirl of ideas and ambitions was born The Farm at Brush Creek.

> "Dad was a visionary," said Corinne White Troise. "When he first rolled out the idea of The Farm, I thought, 'This just can't be done! This is crazy! We already have so much going on.'"

"Dad was a visionary," said Corinne White Troise. "When he first rolled out the idea of The Farm, I thought, 'This just can't be done! This is crazy! We already have so much going on. We have these problems and these issues, and we've got to take care of that first. Plus, it's so much money.' All the reasons you shouldn't do it. But he had this remarkable ability to—not ignore those reasons—but to look past them to the bigger picture. He was always more excited than bogged down by big challenges."

The Farm at Brush Creek: an exterior view of the Cheyenne Club, a pasture-to-place luxury dining destination.

Between June 2017 and December 2019, Jean-Luc Barone and Chris Anderson turned White's vision of The Farm into reality. Located on the other side of Route 130, a short drive from the core of Brush Creek's operations, the complex is a foodie paradise and a wine-and-liquor connoisseur's dream come true. The original 2016 greenhouse that supplied fresh greens and herbs to the main lodge and dining rooms was joined by a second greenhouse in 2019 to create 20,000 square feet of growing space. The new Saddle Barn, constructed from vintage barn boards, provided an elegant indoor space for wedding receptions and other events. The lower level became home to the Ranch's bakery, a secret speakeasy-style 'spirit vault', and a 94-yard wine cellar housing 30,000 bottles. The Brush Creek Brewery and Distillery complex opened in September 2019. (The brewery closed a year later.) A creamery joined the line-up. The *piece de resistance* was the Cheyenne Club, the most upscale of the restaurants at Brush Creek Ranch. In August 2019, the Cheyenne Club greeted its first diners.

"Every summer, I would come back to the Ranch and there would be something new," said Lynn Bird, wife of White's cousin Terry Bird. "A new building. A new feature. Every time!"

Terry Bird agreed: "It has been fascinating to see the growth and the evolution of the Ranch, because we all remember it when it was just some old, haunted shacks. To see how Bruce and Beth's vision for the ranch has evolved and become a reality out of nothing is extraordinary."

> Begin with the end in mind.

The Farm helped extend the Ranch's peak season and helps the property make money during periods outside of the prime times when Brush Creek is sold out.

"Our tenets are educating, enhancing, and enjoying," said White in a 2017 interview. "We're always looking to enhance our guests' experience, whether it's the ecology or the outdoor activities we offer. I'm not sure that adding more necessarily makes us better. But to improve the ecology of the ranch, we want to work towards 100 percent sustainability. So, we'll be growing our own vegetables."

White was particularly committed to restoring Brush Creek's stature as a cattle ranch. After Ron Hawkins and his team repaired the Ranch's fencing, irrigation system and waterways, it was time for Brush Creek to have its own herd of cattle. But not just any cattle. White became fascinated by a particular breed of Japanese beef cattle prized for its marbled meat: Wagyu. Unlike ordinary beef, which can be high in unhealthy saturated fat, Wagyu's mono-unsaturated fat to saturated fat ratio is higher than in any other kind of beef. Besides being healthier, the taste and tenderness of Wagyu beef are coveted traits for serious chefs and gourmands.

> "I think having the ranch operations here is what keeps it authentic," said Hawkins. "I explained to Bruce early on that for most of the ranchers around here, it's not the money that keeps them here. It's about the lifestyle. They're not going to leave this lifestyle. It's what they do and who they are."

Wagyu cattle were first imported from Japan into the United States in 1975, according to the American Wagyu Association. The first to arrive were four bulls, whose semen were studied at Colorado University. The 1990s saw a small number of importations of Wagyu cattle into the U.S., including—at last—three females in 1993. But by the late 1990s Japan deemed the Wagyu breed a national treasure and banned export of anything related to Wagyu—including semen, embryos, and live cattle. U.S. ranches saw the door closing and doubled down on carefully maintaining and increasing the herds they had. One ranch in Texas that raised the coveted "Japanese Red" Akaushi strain hired off-duty Texas Rangers to guard their herd.

"A couple of Bruce's friends bought him an Akaushi bull and named him Bruno, for 'Bruno Blanco'," said Ron Hawkins. "So Bruce comes to me and says, 'So, what I do?' I said, 'Well, I guess you're going to have to get him some cows, or you're just going to have a bull standing around.'"

In June 2017, the first Wagyu cattle arrived at Brush Creek Ranch. Establishing a herd is not a small undertaking; it can take years before the cattle are ready for market. Following Japanese methods, the cattle are coddled to reduce stress. By taking stress out of the equation, the Akaushi beef attains the qualities that make it a delicacy. Recognizing a business opportunity, Brush Creek began offering its Ranch-raised Wagyu beef through an arrangement with an online meat retailer.

The Brush Creek Distillery is another Ranch operation that extends its reach beyond Brush Creek's guests. The facility's premium gin, rye, bourbon, and vodka are available for retail sale in Texas, Colorado, and Kentucky. The spirits can also be found in White Lodging hotels. In

American Wagyu is a breed that brings the best of America's Angus cattle and Japanese Wagyu cattle.

Brush Creek Distillery features its own premium gin, vodka, rye, and bourbon.

keeping with the Ranch's goal of sustainability, the distillery uses certified-organic greenhouse botanicals, mountain water, and ingredients foraged from the Ranch. The spent grains from the rye and bourbon are shared with local ranchers and used in Brush Creek's bakery for the aptly named Spent Grain Bread. Guests are welcome to schedule a tour of the distillery to learn more about its crafting and sustainability practices.

Just a few months after The Farm was up and running, the world shut down. In early 2020, the COVID-19 virus began its race across the country and around the world. Millions of people fell ill; many died. Mask mandates, 'social distancing', and vaccines dominated public discourse for more than a year. Hotels and restaurants were especially hard hit, along with performance venues, stores, offices—anywhere that people gathered. White Lodging's hotels were no exception.

> "COVID was the single most devastating event in the history of the hotel industry," said Bruce White. "And that includes 9/11, the financial recession, and even World War II."

"COVID was the single most devastating event in the history of the hotel industry," said Bruce White. "And that includes 9/11, the financial recession, and even World War II. We obviously had to renegotiate debt with our lenders, but the federal government had given them backstops, so they were cooperative. We had to change our operating models radically. And we had to ask an awful lot from our people, particularly our hotel general managers. The real difficulty with the pandemic was, if you tell an entrepreneur that there are roadblocks and obstacles, the overwhelming majority of entrepreneurs will say, 'Well, that's okay. I'll figure out how to get around them. Just let me know where the finish line is. I'll get to the finish line.' But with the pandemic, nobody knew where the finish line was. And people didn't know if it was going to get better. Is it instead going to get worse? You basically had to plan for the absolute worst.

"The survival of the whole company was at stake," continued White. "We laid off an incredible number of people, the majority of our workforce. We actually had to lay off people from the home office. Our sales went from averaging about $3.5 million a day to less than $150,000 a day. So, we had no sales coming in at all. And this lasted for an extended period. We'd have 1,000-room hotels that only had six occupied rooms in them. We had general managers that were used to having 600 employees, having to make do with maybe 12 employees on staff. The GMs would be working the front desk or laundry or making up rooms themselves. So, the pandemic was traumatic, but we did what we thought was right."

Thanks to an assortment of measures taken by the federal government and the White family's charitable foundation, many laid-off employees stayed afloat financially, waiting for the sun to come out again. Like White Lodging's hotels, Brush Creek Ranch had its share of trials during the pandemic.

"We closed here at Brush Creek on March 20," said Mike Williams. "The governor shut us down. He called me personally. 'Mike, you got to shut your business down today at 5 p.m.' We had just checked in a wedding party. So, we scrambled and pulled off the wedding at midnight in the Saddle Barn. The party and newlyweds left the next morning with a to-go breakfast and that was it.

"The next two months were really hairy," continued Williams. "We had to lay off everyone, except about seven staff members. And we were thinking that, without guests, we would all be spending the summer staining cabins and mowing the lawn."

Then, to Williams's surprise, the phone started ringing.

"People wanted to know if we were open. And they kept calling. And we had to keep telling them that we didn't know yet. Finally, we got a call from someone who wanted to rent out the entire Magee Homestead for a month. That was great. And it got us thinking."

Williams and his team ran some numbers to see if it might be feasible to open just the Lodge and Spa on a limited basis. Staff would all wear masks. Other sanitary precautions would be taken. A smaller than usual number of guests would allow them to be spread out in the dining room; and of course, the sheer size of the Ranch meant that people could easily keep their distance from one another. Williams arranged a Zoom call with Jean-Luc Barone, Chris Anderson, and the Whites. White thought the plan sounded doable.

"We ended up opening on June 8," said Williams. "That was only about three weeks later than our usual opening date. One thing that Bruce wanted to know was when we were going to open the Cheyenne Club. I told him that the plan only covered the Lodge area, not the other side of 'The Street'—our nickname for the public road that you have to cross to get to The Farm. I said, 'Bruce, we're only going to hire enough people to take care of one side of the street.' I think it was Jean-Luc who suggested that we could serve dinner on the Lodge side one night, and at the Cheyenne Club the next night. And keep rotating. So, we opened the Cheyenne Club three days a week: Tuesday, Thursday, Saturday, a schedule we still follow."

As the pandemic waned, White Lodging began to get back on track. Hotels reopened. Associates returned to work. Guests came through the doors, suitcases and smiles in tow. Hotels in the construction pipeline picked up pace again.

As the world began to return to normal, Brush Creek was kept busy nonstop for two years. People who had been cooped up during the worst of the pandemic wanted to be outside. Employees were welcomed back with open arms. The Whites—both of whom had gotten COVID on the early side of the pandemic—were able to go back to greeting guests, one of Bruce's favorite 'jobs' at the Ranch.

White was always quick to credit White Lodging with the ability to pull off something as grand, yet authentic, as Brush Creek Ranch: "Without the support and resources of White Lodging, we wouldn't be an operating guest ranch. Because I pity the poor person that would get into this business without having the type of resources that White Lodging brings to bear.

"Conversely, the Ranch is very important for White Lodging, because of the recognition it has received on a global basis from Conde Nast, Forbes, and others," continued White. "It has demonstrated within the industry that White Lodging can do things outside the norm and do them very successfully. It was really our first entrée into the luxury segment of the hospitality marketplace. So, while Brush Creek utilizes the resources of White Lodging, White Lodging has really benefited from the halo and the experience and our engagement in the development and growth of Brush Creek Ranch."

As the pandemic waned, White Lodging returned to business as usual. Hotels reopened. Associates returned to work. Guests came through the doors, suitcases and smiles in tow. Hotels in the construction pipeline picked up pace again.

"If there's one thing White Lodging has demonstrated, it's the ability to adapt and pivot at the right times," said Deno Yiankes, who weathered 9/11, the Great Recession, and COVID with the company. "Adapt. Pivot. Keep growing. Bruce has certainly shown his ability on that score over the years."

But even Bruce White's legendary ability to manage his way through any challenge Life might throw at him could not prepare him for what lay ahead.

CHAPTER 10

A Brand-New Star Up in Heaven Tonight

> *There's a brand-new star up in heaven tonight, shining down on us glorious and bright. I'm gonna miss you every day, but I know that you're all right.*
>
> **The Oak Ridge Boys**

Lightning never strikes twice, so the saying goes, but Bruce White was—as ever—an exception to the rule. In his case, lightning struck six times: discovering his love of hospitality at 16 . . . meeting and marrying Beth Maloney, the love of his life, and creating a family together . . . running into Mike Ruffer of Marriott in 1990 . . . the $1.7 billion RLJ deal in 2006 . . . and finding beautiful Brush Creek Ranch.

Lightning hit one final time in April 2022: White was diagnosed with inoperable pancreatic cancer at age 69.

On Easter Sunday 2022, Beth and Bruce White were at River House on Brush Creek Ranch, sitting side by side on a sofa, reading and enjoying the morning quiet. Beth's mobile phone lit up. Son Conner was calling from Colorado. His worried voice came down the line.

"Is Dad OK? He just sent a text that doesn't make any sense."

Beth looked at the family's group chat and immediately saw what Conner was talking about. The text was all caps in parts and garbled—totally out of character for White. Her husband was always meticulous about punctuation in his emails and texts.

Puzzled, Beth looked at his phone and checked to see if he had sent any emails to his executive team that morning. Sure enough, a note to CEO Jean-Luc Barone was also garbled.

Beth became concerned. She thought back on the past few weeks. A month earlier, White had complained about swelling in his ankles that prevented him from wearing his beloved cowboy boots. A scan revealed blood clots in both calves. A blood thinner was prescribed, and life went on as usual . . . until the odd Easter Sunday morning texts.

At Beth's urging, the couple returned to the Chicago area two days later. White forged ahead with a four-hour interview with a candidate to head up White Lodging's human resources. When he emerged from the long meeting, he told Beth that he felt "a little fuzzy" but otherwise fine. She was relieved but also glad that they had already scheduled an MRI for two days later.

On Friday, the couple arrived at Chicago's Northwestern Memorial Hospital for the MRI appointment. A doctor took one look at the images and sent them straight to the emergency room. White's lungs were covered with embolisms—small obstructions in the blood vessels. The most common cause is blood clots, but other substances can also be the culprit. In White's case, the embolisms were made of cancer cells originating in his pancreas. More exploration revealed that he had pancreatic cancer. The cancer was in the tail of the pancreas, rendering it inoperable. It was also far advanced.

> White had lost several friends to cancer, including one of his favorite Marriott executives: Arne Sorenson. Sorenson, who was Marriott's CEO at the time, was diagnosed with pancreatic cancer in May 2019 and died in February 2021 at 62.

"We both were so shocked," said Beth White. "We got the news on Friday, April 22, and decided to keep the diagnosis to ourselves for a couple of days. Our three kids happened to be in Chicago to attend a close friend's wedding that Saturday and we didn't want to take anything away from the celebration. We just digested the news ourselves."

Cancer was no stranger to the family. Twenty years earlier, White had gone through a bout of prostate cancer and beaten it. Beth's older brother James was diagnosed in 2019 with lymphoma of the brain. White had lost several friends to cancer, including one of his favorite Marriott executives: Arne Sorenson. Sorenson, who was Marriott's CEO at the time, was diagnosed with pancreatic cancer in May 2019 and died in February 2021 at 62. Sorenson's loss was still fresh when White received his own diagnosis 14 months later.

"When we got the cancer diagnosis, the first thing Bruce said was, 'I'm not going to be able watch Timothy grow up,'" said Beth White. "Our daughter Corinne had given birth to Timothy—who is named after my father—in 2021. The second thing he said was, 'So many people depend on me.'"

White's second comment called to mind Dean White's funeral in 2016. When Bruce's father died at age 93, condolences poured in from dozens of high-profile politicians and business peers. Officialdom's praise of the elder White was gratifying, but Bruce had been particularly touched by longtime Whiteco employees who approached him to express thanks for the opportunities that Dean White had provided. Many had been able to buy houses and put their kids through school, thanks to their jobs working for "Mr. White." Their gratitude had inspired Bruce and Beth to begin thinking about how to ensure that White Lodging could continue after their time at the wheel. Up to that moment, White had assumed that he would sell the company at some point and retire.

Bruce White with then Marriott CEO Arne Sorenson.

On Sunday, April 24, the couple gathered their children in the family's Chicago apartment and shared the diagnosis. All three kids knew something was amiss, but they had chalked up their father's odd text messages the previous Sunday to a small stroke.

"Our friend's wedding was the last night of normalcy," said Corinne White Troise. "When our parents told us the following morning, it was the most awful news you can ever get."

The couple began making calls to friends and family to share the bad news. White's youngest brother Craig and cousin Terry Bird flew to Chicago to be at White's bedside in Northwestern Memorial Hospital. Other relatives, close friends, and colleagues checked in and visited whenever White was up for company, at the hospital or at home. Old friends came by or called regularly to get updates and shoot the breeze. Mike Williams—who had worked with White for forty years—flew to Chicago from Brush Creek Ranch, where he was chief operating officer.

"We sat there for four hours and just talked," said Williams. "It was really nice. And I'll bet we didn't talk about business more than twenty percent of our time together. We talked about basketball and everything else under the sun."

White began chemotherapy immediately, game for buying himself as much time as possible. At least one scan showed slight shrinkage in the cancerous mass. Beth—a devout Catholic—prayed for a miracle, but her pragmatic, no-nonsense side recognized the inevitable.

As for White, he accepted the situation with few complaints and made a point of carrying on as normally as possible, except for going to White Lodging's Merrillville office. He never set foot again in the company's headquarters.

"He still received daily reports and talked to his team regularly," said Beth White. "We had a lot of hotels in the construction pipeline then so there were lots of online four-hour meetings. He was on his A-game then because he was doing what he loved. But afterward, he was exhausted."

Jean-Luc Barone had already been appointed White Lodging's CEO in January and could pick up the responsibilities that White knew he could not handle. Barone had joined White Lodging from Starwood in 2016 as Vice President of Food and Beverage and quickly won White's full confidence. Barone was instrumental in developing White Lodging's upscale hotel restaurants and bars. His elevation, first to COO in 2018 and then CEO in 2022, was seen as a major plus for White Lodging's executive bench strength.

Despite dealing with 'chemo brain' and bouts of extreme fatigue, White managed to get in a few brief trips in the time that remained.

Beth drove him down to tiny Shelby, Indiana, where he had spent many happy times as a kid with his grandmother Mary White. While Beth videotaped him, White reminisced about his beloved grandmother, talked about the old Whiteco sign factory, and pointed out vintage landmarks in the small town.

In late June, the couple flew to Austin, Texas, to visit White Lodging's ever-expanding collection of hotels in the city. Four new properties had opened in 2020 and 2021, including the 31-story, 600-room Austin Marriott Downtown, located across the street from the city's convention center. A bar in the hotel was named Corinne. One of the other recently built hotels in Austin was The Otis, a new addition to Marriott's Autograph Collection. (Conner has a restaurant named for him in the Indianapolis Marriott Downtown. Years earlier, a small chain of eateries run by White Lodging was named T. J. Maloney's Authentic Irish Pub, after Beth's father Timothy.)

The Otis hotel in Austin, a new addition to Marriott's Autograph Collection, was one of four new properties built in Austin in 2020/2021.

> **"Bruce called me over before the dinner and told me that his diagnosis was not looking good. He said, 'The thing I value the most is the relationships I have with people like you. All the success and everything, that really doesn't matter. It's just about the people I've have worked with and known along the way that have given me the greatest joy in life.'"**
>
> Liam Brown
> Group President, Marriott

"That trip to Austin was great," said Beth White. "It really put the sparkle back in his eye. He was in his element, walking around in the back of the house and talking to everyone."

Even in phone calls with his younger son Otis, White wanted to talk 'ops,' not illness. "I would call him and ask, 'Dad, how are you feeling?' He did not want to talk about it at all. Instead, it was, 'How are you doing at the hotel? What are you guys doing today? Is the bar busy tonight? What bar activity are you seeing? What cocktails are you guys making?' He loved ops. He loved the energy. He loved the creativity."

The Austin trip with Beth provided White with an opportunity to talk face-to-face with Marriott's Liam Brown about the cancer diagnosis. Brown was one of White's longest-running relationships at Marriott.

"We had a small dinner for our owners and franchisees," said Brown. "Bruce called me over before the dinner and told me that his diagnosis was not looking good. He said, 'The thing I value the most is the relationships I have with people like you. All the success and everything, that really doesn't matter. It's about the people I've have worked with and known along the way that have given me the greatest joy in life.'"

> *Everyone who knew Bruce White knew that travel—especially world travel—was one of his passions. Many had had the good fortune to go on one or more trips with the Whites.*

White's comment was in keeping with something that his younger son Otis noticed during his father's final year. Everyone who knew Bruce White knew that travel—especially world travel—was one of his passions. Many had had the good fortune to go on one or more trips with the Whites. Friends who came to visit during his illness often asked where he wanted to travel before bowing out of this world.

"Dad told them that there really weren't any trips he wanted to do," said Otis White. "He would say, 'I did all of those trips because it was a great way to spend time with friends.' What he really wanted to do was see as many friends and family as possible."

Trips to Brush Creek Ranch were now quiet family affairs. Instead of mingling with Ranch guests—one of White's favorite things to do—the couple enjoyed the summer weather and soothing sounds of French Creek running past their River House patio. Over Labor Day weekend, Bruce's brother Craig and several cousins joined Beth and Bruce at the Ranch. The visit provided a perfect opportunity for the cousins to reminisce on video about their childhoods, share memories of their revered grandmother Mary White, and hint with winks and grins that certain tales of youthful hijinks should go unrecorded.

"Bruce was sharp as a tack until the very end," said his brother Craig. "We went out for dinner one evening while visiting him at the Ranch. I bet if you had asked somebody at the adjacent table which one of us had Stage 4 pancreatic cancer, Bruce would have been the last person they picked. His energy level was amazing. The strength and courage he showed from the moment he was diagnosed with cancer—absolutely amazing. Never complained. We can only imagine what that takes to go day by day, after that diagnosis."

Bruce plays with his grandson Timothy.

One small upside of Bruce's illness was the fact that all three of his children arranged to move back to the Chicago area. Corinne had worked at Brush Creek Ranch for several years, but between Timothy's birth and her father's illness, Chicago looked like the right place to be—particularly to give Timothy and her father as much time together as possible.

Corinne's brothers, Conner and Otis, were general manager and assistant general manager, respectively, at the Denver Marriott Westminster. They also opted to be closer to home.

"The two of us were supposed to stay much longer at the hotel, but we just had to accelerate the schedule," said Conner White. "For

> Just remember: quality doesn't cost, it pays. Simply stated, it costs more to get a guest back than to keep one.

all of the negative, horrible parts of Dad's illness, I think it definitely had a silver lining. We were all together again as a family, having dinners together most nights, not just on holidays. That turned out to be a special part that I wasn't expecting: all of us coming together in the same place."

By Thanksgiving, the cancer was taking a visible toll on White. The family gathered again at Brush Creek to mark the holiday. Six weeks later, on January 19, 2023, White passed away, surrounded by his family. He had made it to Christmas Day—his 70th birthday—but declined quickly after the holiday.

Knowing what lay ahead, Bruce and Beth had put together plans for a memorial service. Each contributed to the program to make it a deeply personal send-off. The couple arranged to hold the service at Old St. Patrick Roman Catholic Church on Chicago's West Adams Street. The substantial brick building was dedicated in 1856 and is one of the few structures in the Windy City that predates the Great Chicago Fire in 1871. In 1977, the church was listed on the National Register of Historic Places.

The crowd that packed the large sanctuary on Friday, February 10, 2023 was joined by hundreds of people around the country who watched a livestream of the service. A slide show of White family-and-friends photographs played on a large screen at the front of the sanctuary while the church filled up. Music featured prominently before and during the service. Beth and Bruce had created a list of songs to include, ranging from ethereal classical pieces to Bruce's favorite country tunes. Representing the latter category, the iconic Oak Ridge Boys—good friends of Bruce since his Holiday Star Theater days—appeared at the front of the church partway through the service to serenade the mourners with an *a cappella* rendition of "Amazing Grace." The song was a classic for the Oak Ridge Boys, who had started their long career singing gospel, before later turning to country.

Monsignor Kenneth Velo, one of the city's senior Catholic clerics, conducted the service. Chairman of Chicago's Big Shoulders Fund,

Bruce (third from right) with the Oak Ridge Boys, who played every New Year's Eve at the Holiday Star Theatre for 25 years.

Monsignor Velo knew the couple from their involvement in the Fund's school initiatives. The Monsignor broke the ice with a tale about White and his extensive wine cellar. During a Big Shoulders fundraiser at the Whites' home a few years earlier, White had invited the priest to the basement for an impromptu private tour of his wine collection. After pulling out a few bottles and describing what made each special, White asked the Monsignor what kind of wine he liked. Without missing a beat, the priest responded wryly: "Well, Bruce, I only drink on the job." The crowd in the sanctuary laughed and relaxed.

Tim Ozark, Craig White, and Deno Yiankes delivered heartfelt eulogies and Beth White did a reading from the Bible. At the conclusion of the service, the Oak Ridge Boys once again stepped to the front of the church. The foursome sang "A Brand New Star (Up in Heaven Tonight)"—lyrics that set tears flowing. As the city and Northwest Indiana's most senior Catholic clergy retreated with solemnity down the center aisle, The Oak Ridge Boys delivered their final salute to their dear old friend Bruce: the infectious, toe-tapping "The Y'All Come Back Saloon"—his special request. It was easy to picture White grinning down from on high as the rollicking musical number closed the service.

Guests were driven to a nearby event space to enjoy a lavish luncheon and a few hours of swapping favorite stories about 'Bruno Blanco.' If the raucous laughter that filled the room was any indication, White's final grand gesture of hospitality was thoroughly enjoyed and deeply appreciated. As friends and family exited the luncheon, everyone was invited to pick up a playlist of White's favorite songs and help themselves to a Yeti thermos, complete with a bag of White's favorite tea.

"The thing that comforts me is, he didn't miss a beat his entire life," said Craig White, Bruce's brother. "I can't think of a person that was more well-rounded than Bruce in every area of life. He was so gifted that he could run White Lodging, yet he still had time for Beth and him to travel the world and really live life to its fullest in every area. I don't know of anybody else who had the whole universe of talents that Bruce had."

Beth White commented that her husband was at peace with himself when he died: "Bruce told everyone who visited him: 'I've been playing with house money for a long time. If you told me that I could live 20 years longer, but not have all the good times and my family, I wouldn't take it.' He had a lot of gratitude for what we've done, what we've had, and what we've shared."

Planning the memorial service together was just one of many joint tasks that Bruce and Beth tackled during White's final months. Naturally, the future of White Lodging loomed large. What would happen to the company without Bruce White at the helm?

Fortunately, the impression left by the well-wishers at Dean White's 2016 funeral had nudged White to reconsider his assumption that he would simply sell White Lodging when the time came. The RLJ deal in 2006 had demonstrated that the company's properties were desirable. The new properties constructed since the RLJ sale were generally bigger and flashier than the original inventory of mostly select-service suburban hotels. Attracting potential buyers would not have been a problem if White ever decided to sell and retire.

But after hearing many of his father's former employees or Shelby residents express their gratitude for Dean White and Whiteco, the idea of selling White Lodging lost its appeal.

> "What he heard at his dad's funeral in 2016 really hit home," said Beth White. "I think that's when he began to change course. He started to talk about wanting White Lodging to be a 'Forever Company'—something that would long outlive us."

"What he heard at his dad's funeral in 2016 really hit home," said Beth White. "I think that's when he began to change course. He started to talk about wanting White Lodging to be a 'Forever Company'—something that would long outlive us."

White also received encouragement from someone he deeply admired: Bill Marriott. Following a quiet dinner at the exclusive Alfalfa Club in Washington, D.C., White told Marriott that he and Beth were likely to sell White Lodging, rather than expect their three children to carry on. Marriott knew enough about the Whites' kids to know that they were smart, capable, and shared their parents' values. He advised the couple to reconsider. Marriott followed up with a written note a few days later.

"That encouragement caused me to think more deeply," said White in a 2022 interview.

White signed up Beth and himself for a family business enterprise workshop at Northwestern University's Kellogg School of Management. There the couple delved into family business topics ranging from succession planning to best practices for philanthropy.

"One of the first things we did was create an outside advisory board," said Beth White. "We had no reason at the time to think we would depend upon it so soon, but when Bruce fell ill, we realized its value."

Among the advisory board's recommendations was a suggestion to sell the remaining select-service properties in White Lodging's portfolio and focus instead on what had become a passion for White: "urban, experiential and lifestyle" properties that offered not only full-service amenities but gave guests a one-of-a-kind experience. Brush Creek Ranch was certainly in that category, as were quite a few of White Lodging's large urban hotels. In 2022, the company sold its last suburban properties and management contracts.

In addition to the new advisory board, plenty of guidance was also available, if needed, from the team of "OWLs"—Old White Lodging associates—who collectively had decades of cumulative experience to offer. Deno Yiankes, Larry Burnell, John Januszko, John Szczepanski, Jan Grabow, Mike Williams and others were not only knowledgeable, but happy to help the Whites in any way they could. White's old YPO forum members were also available to assist. Tim Ozark offered to provide support and counsel to Beth and the family, whenever needed. Purdue classmates Mike Wells and Steve Poe were happy to lend a hand. Business partners with White on several White Lodging projects, the two had been hands-on in developing some of the company's most complex properties.

Internally, White Lodging had plenty of talent and bench strength. When Brush Creek Ranch began to absorb more of White's time and passion in the early 2010s, he knew that the company needed to be able to function without his undivided attention. He still wanted to be in on most decisions, but having Jean-Luc Barone, Chris Anderson, David Lanterman (Chief Operating Officer) and other seasoned executives on board made it much easier to hand off responsibilities even before the cancer diagnosis in April 2022.

One issue that could easily have become a sticky wicket was the precise role of White family members going forward. Family businesses often falter when the founding generation is no longer leading the charge. The original zeal for the business isn't always passed down to the next generation. Or, as in the case of Dean and Bruce White, the founder might have a tough time refraining from micromanaging the younger generation. After several dust-ups in the office—and one candid psychological profile—father Dean and son Bruce had wisely concluded that they were better off not working together. Instead, Bruce founded White Lodging, and the two men became occasional business partners. The arms-length collaboration was the ticket to peace and prosperity.

For years, Beth and Bruce had been telling their three children not to expect that jobs would be waiting for them at White Lodging simply because of their last name. The couple actively encouraged their kids to pursue opportunities outside of the family company.

"We were always told growing up that there was no way we were getting into the family business," said Otis White. "It wasn't an option. I think they really wanted to avoid any sense of entitlement. So, it forced us to get out and find out what we wanted to do versus just knowing that we had this family business that we could fall back on. Our parents wanted each of us to find our passion because they knew that doing so would be the path to the happiest life."

White often expressed his belief that the business would be "way harder for G2 (Generation 2) than it is for G1 (Generation 1)," said Otis White. "Dad wanted us to be sure that working in hospitality was truly the direction we wanted to go. When the three of us were growing up, the business was always part of our lives, but never the focus. Our family dinners weren't about the latest hotel or how White Lodging was doing. The conversation was always about school, what we had learned today, or about travel."

White had another reason for cautioning his kids against assuming that everything would be smooth sailing if they came aboard. In his YPO forum and in his business dealings, he had seen or heard about infighting that destroyed not only family harmony, but the business as well.

Tim Ozark, one of White's YPO forum peers, recalled one fellow member who ran a large family business, only to lose control of it because of "cousins and people who were hangers-on who weren't working. He ended up having to sell the whole thing.

> *Ironically, the parental discouragement campaign had a reverse psychology effect: After completing college, all three White children migrated back to White Lodging in positions that genuinely interested them.*

"The concern of many founders is that the second or third generation won't have the same value set or passion," continued Ozark. "The younger generation might look at reducing risk, or monetizing, or taking a totally different path from what the founder envisioned."

"When kids get involved in a family business, there can be a serious downside," said White in 2022 interview. "It can create conflict. That happened in my father's generation. My dad and his siblings—and their mother—all had a stake in the business when G. W. White passed away. At certain points in time there was incredible conflict in the family."

Dean White ultimately bought out his siblings and mother, which helped to diminish family discord. Bruce's generation was a different story. None of his three siblings had ever been involved with White Lodging, so there were no grounds for conflict. But the next generation—Corinne, Conner, and Otis—could be a different story. Although conflict was unlikely, Bruce and Beth wanted to avoid setting up a situation that could lead to serious disagreements among their three offspring.

Ironically, the parental discouragement campaign had a reverse psychology effect: After completing college, all three White children migrated back to White Lodging in positions that genuinely interested them. A graduate of Northwestern University, natural organizer Corinne customized ranch stays for prospective guests at Brush Creek Ranch and set up tours for wedding planners and other providers of specialized services. After graduating from Northwestern with an MBA in Real Estate, Conner elected to focus on White Lodging's investments and real estate portfolio. The youngest of the trio, Otis realized how much he adored 'ops' and was very happy to work at various White Lodging properties after graduating from Butler University. When his father passed away in January 2023, Otis was assistant manager of Purdue's Union Club Hotel. Since

Beth White

Conner White, Corinne (White) Troise, and Otis White

then, he has become one of White Lodging's specialists in training and talent development.

"Dad made it clear to us that none of us had to be CEO of White Lodging," continued Otis White. "His message was more along the lines of the family being *stewards* of the business. The family will be involved, but not have to be in the most key roles."

After Bruce's passing, Beth White was named Chairman of White Lodging, succeeding her husband. She had often attended board meetings in the past, but now she was in the driver's seat. A student by inclination and habit, Beth dove into learning her new job while still processing her grief for the loss of her life partner.

Philanthropy was another area that called for ongoing stewardship by the White family. Bruce's parents led the way when they set up the Dean and Barbara White Family Foundation in 1998, after Dean sold his billboard operation to Chancellor Media Group for $960 million. Retired but still involved in White Lodging deals, Dean wanted to use some of his wealth to boost the quality of life in Northwest Indiana—The Region. The loss of much of the steelmaking industry that once employed thousands of workers in Gary and nearby communities had hit families hard. At the peak, more than 30,000 people worked at the steel mills; by 2024, that number had dropped to around 3,700. Gary's population fell from a high of 180,000 in the 1960s to half that number. More than 10,000 buildings in the city stood empty.

Dean and Barbara White tapped their sons Bruce and Craig to be trustees of the Foundation, but gave them no guidance, leaving it to them to decide how to disburse money wisely.

"Craig and I begged them to give us direction," said Bruce White in 2022. "They wouldn't. Our dad was opportunistic, and that applied to his business and the foundation. So, every time we made a decision, we asked ourselves, 'How would Mom and Dad feel about this?'"

The two White brothers focused on investing in community centers, especially YMCAs, which can provide not only sports facilities, but a variety of support and services to a community. Crown Point's Crossroads YMCA benefited from the Whites' generosity, as did youth sports programs in The Region.

"Our parents' love for Crown Point was a focus point for us," said Craig White. "Then Lake County, second. Then Indiana, third. While they were still alive, we decided that updating and expanding Crown Point's YMCA was a good investment by the Foundation. So, we gave the manager of the existing Y an assignment: find the best YMCAs in the country. He did a great job and led us to Wichita, Kansas. We flew out to Wichita, not knowing what to expect. We were given a tour of what's called a 'destination YMCA'. Dad liked the idea, so he told us to take a few Crown Point community leaders out there to see it for themselves. It was easy to see that Lake County had room for at least one of these destination YMCAs. So, we built one in Crown Point. The old Y had 6,000 members; today, they're up to 42,000 and counting."

"When I first came here, there was a lot of talk about the Crown Point Y," said Bill Hanna, who became executive director of the Dean and Barbara White Family Foundation in March 2021. "I pictured what I grew up with: a dark rubber floored gym with flickering fluorescent lights. But if you go to the YMCA in Crown Point, you're going to find a water park. Cabanas outside. The Y's CEO likes to call it a cruise ship that is anchored in Crown Point."

Craig and Bruce White didn't limit themselves to YMCAs. They chose four areas to focus on: health and wellness; quality education; public safety; and community development. Grants have been given to the tiny town of Shelby, where Dean and Barbara started their life together after WWII. A $2,000,000 grant was earmarked in 2016 for the U.S. Merchant Marine Academy—Dean's wartime alma mater—for an alumni foundation. The Latin School of Chicago—where Bruce and Beth's three children went to high school—has received support. Dozens of grants have gone to other community organizations.

In late September 2024, the Dean and Barbara White Family Foundation gave $30 million toward a new cancer center in Crown Point. The three-story facility is part of the Franciscan Health Crown Point Hospital. Craig White attended the groundbreaking ceremony where Diocese of Gary Bishop Robert McClory blessed the building site for the 71,000-square-feet center. When completed, the center will consolidate Franciscan Health Crown Point's cancer care services into a single location adjacent to the main hospital.

The largest single Foundation gift, by far, was a $150 million award in June 2024 to the Indiana arm of the Big Shoulders Fund, the Chicago-based education-focused organization that the White family has supported for many years.

The Big Shoulders Fund's story began in 1986 with one man: Joseph Cardinal Bernardin, head of Chicago's Catholic churches for many years. Bernardin worried about the number of parochial schools struggling or closing in the wake of demographic shifts in some of the city's less-prosperous neighborhoods.

"Bernardin believed that every child deserved an education in a safe and structured environment," said Josh Hale, president and CEO of Big Shoulders. "He didn't

Bruce and Beth White speak at a Big Shoulders Fund event.

Supporters of Big Shoulders, Bruce and Beth White interact with children on a school tour.

care whether they were Catholic, Protestant, Jewish, black, brown, white, whatever. But he had a funding issue. He didn't have the money to keep those school buildings open. So, he gathered a group of Chicago business leaders who raised millions of dollars for the Fund. They gave scholarships and offered some financial support to the schools but soon discovered that many of the schools didn't have the expertise to manage their finances, market themselves to parents, and so forth."

After the Fund brought Hale on board in 2005, a strategic vision took shape—one that embraced a more business-oriented approach to the problems the schools and students faced. Participating schools that wanted to work with Big Shoulders signed legal agreements, usually through the diocese. The schools vowed to implement better management practices and adhere to certain standards. In turn, the Fund provided some financing and advice to boost the school's services. Thanks to the $150 million White family grant in 2024, the program will be able to expand its existing small footprint in Northwest Indiana.

> "Bruce and Beth don't know a stranger," said Hale. "They're friendly and put people at ease right away. Bruce even managed to squeeze himself into one of those little pre-school chairs so he could talk to the kids on their level."

"We have summer programs, before-and-after school care, field trips, test prep support, all the things that any parent would want for their children," said Hale. "Tutoring. Mentoring. Support for kids transitioning to high school or thinking about college. Then we also have a whole program that is focused on the business side of running a school, from marketing to finance. So, in short, Big Shoulders has evolved from its original mission of fundraising for scholarships to children, to an organization that much more resembles a group managing a group of schools."

Hale recalled the first time he took Bruce and Beth White on a Big Shoulders school tour.

"Bruce and Beth don't know a stranger," he said. "They're friendly and put people at ease right away. Bruce even managed to squeeze himself into one of those little preschool chairs so he could talk to the kids on their level. At the end of the tour, we were joined by Jim O'Connor, who was really the founding chairman of Big Shoulders. Mike, the school principal, joined us. Mike and Bruce started talking football, including specific games. Bruce's knowledge of sports was encyclopedic. By the time they were done swapping stories, the whole room was in laughter. Bruce made friends like no one else I've ever met.

"Before Bruce and Beth left, they committed—then and there—to fix up the gym, which was just a dingy large room in the basement. It couldn't be used for much because there was a leak. They became patrons right on the spot."

In keeping with Bruce's longstanding 'Go big or go home' mindset, combined with Stephen Covey's 'Begin with the end in mind,' the Whites' support of Big Shoulders and other community programs is predicated on kicking in substantial money up front.

"Our philosophy is really simple," said White in a 2022 interview. "If something's worth investing in, it's worth investing in big today, as opposed to just letting resources—money—sit around. We believe, as Warren Buffett does, in compound interest. If you invest early and correctly, you're going to have much bigger impact down the line."

The Whites set up the White Family Scholarship Program, joining other local leaders in providing direct financial support to hundreds of kids in Big Shoulders schools. But the couple's most breathtaking commitment—before the $150 million gift in June 2024—was the creation of a special summer camp at Brush Creek Ranch: Staddle Camp.

"Bruce was sitting at the back of the room during a Big Shoulders board meeting," recalled Hale. "He was listening and jotting down notes on his iPad. At the end he came up to me and said, 'I have an idea for something that I want to talk to you about. I'll send you something shortly.' So, he left and headed home. On the way, he pecked out a two-and-a-half-page memo on his little iPad that clearly defined the patron program and the scholarship program, including how many students, what it would look like, some of the programmatic things that they want to include, mentoring, outings, experiences, what he wanted the scholars to take from this experience. Then he talked about how he and Beth bought this ranch in Wyoming and 'I have an idea for a camp out there.' And I just shook my head as I'm reading: 'When did he write this thing? In the car?!'"

White's idea was to bring middle schoolers from Big Shoulders schools out to Wyoming to Brush Creek Ranch for a week at a time in the summer. Typical of his 'Begin with the end in mind' approach, White knew exactly what he wanted to do with the camp. He invited Hale and a few others out to Brush Creek to show them what he envisioned.

Bruce and Beth talk with kids at the Staddle Camp chuck wagon. The camp is focused on STEM (Science, Technology, Engineering, and Math) activities.

"Bruce saw the world in three dimensions, his vision was 3D," said Hale. "He was able to conceptualize and see things in different parts, whether it's partnerships or how you implement and build something. He saw all the different pieces. So, we all went out the next morning to the site on the Ranch where he had envisioned this happening. He had his general contractor there. I thought, 'This is getting very real, very quickly! How's this all going to happen?'

"I remember it was a warm early summer day and I can still see the tall brown grass swaying in the wind, and the trees. We're walking through the site and he's waving his hand to point things out, telling us, 'This is where we'll have platform tents and this is where we'll put a chuck wagon kitchen. And Medicine Bow National Park (next to Brush Creek) will be the classroom.' He had this whole vision. And if you walk out there today, it looks exactly like that."

In 2011, Staddle Camp at Brush Creek Ranch launched. The students who want to attend camp must fill out an application form and be nominated by a teacher or principal at their school. If accepted, they're flown to Wyoming courtesy of United Airlines. The camp runs from Sunday afternoon through Friday afternoon. The first year, Otis White and a longtime friend handled chuck wagon duty.

"I think we have a little over three hundred kids come through, every summer," said Beth White. "They prepare beforehand by going on field trips to Adler Planetarium, Peggy Notebaert Nature Museum, The Field Museum, and North Park Nature Center. The camp is focused on STEM: Science, Technology, Engineering, and Math. So, they might test the Chicago River and then when they get to Brush Creek, they'll test our water and compare. Every year, they do something a little different."

> **The kids stay in tents and are often scared to death when they first get to the Ranch, because it's too quiet," said Bruce White. "Many have never seen a starry sky."**

"Each school that sends kids to Staddle Camp also brings chaperones," continued Beth. "And then we have our own camp counselors. We've been doing it long enough that some of our early Staddle Camp kids are now counselors."

For most participants, Staddle Camp is radical departure from their daily experience in urban Chicago.

"The kids stay in tents and are often scared to death when they first get to the Ranch, because it's too quiet," said Bruce White. "Many have never seen a starry sky. We have to teach them the whole bear awareness thing, because it's in an area where if they leave their food out, the bears will show up. Most of these kids have never ridden a horse. We even had to stop them from riding bicycles because there were too many accidents, because they don't know how to ride bikes. And of course, the people they're working with locally are cowboys from Wyoming. So, it's a cultural learning experience for everybody."

Now more than ten years old, Staddle Camp has hosted thousands of sixth and seventh graders.

"The Camp definitely reflects the motto that Bruce and Beth promote, especially at Brush Creek Ranch: 'Educate. Enhance. Enjoy.'" said Hale. 'The kids are constantly learning, constantly growing. And they're having fun doing it."

Another institution that has benefited from the Whites' commitment to education is Purdue University, the couple's alma mater. When the family moved back to the Chicago area after living in Colorado for several years, Bruce became more interested in his old stomping grounds: Purdue and Northwest Indiana. In 2005, then-Governor Mitch Daniels appointed White to the board of the Indiana Economic Development Corporation (IEDC)—a position that gave White an opportunity to weigh in on initiatives to bolster the state's economy long-term.

Six years later, after seeing White's performance on the IEDC, Daniels appointed him to Purdue University's Board of Trustees.

"I'd gotten to know Bruce at the quarterly meetings of the IEDC, which I was chairing at the time," said Daniels. "So, I got to see him in action: brilliant, outspoken, always willing to challenge somebody's accepted beliefs.

"I used to give a little speech to newly appointed members of our major university boards," continued Daniels. "I was always trying to upgrade those boards. I thought our big public schools deserve the best. I didn't want another booster club or people running around here with a tin cup. I wanted them to love the school but demonstrate that affection by constantly pressing to make it better. That was Bruce. By the time 2011 came around and there was the vacancy on the Purdue Board, I knew he'd be exactly that kind of trustee and he was. It took a couple of tries to get him to agree."

White accepted the honor and quickly dove into learning everything he could about land-grant universities like Purdue. Purdue is one of more than 100 public universities in the nation launched by the federal 1862 Morrill Act, which gave land to each state to establish a higher education institution focused on agriculture and "mechanic arts." The University of Nebraska, where White's grandparents and five aunts and uncles matriculated, is a land-grant school. In 1869, Indiana's state legislature accepted John Purdue's offer of $150,000 and 100 acres of land. The school welcomed its first students in 1874.

White Lodging's Deno Yiankes recalled getting on the company plane at one point and spotting White with a stack of binders.

"This is 2011 and we're busy opening these big hotels. We're flying to meetings that are very critical. I look over at Bruce and he's got four jumbo three-ring binders. He didn't volunteer what they were, so I finally asked. 'Oh, I'm reading up on land-grant universities. I'm getting ready for my first Board meeting'. I see him with these binders and other books for the next month. They're covered with Post-it notes and he's highlighting things. Every so often he would comment, 'There are so many opportunities! I'm going to do everything I can to contribute to make things better.'"

One of the 'contributions' that White brought to the Purdue Board was a level of enthusiasm that astonished some of his fellow board members and supporting staff.

> *One of the 'contributions' that White brought to the Purdue Board was a level of enthusiasm that astonished some of his fellow Board members and supporting staff.*

"I got to hear about it secondhand for a couple of years," said Mitch Daniels. "People said, 'Boy, Bruce White hit the Board like a tornado.' He was now and then brash, brazen,

> Be a leader,
> be a learner,
> be a friend.

blunt, but always constructive. Bruce broke china, but afterward he helped everybody else pick it up and move forward."

Because Daniels had tapped White in part for his financial prowess, White focused on bringing a more rigorous approach to financial accounting and planning. He was happy to be involved with the hiring of a new chief financial officer who, to White's satisfaction, "revamped the accounting processes and uncovered millions upon millions of dollars of cash that was sitting unused, basically being hoarded by various departments."

Another area that attracted White's attention was facilities. His experience acquiring real estate and constructing hotels was a major plus. He could easily visualize the best use of a parcel of land.

"Bruce was working to set us up for future success," said Mike Berghoff, a fellow Board member. "Everything from master planning the campus to acquiring vacant land on the perimeter of the campus that would set us up for future expansion. Even if it didn't really seem necessary at the time or maybe it was a little bit more than we wanted to pay, Bruce saw the strategic advantage and he would push."

White's interest in Purdue's facilities included one building that was near and dear to his heart . . . and very much out of date: Beta House. Separate from his Board duties, White set in motion a major renovation of his old fraternity's digs.

"Bruce called me one day and said, 'We really need to do a capital campaign to refurbish the Beta House'," said Mike Wells, fellow Beta. "By the time we were done with the renovations, we had spent $5 million, instead of the $4 million we had proposed. So, Bruce said, 'OK, I'll front the money.' So, he fronted the $1 million. But with a caveat: He expected me to raise the $1 million to pay him back. We did it and paid him off. Then he gave a $2 million no-strings gift. But he was absolutely not going to forgive that first million-dollar loan. As a matter of principle. 'A business deal's a business deal. I want that money back.'"

Fixing up Beta House was gratifying, but small scale compared to White's ambitions for the University. White worked on financial and facilities issues for most of the four years that he was on the Board. Improvements were made, but at a pace that he found frustrating.

"Some boards are dog-and-pony shows, and that was just not in Bruce's character," noted Tim Ozark, a friend from YPO. "He wanted to get to the heart of the matter. He was competitive. He loved challenges. And he loved 'disruptive debates' and trying to come up with a better solution to a problem."

As an entrepreneur and head of his own company, White was used to putting money where and when it was needed and seeing major progress soon thereafter. Staddle Camp at Brush Creek Ranch was a perfect example of White's ability to get things done at a quick clip. So was Brush Creek Ranch, for that matter. But his involvement on organizational boards often required more time and patience to see results.

"I know that was one of his frustrations with being on a board was that things didn't move at the pace he wanted them to move at," said Beth White. "He loved his work on University of Chicago Medical Center, for example, where he was a trustee for I don't know how many years. He loved it from the aspect of learning and being able to make a difference. But then I think the pace and the bureaucracy would get to him. Purdue was better because Purdue was a smaller board, so he could see more immediate impact."

Even so, by February 2015, White decided that he had contributed as much as he was likely to as a member of Purdue's Board of Trustees. Also, Beth's father was seriously ill at the time and Bruce needed to be on hand to help.

"My personal rule is if I'm involved in something, I show up to the meetings. And I missed two consecutive meetings of the Board because of being with Beth's father in the hospital before he passed. And I just said, 'If I can't attend the meetings, then I have to resign.' So, I reluctantly resigned."

As honored as he had been to be appointed to the Board by Daniels in the first place, White was happy to be a free agent again. He identified two areas where he felt his business expertise could have a tangible and lasting impact on the school: Purdue's existing hospitality program and the university's Union Club Hotel.

The latter was a bricks-and-mortar project tailor-made for White Lodging. During his time on Purdue's Board of Trustees, he had tried to dissuade Mitch Daniels from pursuing a proposal by a Chinese company to build a new convention center on campus. White had waved away the idea, counseling Daniels that the project was not a good fit for the school.

The proposed deal never went anywhere, leaving White free to offer to renovate the century-old Union Club Hotel at the heart of the campus. The hotel had originally been built in phases and opened in 1929 as an addition to Purdue's Memorial Union. A second wing was added to the hotel in 1939, and in 1955 a five-story, 130-room north wing was added. The place had not changed much since then.

> **"The Whites turned our 100-year-old hotel into a destination. The University wouldn't have taken on such a project. It was like remodeling a historic house. You have to have the right people to make that happen."**
>
> Mike Berghoff
> Board of Trustees, Purdue University

White had stayed at the Union Club Hotel while attending Board meetings and wasn't impressed. "I thought, 'How in the world could a school that wants to have a nationally recognized hospitality program operate a hotel on campus that was so poorly run?'"

"Bruce always made the point that the Union Club Hotel, as it was, was a dreary place, not just physically, but in terms of the responsiveness and friendliness, hospitality of the staff," said Daniels.

"I think the overall cost for the update was $35 million and the Whites' contribution was $30 million," said Mike Berghoff. "The Whites turned our 100-year-old hotel into a destination. The University wouldn't have taken on such a project. It was like remodeling a historic house. You have to have the right people to make that happen."

On August 5, 2020, the restored and updated 182-room hotel opened its doors. White's experience at Brush Creek Ranch, carefully restoring historic buildings, was on full display at the Union Club Hotel. Original Purdue architecture and academic-flavored design can be seen in carpet patterns, upholstery, room fixtures and other elements in the hotel. The renovation entailed a complete overhaul of all guest rooms and public spaces, including a stunning transformation of the lobby to create a much grander entrance.

"The University then took on the complete redevelopment of the lower level," said Berghoff. "That was a $47 million renovation. So combined, it was roughly an $85 million project. That did not happen without the White family. So that was a big change. Big change."

The Union Club Hotel joined Marriott's Autograph Collection and quickly became one of the brand's best-rated hotels.

"The hotel has an outdoor courtyard and we're going to try to make it the coolest courtyard in the Midwest," said White in a 2022 interview. "When people come back for games or graduation or orientation, our rates are $700 per room per night. People in my age group were used to paying $12 of room back in the day at the Union! We need to expand the bar because it has become so popular. The mostly student-run bar and restaurant are the busiest, most popular restaurant and bar in Lafayette.

Left to right: Mitch Daniels, Liam Brown, Bruce White, and Michael Berghoff.

We feel great about our investment because it's playing out just the way we wanted it to."

Lovely as the new hotel was, White had more ambitious plans for the facility. He wanted to see the Union Club Hotel become a training center for the University's hospitality students. With characteristic bluntness, White had told Daniels and the Board of Trustees that he "wouldn't hire anybody from your hospitality school."

"Bruce being Bruce, the hotel project wasn't just about upgrading the physical facilities," said Daniels. "He wanted our young people, our Hospitality and Tourism Management (HTM) students specifically, to have more apprenticeship type opportunities. And so as thrilled as we all are with the physical enhancements, frankly, I'm more excited when I go in there to see all the Purdue students getting hands-on experience. It's going to give them a further head start when they get out in the world of work."

In 2020, White Lodging created the LAUNCH Hospitality Immersion Program at the Union Club Hotel. The program is designed to provide a paid hands-on experience across all hotel and restaurant operations. LAUNCH is an echo of the valuable training that Marriott provided to tiny White Lodging in the early 1990s when White landed the first Fairfield Inn franchise.

"The students are learning all the Marriott systems," noted White. "If they go to work for Marriott or White Lodging in one of our hotels—or in any company that operates a Marriott hotel—they're already familiar with all the systems, the standards. They've worked in an environment that has high standards and for a brand that has high standards. They're getting a great experience. The guests love knowing that the students are their server, their cook, their front desk agent, their housekeeper."

Hand-in-hand with the LAUNCH program, the White family gave $5 million to boost Purdue's existing hospitality program. The $5 million pledge was earmarked for an honors program in hospitality, an endowed scholarship for top achievers among hospitality students, and a named headship. In recognition of the gift and their ongoing commitment to making the hospitality program the best in the country, the school was renamed the White Lodging-JW Marriott, Jr. School of Hospitality and

Tourism Management in October 2021. White insisted that Marriott be included in the school's new name.

The following year, the White family foundations together gave Purdue $20.8 million to establish the Dean V. White Real Estate Finance Program within the School of Management. In 2023—just a few days after White's memorial service in Chicago—the family gave an additional $50 million to Purdue to establish the Bruce White Undergraduate Institute, within the newly-renamed Daniels School of Business. The gift helped to draw in another $80 million in gifts to the business school.

> If you don't have time to do and invest in the important things, you don't have time to succeed..

"I had always thought there was a big void in hospitality education," said White in 2022 interview. "Cornell is, head and shoulders, number one. But to a degree, Cornell has become more of a school to train investment bankers. Not nearly as many Cornell graduates go into hotel operations anymore. I thought that there was space for a #2 hotel school in the U.S. that wasn't as selective as Cornell and that had found the right balance between hotel operations and the hotel business."

"Bruce was discontented with the nature and direction of business education in so much of the country," said Daniels. "And he was, as he should have been, incredibly proud of what he had done. Not for what it did for Bruce and Beth White or their family, but for what it had done for all the people they employed and all the people who were leading better lives because of it. And he wanted our business school students here to have that same understanding, that same aspiration, and to know that if they go out and do things nearly as well as Bruce White did, sure, they'll do well themselves, but it's what they'll do for so many others in businesses they build or start."

> Plans for the Bruce White Undergraduate Institute were in the works before White passed away. He bristled at the idea of the program being named for him, but he was overruled by his family and Daniels.

Plans for the Bruce White Undergraduate Institute were in the works before White passed away. He bristled at the idea of the program being named for him, but he was overruled by his family and Daniels.

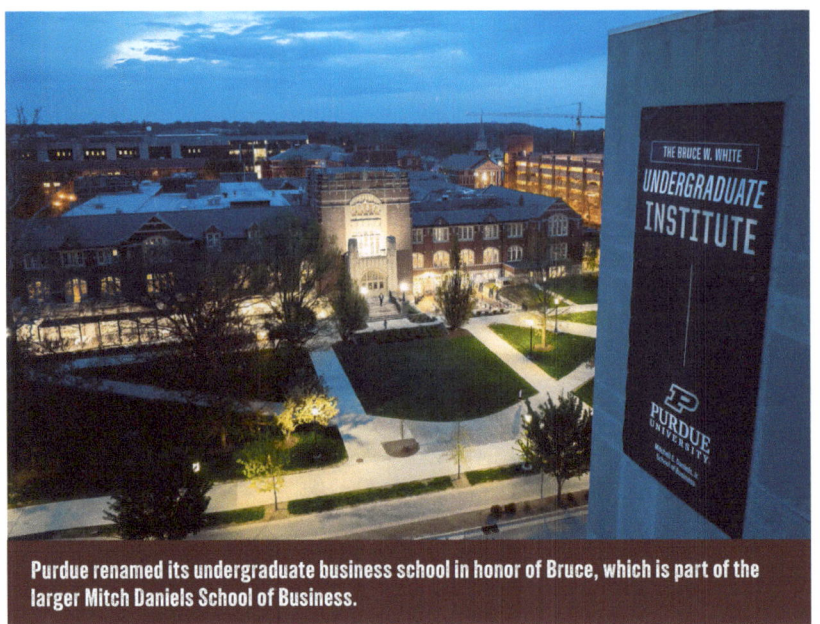

Purdue renamed its undergraduate business school in honor of Bruce, which is part of the larger Mitch Daniels School of Business.

"He wanted to name things for everybody but himself," noted Daniels. "His dad. The White family. And it was quite an arm wrestle to get him to agree to the only appropriate name for the undergraduate program. I know Bruce would say that if there's going to be a legacy, it has to be the people. It has to be the young people that are produced, that are benefited, that get their first job in that hotel, that learn the tools that they will take into the business world better here because of the investments. Bruce was somebody who was all about results, real impact, all about changing things for the better. As I said, if he broke some china, he was happy to help sweep it up, as long as things came out better. Not because he was trying to bully anybody, not because he enjoyed arguing with people. But because he was trying to move something forward, whether it was the business or Northwest Indiana or this University. And he was always in a hurry to make something real big happen, so he didn't mince words."

"Bruce had a commitment to excellence, both in people and product," noted Mike Berghoff. "He was unwavering in that commitment. His attitude was if you can't be the top one, two or three, why are we doing it?"

Another large piece of White's legacy is Brush Creek Ranch in Wyoming. Almost the entire 30,000 acres of ranchland owned by the Whites are held in a conservation easement, a reflection of the family's view of themselves less as owners, more as stewards of the property.

"That means it can never be developed," explained White. "It's going to remain as pristine in perpetuity as it is today. We also have an ownership structure called a family residential trust in perpetuity. The Ranch is technically owned by the trust but controlled by the family."

While the conservation easements protect the land from development, the White family's commitment to prudent ranching and environmental practices will help to preserve the soil, river, watershed, flora and wildlife on Brush Creek.

"If you look at the West, the number of ranches is going down because it's so tough to make it agriculturally," explained White. "The economy has had to diversify and tourism is part of that diversification. People come here from all over the world to learn about the American West and cowboy culture."

Guests contribute to Brush Creek's long-term health by helping to make the Ranch economically sustainable. White's long-term vision for Brush Creek Ranch has been to preserve the land and the history but share it with people who are open to experiencing the West's rugged terrain, beauty, and authentic traditions. The fact that Brush Creek hosts many returning guests suggests that White and White Lodging have figured out a winning formula.

White also saw the Ranch as a great opportunity for family members to work together.

"I think keeping Brush Creek sustainable will be great discipline for future generations. They're going to have to work in a collaborative and productive fashion to make sure that the business of the Ranch can sustain the operation of the property.

"Looking at the past decade or so, what we've done is just the beginning," noted White. "My generation's job was to build the foundation. The next chapter of Brush Creek is yet to be written."

❖❖❖❖❖

Another legacy that can't be measured in acres or dollars is the large circle of friends that Bruce White created in his 70 years. His knack for connecting with people—and staying connected—dated from his devil-may-care days growing up on South Park in Crown Point. Seventy years later, Bruce was still in regular touch with his childhood buddies.

During his undergraduate days at Purdue, White cultivated bonds with fellow Beta House fraternity members such as Steve Poe and Mike Wells, who ended up being not just lifelong friends with White, but business partners on several hotel projects.

"It's not unusual for some of these fraternities to have two or three people in the real estate business who are successful," noted Wells. "But they're not partners. Steve, Bruce, and I were partners. I think that's pretty rare. We made a lot of decisions together. We made our share of mistakes. But for the most part, we recognized our mistakes and moved on. We made a great team and enjoyed working together. I go to meetings now and look around: 'Where's Bruce?'"

> **"** In 1995, I was very ill with prostate cancer," said Johnson. "Bruce came to visit and basically said, 'Whatever you or your family need, I can provide it.' And he meant it. **"**

Lacy Johnson was another lifelong Purdue friend. Johnson and his wife traveled with the Whites on worldwide trips and became friends with others in Bruce and Beth's circle. The Johnsons were also among the many delighted recipients of bottles or cases of wine selected by White, whose knowledge of oenology was both deep and wide. But most important to Johnson was White's willingness to support a friend who found himself in a bad place.

"In 1995, I was very ill with prostate cancer," said Johnson. "Bruce came to visit and basically said, 'Whatever you or your family need, I can provide it.' And he meant it."

"A few years ago, we were flying back from somewhere and he said he'd drop me off in Indianapolis," recalled Mike Wells. "We had been on the go for 16 hours. We had a friend who had cancer and Bruce said he was going to drop by to visit. The man didn't live in Indianapolis, so

"BE A LEADER. BE A LEARNER. BE A FRIEND."

Naturally, the three White children were more influenced by their parents than by anyone else. Asked to identify their father's values, the trio put their heads together and came up with a list:

Human connection. Genuine connection is the lifeblood of a loving family and the backbone of the hospitality industry.

Hard work is non-negotiable. "Dad would say, 'Hey, when your boss hands you your paycheck at the end of the two weeks, you need to be able to look him in the eye and shake his hand and feel that you really deserved it.'"

Wholesome Midwestern humility is at our core. We are never above anyone or below anyone. We treat everyone with respect and commit to taking the high road in all situations.

Lifelong learning. Education and lifelong curiosity are key to personal development.

Humor. Have fun and always maintain the ability to laugh at yourself.

Entrepreneurship. For a family-controlled business to sustain itself, it must consistently grow, generating an appropriate risk adjusted return on invested capital.

Philanthropy. Giving back to our communities in ways that make an impact and relate to our values.

Legacy. Providing opportunities for future generations to experience and enjoy the same passion that drives us today.

Self-reliance, personal responsibility, practicality, avoidance of blaming others rather than ourselves.

Bruce got a car and drove to his house. Bruce spent an hour and a half with him, then got back on the plane. He didn't have to do that, at the end of a long day, but the man was his friend."

"One of Bruce's incredible qualities was that of being able to establish and nurture relationships and then have those friends become part of his extended family," said Tim Ozark, one of White's YPO friends. "And it didn't matter if you were from Purdue, or if he met you and became friends in Valparaiso, or Vail, or Chicago or Denver. You became part of that extended family."

"I think what brought my dad the most joy was the time spent with friends," said Otis White. "The stories shared. All of White Lodging and the business is nothing if not for the people that you get to share it with."

Besides being fun to be around—karaoke, anyone?—White provided a model for living a good life. Few could keep up with his hard-charging pace, but all could look to him for guidance on how to fashion a meaningful life.

"I've met people who are inquisitive," said Deno Yiankes, who delivered one of the three eulogies at White's memorial service. "I've met people who are innovative. I've met people who are curious about learning different things in this life. But I had never met an individual like Bruce where it's all together, in one person.

"He left a permanent mark on me and I'll be forever grateful for the experience I had with him," continued Yiankes. "I was working with an absolute legend in our industry. The learnings—both personal and professional—can't be matched."

The catchy mantra White had taught his kids—*Be a leader. Be a learner. Be a friend.*—reflected his own aspirations and the powerful influence of his wise and strong grandmother Mary White.

White was far from being a proselytizer or a prig, but he did have strong convictions about what some consider old-fashioned values: distinguishing right and wrong, honoring one's word, being fair, and doing one's best.

Josh Hale of Big Shoulders recalled a long conversation with White about what he and Beth were doing to instill solid values in their three children. The chat left Hale thinking about his own family.

"I remember getting home from that trip and saying to my wife, 'We have got to figure out what values we're passing down to our kids. Like, what the hell are we doing? Why didn't I think about this before now?!' And that conversation still sticks with me today. I think about it whenever I'm talking to my kids. What am I passing on?"

Hale ticked off a list of a few of the values that he saw White put into action.

"Humility, generosity, hard work. No one is above sweeping or digging. Don't lie. Don't cut corners. Don't cheat. Never be afraid of thinking big and beyond what's in front of you. I always thought respect was one of his most important ones, whether it's respect for your elders, dishwashers, storekeepers. Treat people the way you would want to be treated. Bruce didn't say to me, 'This is what matters, Josh.' I just observed him."

In 2017, Johnson & Wales University bestowed an honorary PhD on White. White Lodging was 32 years old that year and White was a well-known and well-respected player in the hospitality industry. White told the graduation audience the story of how bussing tables at Merrillville's Holiday Inn had 'hooked' him on hospitality. How he wanted to skip his Purdue graduation so he could hop into his blue Econoline van and get to California and Hyatt a few days early. (He attended graduation anyway, to please his parents and grandparents.) How none of his classmates or professors would have singled him out as "most likely to succeed."

Then White offered a bit of advice.

Bruce White spoke at Johnson & Wales University in 2017, when he received an honorary PhD.

"If you have a strong enough will, fueled by an overwhelming passion for what you do, over time your vision becomes your destiny. . . . In college, you know the mission, what you have to do and you do it. . . . Life will much more resemble a moving picture, i.e., it is far more fluid and ambiguous and you often don't see the results of your decisions and efforts immediately, as they come to light down the road in the form of some unanticipated consequence . . . sometimes good and sometimes not.

"The real world has no core curriculum but is built on 'core values.' There are no required courses—only 'electives.' The possibilities are endless and the results uncertain. This reality is scary, frustrating, exciting and a test of your values, self-confidence, persistence, and will to achieve your dreams. College is something you complete and is in reality an 'open book' test. Life is something you experience and only you can define how to measure its success. Your parents, professors and friends will no longer be able to help you with that. You will have to determine your own destiny.

> **"Life is something you experience and only you can define how to measure its success. Your parents, professors and friends will no longer be able to help you with that. You will have to determine your own destiny."**
>
> Bruce W. White
> 2017 Johnson & Wales Graduation

"What you do with your physical diploma today is really not too important. What you do with the rest of today is an opportunity not to be missed: letting your friends and family know how much you care for them . . . not only how important they were in your success to date, but more importantly, the impact their legacy will have on your future."

◆◆◆◆◆

Six weeks before he passed away in January 2023, a touch of wistfulness in his voice, White told a friend: "Whenever I'm in Chicago, I can't wait to get back to Brush Creek."

A few months later, the boy from South Park was granted his wish. Beth, Corinne, Conner, Otis, and other family members gathered on Brush Creek Ranch to celebrate the exceptional life of Bruce William White. Husband. Father. Grandfather. Son. Brother. Cousin. Entrepreneur. Hotelier. Rancher. Student. Explorer. Provocateur. Disruptor. Pioneer.

One of Bruce's favorite spots on Brush Creek Ranch.

Yodeler. Prankster. Dancer. Karaoke-meister. Oenophile. Boilermaker. Mentor. Role model. Visionary. Benefactor.

Leader. Learner. Friend.

Together, the White family laid Bruce's ashes to rest on the wild Wyoming landscape he had come to love dearly . . . the landscape of his boyhood dreams . . . the landscape of his heart.

> **"I see myself much more as a steward than an investor. While economic sustainability is an essential ingredient for longevity, you can do a lot of things to make money that leave no legacy for others to build on . . . to contribute to communities and enhance quality of life."**
>
> **Bruce W. White**
> **Founder, White Lodging**

Afterword

by Beth M. White

When I volunteered to write an Afterword for my husband's biography, I didn't expect the assignment to be difficult. After all, we had been married for more than three decades, parented three children together, and navigated Life's ups and downs (mostly ups) as a team. How hard could it be to write a few words about my life partner, a man I adored?

As it turns out, hard. Very hard.

As I pondered the meaning of the term Afterword, I realized that the concept—like the man—is complex. How do you sum up a life as jam-packed and wide-ranging as Bruce's, without leaving out something essential? How could I, who knew him better than anyone, convey how precious our time together was . . . not just to me, but to both of us, and to our kids?

Perhaps the easiest approach is to focus on one of the main themes of Bruce's life: relationships. Long before we met in 1986, Bruce had mastered the art of making and keeping friends. Throughout our married life, he picked up the phone regularly to reconnect with childhood buddies, Purdue fraternity brothers, his tight circle of cousins, his beloved grandmother Mary White, and even some of the celebrities he got to know when he ran the Star Plaza Theater in the 1980s. It was pure pleasure for Bruce to hang out with others, whether he was playing a pick-up game of hoops on the road, teaching our kids to ski, taking friends on whirlwind trips around the world, belting out a karaoke tune at a party . . . or sitting quietly next to me on the sofa, his readers perched on his nose, his eyes glued to a book or his iPad.

Anyone fortunate enough to be in his vast circle of friends can attest to Bruce's loyalty and knack for connecting people. As our friend Josh Hale has said, Bruce White "never met a stranger." It's true! It always amazed me how easily Bruce could find some common thread that endeared him to whoever he was talking to. It didn't matter who the person was or where they came from. He could talk seriously to an academic one minute and then be silly and playful with a child the next.

When I accompanied Bruce on hotel walks, I marveled at his ability to put people at ease within seconds, whether he was asking about their kids, surprising them by rattling off their high school basketball record or cracking a joke. He was genuinely interested in others and loved learning what made people tick. And people FELT his sincerity. Bruce simply possessed an uncanny talent for making people of all walks of life feel heard and important.

I learned early on that Bruce couldn't bear to keep his friends to himself! Many of our parties and travels through the years brought together people from every era and sector of his life and mine. He truly loved watching old pals meet for the first time and forge new friendships. Bruce also reveled in being the point person for family reunions, sometimes (quite wisely, I think) using the gatherings as a chance to record reminiscences before the memories were lost forever.

Bruce claimed to be an introvert and I used to joke (with an accompanying eyeroll!) that I always had to worry about him being the "wallflower" of the party. Nothing was further from the truth. He was the life of the party; everyone wanted to be around him. He sang with gusto, put even the shyest guest at ease, set whole rooms laughing, and could be picked out of the noisiest crowd based solely on his infectious belly laugh. When we hosted friends at Brush Creek Ranch, Bruce was thoroughly in his element, shepherding them around the property, taking them on hair-raising rides in his Razor, and—above all—making sure that everyone thoroughly enjoyed themselves.

The relationships he held most dear, of course, were with me and with our three kids. Right up to his final day, he wrapped the four of us in a loving bear hug that only grew stronger as the years passed. Whether he was with us at home or halfway around the world, we always knew we were his first priority and his last thought when he closed his eyes at the end of a long day.

One of the many tragedies of losing Bruce in January 2023 was how little time he had to enjoy being a grandfather. Bruce and our grandson Timothy had only eighteen months together, and Bruce treasured every moment. Timothy and his parents moved in with us shortly after Bruce's cancer diagnosis, to give them as much time together as possible. Little Timothy was the best medicine Bruce ever had. The first question he would ask upon waking was "Where's Timothy?" In turn, little Timothy would light up when he heard his grandfather whistling the theme song to the old *Andy Griffith Show*. Together they would conduct music, each waving one finger in the air to mark the rhythm. (I suspect he was trying to turn Timothy into a pint-sized rock music fan.) Although Bruce was by and large at peace with his cancer diagnosis, the one thing that caused him visible pain was the thought of leaving Timothy behind.

Bruce and Beth enjoying a Brush Creek Ranch evening.

Since his death, the kids and I often lament how much Dad would have loved trick or treating, playing Santa or simply hanging out with his (now three) grandchildren.

Bruce and I were united by a deep bond of trust, respect, common values and genuine love. Ours was a true partnership; we shared a mutual and unwavering commitment to our union. A friend recently relayed a memory of Bruce and me that I had forgotten; her story was such a gift to hear. For years we hosted Christmas parties that included live entertainment. My friend said, "I remember being at one of the December parties and Bruce asked the musicians to play "Beth" by Kiss. I saw him look at you when the band sang the line, 'Beth, I hear you calling but I can't come home right now.' I have tears in my eyes remembering that moment and the love in yours and Bruce's eyes."

What that dear friend saw at the party was something I lived with every day. Bruce and I adored each other. Even though he has been gone more than two years now, I can feel his spirit supporting me. I always felt that I understood the depth of our relationship . . . yet now in his absence I am reminded again and again of the deep and special bond we shared. We had fun. We danced. We made up rhymes. We hugged. We talked. We planned. We could also just enjoy the quiet of being together on a lazy Sunday morning. Bruce wasn't just my husband; he was my best friend.

I could go on and on, but I'll stop here. I was the luckiest woman on the planet during our 35 wonderful years together. One simple line perhaps captures how I feel about the man: Bruce White was easy to love . . . and hard—oh so hard—to lose.

Finally, I want to thank Kathi Ann Brown for her personal commitment to capturing Bruce's "story" in book form, a feat in and of itself. She immediately understood the urgency of interviewing Bruce and connecting all the dots in family, friends and business when I first engaged her in the fall of 2022. She quickly became part of the expansive circle of Bruce's colleagues and large circle of friends. Thank you, Kathi.

Beth Maloney White
January 2025

Acknowledgments

Beth White, Wife
Bill Hanna, Dean & Barbara White Family Foundation
Bill Marriott, Jr., Marriott International
Carol Smith, White Lodging
Caryn Kawka, White Lodging
Chris Anderson, White Lodging
Craig White, Brother
Chris White, Brother
Chuck Collins, Brush Creek Ranch
Cindy White, Sister
Conner White, Son
Corinne (White) Troise, Daughter
Dan Kozlowski, Big Shoulders Fund
Deno Yiankes, Strategic Advisor, Board Member
Douglas Bird, Cousin
Fuel Hospitality, Documentarian + Photographer Jacob Keller, Brush Creek Ranch
Jan Grabow, White Lodging (Retired)
Jean-Luc Barone, White Lodging
Jeannette Biser, Brush Creek Ranch
John Januszko, White Lodging Executive (Retired)
John Szczepanski, White Lodging Executive (Retired)

Josh Hale, Big Shoulders Fund
Kathi Ann Brown, Author + Historian
Lacy Johnson, Friend
Larry Burnell, Strategic Advisor, Board Member
Larry Deandrade, Saratoga Jet Center
Liam Brown, Marriott International
Linda Mueller, White Lodging
Lynn Bird, Cousin
Lynn Spannen, White Lodging (Retired)
Lynn White Rader, Cousin
Michael Berghoff, Purdue University
Michael Williams, Brush Creek Ranch
Mike Banas, White Lodging
Mike Braughton, Purdue for Life Foundation
Mike Wells, Friend + Business Partner
Mitch Daniels, Purdue University, Former Indiana Governor
Patrick 'Otis' White, Son
Pat Costin, Friend
Ron Hawkins, Brush Creek Ranch
Spectrum Creative, Book Designer
Steve Poe, Friend + Business Partner
Terry Bird, Cousin
Tim Ozark, Friend + Business Partner
Wendy White Fileti, Cousin

All photography in this book is provided courtesy of the White Family and White Lodging with the following exceptions:
Page 15. Photo: Town of Shelby Archives
Page 38. Photo: *The Purdue Exponent*
Page 114. Photo: *Hotel Business* Magazine
Page 164. Photo: *Hotel Business* Magazine

www.ingramcontent.com/pod-product-compliance
Lightning Source LLC
Chambersburg PA
CBHW041134130526
44582CB00028B/115